ALASKA

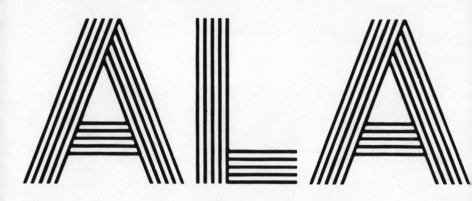

THE COMPLETE TRAVEL BOOK

Revised and Updated

Photographs by Bob and Ira Spring

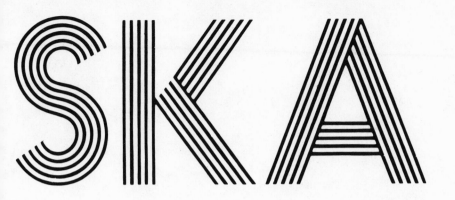

SKA

Norma Spring

COLLIER BOOKS

A Division of Macmillan Publishing Co., Inc.

NEW YORK

COLLIER MACMILLAN PUBLISHERS

LONDON

Library of Congress Cataloging in Publication Data
Spring, Norma.
Alaska: the complete travel book.
Includes index.
I.   Alaska—Description and travel—1959
Guide-books.
[F902.3.S67   1975]   917.98′04′5   75-20229
ISBN 0-02-098650-5

Alaska: The Complete Travel Book was originally published in a hardcover edition by
Macmillan Publishing Co., Inc.

First Collier Books Edition 1979

Macmillan Publishing Co., Inc.
866 Third Avenue, New York, N.Y. 10022
Collier Macmillan Canada, Ltd.

Printed in the United States of America

Acknowledgments

IT would take another chapter to acknowledge fully all the friends, acquaintances, companies, and individuals involved in various phases of the growing travel industry who helped us with this book. The interest they have shown throughout its progress, and contributions they have made through letters, travel and news releases, brochures, as well as personal conversations, have been invaluable as well as encouraging.

All the photographs, both black and white and color, were taken by Bob and Ira Spring. (Ira is Bob's twin brother.) Since I travel with Bob, almost all of the pictures for this book were taken by him. Alaska Airlines furnished all of Bob's color photographs and the color separations.

Many contributors are mentioned in the book, I hope readers who are stimulated enough to plan a trip to Alaska might someday cross paths with them. Outstanding help has come from Mike Miller, a fellow member of the Society of American Travel Writers, members of the Alaska Division of Tourism, past and present, and various transportation media serving Alaska.

Many travelers in Alaska, singly and on tours, have been part of the research. Their comments—good and bad—whenever and wherever we had occasion to meet and discuss Alaska, have contributed more than they realize to shaping and sharpening our perspective of the ever-changing travel picture.

We hope this book will remain useful as a "travel preparation" piece, even though Alaska continues to develop at jet speed. We have tried to depict the state "the way it is," a place where people can visit, choosing their own means and style, and come away feeling they have had a wonderfully warm, personal travel adventure in a unique setting.

We are convinced that Alaska's charm is intrinsically tied in with the basic ingredients that make up the "Great Land" and shape up its friendly people. We are optimistic that Alaska might be able to maintain this pleasant "travel climate" for some time to come.

Finally, I wholeheartedly acknowledge that without the Alaska-sized support, encouragement, and assistance proffered by my family—Bob, Terry, Jackie, and Tracy—this book might not have "accumulated."

I hereby dedicate it to all of them, with love.

NORMA SPRING

Contents

Prologue

In our family, "Alaska" is a magic word. Whenever evoked, it has the power to lift our spirits. It also loosens our tongues and causes a strong side reaction—itchy feet. All five of us get an immediate urge to head north to that huge and varied state up in the far northwest corner of our continent.

Our favorite people are relatives, friends, acquaintances, and strangers who happen to let drop our magic word. We like them to lead out with: "Alaska? What do all of you find so fascinating about Alaska?" That's when we cut loose and let them have it—right in the ears.

To us, Alaska is unsurpassable, and so is a travel experience there—our personal conclusion as chronic Alaska travelers. And so we start with the scenery, created on the grandest scale imaginable, and then we point out how amazingly varied it all is. There are vistas of snow-capped mountains, sparkling blue-hued glaciers, smoking volcanic cones. We find solitude and beauty both in the vast green Southeast Alaska forests and in their opposite, the seemingly endless stretches of low-growing Arctic tundra. In the relatively few places that man has so far settled, nature has quickly adapted to the artifacts of civilization and blended them with the background. And each gold rush ghost town or tiny isolated hamlet or native village or booming new city has its own all-Alaskan but unique flavor.

As we warm to our subject we begin to present a few superlatives. Within Alaska are the northernmost projection (Point Barrow) and the highest mountain (Mount McKinley) of North America. In midsummer the days are the longest, up to twenty-four hours in the Arctic. With its 586,412 square miles—more than twice as many as Texas—Alaska is easily the largest state in the Union.

Alaskans have mixed feelings about a diminutive: Alaska is the smallest state in population—about four hundred thousand recent estimate (and growing fast). To visitors like us this is an attraction. We delight in the feeling that here is almost infinite space for roaming, for pursuing a hobby, for developing a project. The possibilities are endless, for Alaska still has room for individualists —which leads nicely into our next point.

It is not scenery, superlatives, or space alone that make Alaska a fascinating state to visit. It is also the quality—if not the quantity— of the people. Hard-working, outgoing, and hospitable, they give the state its mood, its tempo, and its vitality. They welcome the visitor and want him to like Alaska. They take time to answer his questions, give him directions, and tell him about their state. They have helped us find accommodations for the night when necessary, or directed us to their favorite bush pilot or guide. Some of our happiest memories result from occasions when our Alaskan friends have dropped everything and come along with us.

This brings us to the purpose of this book. We have tried to catch the mood of Alaska by giving the reader a wide variety of impressions: our own, those of other travelers, and those of residents. It is our intent to prepare the would-be Alaska traveler for what he might encounter in our 49th state and give him practical tips on getting around up there. We hope our words will put the prospective traveler in a frame of mind either to cope with or to endure (and enjoy!) whatever the unpredictable land has to offer.

We would like to reassure the hesitant visitor, to whom Alaska may yet seem remote and inaccessible. Her largest cities, Anchorage and Fairbanks, are on the international jet routes. Cruise ships and ferries ply regularly scheduled routes along her southern coastline, beginning from Canadian ports as well as from Seattle, Los Angeles, and San Francisco. Paved highways connect inland cities. Travel, especially by air, is an addiction with Alaskans. Visitors soon get "hooked" and find themselves on every type of aircraft from jets down to small charter planes. Plane travel within Alaska is probably much more popular than in other states. We know at least one Eskimo, for example, who cannot drive a car but flies his own plane.

In Alaska's open spaces there seems to be something appealing to everyone. You can just relax, or you can fish, hunt, ride, swim, golf, ski (both snow and water), cruise, pan for gold, photograph, birdwatch, and beachcomb. We especially enjoy exploring beaches. Alaska, with its thousands of miles of sea-nibbled coast, is a beachcomber's delight. Sea gifts are abundant in the form of driftwood, round glass or plastic floats borne by the warm Japan Current from Japanese fishing nets, wood burls to be polished for table tops, and shells: abalone, crab, clam, and starfish. We pick up rocks, all shapes and sizes, from beaches all the way up to and including the Arctic. The best ones we enhance by polishing and we toss the culls into flowerbed borders around our house for some geologist to ponder a thousand or so years hence.

Experiences "off the beaten track" are encouraged. We feel that if some remote spot sounds intriguing, it is worth the extra time, effort, and expense to get there. Chances are others have wandered there already, and there are many bush flying operations that cater to more adventuresome travelers. If you ask around you will always find someone who goes there.

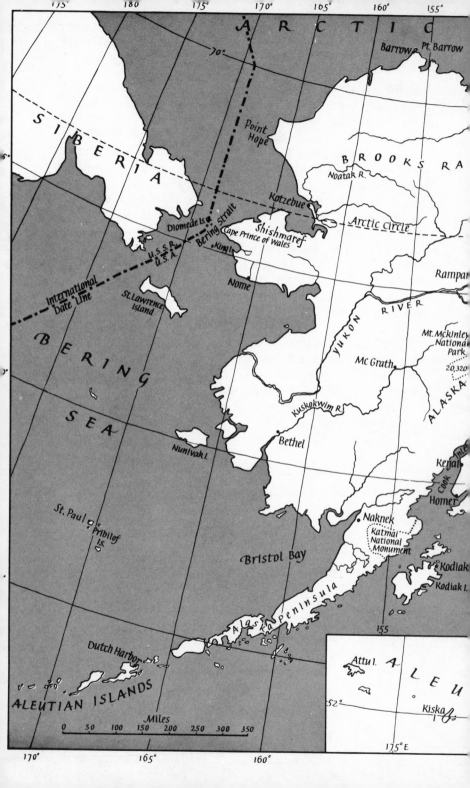

ALASKA

1 Some Facts of Alaskan Life

OUR facts of Alaskan life will have to start with a true confession: we have not seen *all* of Alaska yet, though we have been working on the project for over twenty years. We estimate that it would take more than a lifetime, partly because we can't resist revisiting our favorite places as we add new ones.

"We" is our family group: my photographer husband, Bob, and our three children: Terry, Jacqueline, Tracy Ann, and Alyeska, our Alaska-born husky dog. Bob and I work on a freelance basis. Because we are all willing to put Bob's picture-taking work first, we have been allowed to go along most of the time and "help." We enjoy traveling and working together as a family; it has been our recreation and our way of life.

Since 1952, we have made scores of trips to Alaska at all seasons, using every type of conveyance, sleeping in various shelters from luxury hotels to isolated forest huts to our own tent. Some of our trips have lasted three months, reluctantly terminated just in time to meet school and other deadlines. The shortest was a jet flight from Seattle to Sitka for lunch, returning the same day.

The cautious decision to make our first picture-taking trip to Alaska in 1952 was based on economics. At that time, anywhere outside our continent and anywhere we could not drive was definitely out, but we needed to expand our scope of travel. We gambled that we could travel in Alaska in the style to which we were accustomed (camping) and keep within our limited budget. Our only child was three-year-old Terry, already an enthusiastic veteran camper, and he quickly caught "Alaska fever" through exposure to us. (We think the girls contracted it prenatally.)

All three children still consider Alaska one big, wonderful campground. For years they didn't realize there was any other way to travel in Alaska. If you ask them today they will tell you that car camping is their favorite mode of family travel. A family can car camp their way in Alaska very enjoyably, and also relatively inexpensively, thus saving money for those fascinating areas such as the Arctic, Glacier Bay, and isolated forest camps that are still inaccessible by car.

On our first trip we followed the same plan that we advise today: we used as many types of transportation and routes as we had time for and could afford. Our first trip was in pre-ferry days, so we started from Seattle on an Alaska Steamship Company ship, then carrying both passengers and freight. We intended to see as much of the country as possible, then drive back on the Alaska Highway.

Our station wagon, full of camping gear, food, and photographic supplies, was shipped as freight, and we sailed in comfort up the beautiful Inside Passage route, a perfect introduction to Alaska. Pampered and relaxed by shipboard luxury, we disembarked at Seward, scenically situated at Resurrection Bay on the Kenai Peninsula. We were quickly initiated into the hazards of early-in-the-season (May) car travel on the Kenai Peninsula. No one had told us that during a certain period of the spring thaw dirt roads became jelly. That is how we learned firsthand about the friendly, helpful, hospitable side of Alaskans. We set up our camp and visited with our Alaskan neighbors each time we had to wait while road crews rebuilt the road.

Road conditions have greatly improved since those days. Though surprises are always possible to test the derring-do side of your nature, for the most part roads are paved and gas stations and places to stay are adequately frequent. Though Alaskans have already celebrated the passing of a century since the Purchase from Russia, the image of Alaska that arose from ancient congressional debates still haunts the Alaska Division of Tourism (the state's official dispenser of information). Visitors, the number per year almost equal to the population, are dispelling the idea that Alaska today is isolated, hard to reach, and difficult to get around in. It may still take considerable stamina to live in Alaska, but you don't have to be rugged to travel there, especially in the summer.

The fact is that ways and means of travel and access routes are becoming more numerous and less demanding all the time. An inquiry at any travel-connected company or travel agent serving Alaska will bring a deluge of excellent brochures capable of keeping you in a happy state of planning for weeks. Your choice of accommodations and mode of travel will depend on how independent or gregarious you are and will be limited only by the time and, of course, the money you have.

As for Alaska being rugged, the "little old lady with sneakers" could have been invented in Alaska. We have seen many of her for years all over the state, and in some real fortitude-testing situations. We remember one mild-looking soul in her mid-seventies whom we met on a state ferry deck. She was headed for her home in California. She had already been all the way to Point Barrow, at the top of our continent, carrying nothing but a bulging and battered valise and using only public transportation. Typically, she was loaded with literature and enthusiastically planning her next trip. One of our favorite characters is a middle-aged, one-legged woman who periodically makes the rounds of the state, over rough terrain or smooth, with little more trouble than on home ground.

Statistics show that a surprising number of retired people are attracted to Alaska. They may winter in Florida or California, but they head for the promise of adventure and wide-open spaces in the far north in summer. Some travel independently in campers, cars, boats, or planes. Others go along in caravans or tour groups. Regardless of how they travel, they seldom express other than complete enthusiasm for both country and people.

Being able to drive to Alaska from the "lower" states is as important to many family travelers as it is to us. It is also intriguing to add an international flavor to your trip without going outside of the continent. By car you have to go through about two thousand miles of Canadian territory; by boat through Canadian waters. Though it is necessary to go through customs, it mostly is just a formality, and some sort of identification is all that is required.

Boundaries are harder to define by air, but the pilot usually alerts his passengers to approximate aerial borders.

Another travel advantage in Alaska that most Americans find appealing is the lack of a language barrier. Alaskans sound just like westerners, or southerners, or easterners, depending on their origins. They have been developing some colorful idioms, including words from native tongues, that are particularly apt for their communication needs, and that are easily adopted by "Cheechakos" —a cheechako is anyone fresh from "Outside," which means anywhere beyond Alaskan borders. You are bound to come back with your speech spiced with some Alaska jargon, especially if you have children.

Even natives in far Eskimo outposts have been exposed to English. Except for some of the older people, they use the language well, though sometimes in a more literal sense than we do. Though friendly, they are not inclined to be chatty. Eskimo children may understand Eskimo, having been exposed in preschool years to Eskimo-speaking grandparents, but once they start school, they usually want to forget their native tongue and go along with the crowd. It will probably not be many years until the native languages are obsolete.

So there is no language barrier, and there are no racial barriers, either. Alaska today, like Hawaii, seems to be a well-integrated state. It is a melting pot of many races and people from other parts of the United States as well as other countries. As far as we have been able to observe, there is no discrimination because of age, language, or physical handicap. Eskimo, Indian, Aleut, Japanese, Negro, German, Scot, Irishman, Scandinavian—whatever—all happily share their vast state.

We hope all this encourages you to travel in Alaska. Now let us tell you about the state in more detail.

THE LAND

"Everyone has a map of Alaska on his right hand," says Mike Miller, Juneau, freelance writer and state legislator. "Stretch your thumb down for the Panhandle of Southeast Alaska, leave your forefinger extended for the Gulf of Alaska and on to the Aleutian

Island chain, then bend over the top three fingers for the swing around the Arctic Coast and the huge Interior."

Size

Alaska's distinctive shape is easy to describe; indicating size is another matter. It is big—even Texas, relegated to second place, will admit that. In fact, "Alaska" was derived from the name the Aleuts gave to the juge peninsula jutting into the Arctic seas, and it means "the Great Land." It is hard to describe the magnitude of this land. Statistics are useful only in comparisons; the idea is to gain a perspective on size so that travelers will allow enough time to enjoy their visit. One way is to give as many types of measurement as possible.

Alaska's 586,412 square miles could hold several European countries. One of its glaciers, the Malaspina, is larger than Rhode Island. Parceled out in lots, each state resident could have over a square mile to himself. We'll have to qualify this by mentioning that the state population is the smallest in the United States, and that some land parcels are tied up in unusable mountain ranges and muskeg. But so far, for both living and visiting purposes, there is plenty of elbow room in Alaska.

Alaska wins the vertical award, too, playing king of the mountain with 20,320-foot Mount McKinley, highest peak on the North American continent. There are several other peaks, not quite so high but equally impressive, among Alaska's perpetually snowclad mountain ranges. Bounded by oceans and seas on three sides, Alaska is a sailor's paradise, with thousands of islets, inlets, and bays that add up to a coastline one and a half times as long as the combined coastlines of the "South 48" states.

Time zones

Another sort of measurement is quite confusing in Alaska—time. Alaska is big enough and western and northern enough to include four time zones within its boundaries. The clock is set back an hour for each fifteen degrees of longitude westward. To the north, where the lines of longitude converge toward the Pole, this means there are

Mount McKinley, 20,320 feet in elevation, is the highest peak on the North American continent. The view is across Wonder Lake, near public campground and Camp Denali, Mount McKinley National Park.

Pacific, Alaska Yukon, Alaska-Hawaii, and Bering Sea time zones. The farther west you go the earlier it gets, and it is possible to approach the point (called the International Dateline) where you can actually look into tomorrow and Asia.

If you start for Alaska from the east coast of the United States, you will have to allow for the appropriate time changes across the country, and also allow for daylight saving time when in effect. Set your watch back an hour for every time change as you move westward. Juneau, representing Southeast Alaska, is on the same time as Seattle, Pacific Time. In Anchorage, which is almost as far west as Hawaii, it will be two hours earlier than in Juneau. At Nome, on the Bering Sea, it will be three hours earlier than in Juneau. Next zone to the west is tomorrow, across the International Dateline. But rather than strain our brains, we just check our watches with the first local clock we see on arriving at a new destination. Our youngsters were amused to discover that on a direct flight to Anchorage from Seattle, according to the airport clock, which was on daylight saving time, we arrived five minutes before we left.

Related to time we should mention here the Alaska-sized days. In summer the hours of daylight stretch, depending on how far north you are, to almost twenty-four hours, a wonderful dividend for the summer vacationist. At Fairbanks on the longest day of the year, June 21, there is a baseball game through midnight, using only the midnight sun, no electric lights. Of course the reverse is true in the dead of winter; and at Point Barrow, the sun doesn't rise in midwinter for the same number of days that it doesn't set in midsummer.

Five physical regions

Descriptions of the shape and size of Alaska give no indication of its real character, the diversity of its physical characteristics, and its sometimes violent nature. Geographical features divide it into five sections, each presenting such a different face that it is hard to believe that all are parts of the same state. The beautiful verdant Southeast Panhandle, the more populated Gulf of Alaska area, the dry Interior, and the barren Arctic, frozen for eight months of the year, are rapidly becoming year-round visitor destinations.

The fifth region, the Aleutian chain dribbling far to the west, is the least visited. This fact may send certain adventuresome people rushing to buy a ticket. It is possible, too. The area is served thrice weekly by pioneer bush Reeve Aleutian Airways, based in Anchorage. The Aleutians are a great place for sea and bird life. My husband and Mike Frome, an internationally known writer on travel and conservation subjects, once spent several fascinating days there observing and photographing sea lions and bird life. If you are prepared for unusually severe weather conditions, with roof-lifting winds, impenetrable fogs, and rain and cold, and for transportation schedules that vary accordingly, there is no problem. It is necessary to make arrangements ahead to be sure you will have lodging. If you talk with someone stationed there voluntarily, a naturalist, or a fisherman, he is likely to be enthusiastic about this unusual face of

Alaska. Otherwise, most people would agree with the original explorers, the Russians, that for visiting purposes most people would be happier farther inland from this element-buffeted barrier between the Bering Sea and the north Pacific Ocean.

Natural resources and economy

Alaska is a very rich land in the first stages of development. Its resources have barely been tapped by the exploitation and sporadic bonanzas of the past. New industries, undreamed of a few years ago, are being developed and explored. Some, like gold and furs, have fallen by the wayside, but may revive someday. Others, like petroleum, fishing, and timber, are expanding.

Commercial fishing, a top moneymaker, includes all types of salmon, halibut, and crab (king-size, of course), and tasty Alaskan scallops and shrimps. Fishing in lake, stream, and salt water is a visitor's delight.

Minerals and oil explorations are going on in all sorts of places: in the Arctic, underwater, in holes in the mountains, and on the Kenai Peninsula near Anchorage. Gas burnoffs from oil wells operating along Cook Inlet are brightly evident at night in the winter months and also show up in summer's dusk. After years of delay since North Slope oil probing and discoveries, the oil pipeline is completed and in use. The distribution of oil is now at the top of Alaska's economy. The natural gas pipeline is pending and the crescendo of activity is expected in the early 1980s.

Though Alaska and Japan feud over fish, they see eye to eye on forests. In twenty-five years Japan has managed a peaceful invasion of Alaska after her abortive attempt to use the Aleutians as stepping stones to conquest in World War II. The weapon this time is money, invested in pulp mills and logs. After a century of looking to the eastern United States for markets and investors with lukewarm response, Alaska has been "Orienting" herself. She is happy to sell her abundant natural resources and allow needy foreign markets like Japan to invest their capital where it will do the most good.

Gold, oil, fish, and timber can be measured and their value backed up or refuted by statistics. What about certain intangible resources? Conservationists are unhappy about the industrial march on the Alaskan wilderness. They would be happy to see a large portion preserved for future visitors, perhaps the whole state as a "state of recreation." It is hard to measure the value of things you have to see and feel to appreciate—wide-open spaces, trees, mountains, lakes, and even fresh pure air to breathe. Tourism, listed third in Alaska's economy, depends on natural resources too. The number of visitors increases fast, perhaps faster than Alaskans are prepared for, and the aim is a flourishing year-round tourism industry.

Agriculture and animal husbandry are last on the list, and so far meager. Attempts have been made to graze sheep on Aleutian grass, and some beef cattle are herded on Kodiak Island. The University of Alaska had a musk ox farm, and it is noted for experimentation in Arctic agriculture. The Matanuska Valley near Anchorage has gained a reputation for its huge vegetables which are displayed at an annual fair. Generally speaking, however, Alaska's terrain and climate are not conducive to many profitable farming ventures.

Volcanoes, earthquakes, and floods

There is another facet of the character of the land to be considered—its occasional violence. Alaska is a subcontinent still in the making, and when creative forces are at work, nature doesn't care if you are resident or visitor. Those who live there take "happenings" in stride, figuring the land is neither for them nor against them; it's up to them to measure up or go elsewhere. Visitors would do well to adopt the same philosophy.

Alaska lies in the Pacific Rim earthquake zone. The 1964 Good Friday quake pinpointed Alaska on the map, once and for all, for those who were not quite sure where our immense forty-ninth state was located. It happened to strike in the most populated area, the Gulf of Alaska and vicinity. One whole town, Valdez, relocated; the others rebuilt. Few residents gave up and moved away, and travelers have continued to come in ever-increasing numbers.

There is evidence of volcanic activity, and there is periodic flooding in certain areas. When a flood occurs in a more populated area, as it did in mid-summer 1967 in Fairbanks, it makes news. The residents simply pitched in and cleaned up and battened down for the usual Interior winter, made tougher by the catastrophe. The tourists continued to come and go, mostly undaunted.

We met a group on tour soon after the flood, in the lobby of the Nome Nugget Inn. They were celebrating someone's seventieth birthday. Knowing they had come from Fairbanks, we asked how they fared. It seemed that a funny thing happened to them on the way to the airport. They were evacuated from the bus by an army "duck" just before all their luggage along with the bus was lost. This cheery bunch had been in the same clothes for five days, but though given a chance to drop out, they all voted to proceed to the Arctic as planned. To them, most of them middle-aged or better, Alaska *was* adventure, and they were not about to miss any of it.

John Hopkins Glacier, one of many in Glacier Bay National Monument.

One thrilled lady bragged she had hit the jackpot. Besides the flood in Fairbanks, she had felt a small earth tremor in Anchorage —"like a truck going by, only no truck!"

There are two Alaskan national monuments that are evidence of the violent, uncompromising nature of the land, but they are molded by directly opposing forces. Katmai National Monument with its Valley of Ten Thousand Smokes, located opposite Kodiak Island and at the base of the Aleutian Island chain as it heads out to the west, was formed by violent volcanic eruptions followed by sand and lava flows as recently as this century. Glacier Bay National Monument, in upper Southeast Alaska, is not much older; it has been exposed by the recession of the area's mighty glaciers in the last hundred years or so. Both monuments are accessible by plane and boat, and each in its own way is worthwhile and fascinating to visit.

TOWNS AND CITIES

Though civilization has steadily been encroaching, it has hardly made a dent in Alaska's vast expanses of land. This is especially noticeable when traveling by air. Alaska still has that fresh, unspoiled, "unused" look.

One might compare a flight over Europe with one over Alaska. Clusters of towns in Europe blend into large cities. Farms of various sizes nudge each other, sometimes separated by an estate with a stand of timber generations removed from its first growth. Even the mountain valleys are peopled or cultivated. You are rarely out of sight of civilization in Europe. But in Alaska the towns are few and far between. Comparing Alaska's terrain to that of comparable northern European countries is like turning back the clock a few centuries.

Southeast Alaska is somewhat like the American West of about a hundred years ago.

Most towns are still small, ranging from a few hundred population to medium-sized ones up to sixteen thousand. Some look roughly like western frontier towns, say a setting for "Gunsmoke." The boardwalks, unpaved streets, and false fronts are there, part of twentieth-century Alaska, yet each town is different enough to have its own individual stamp; it cannot be said of any small town in Alaska that if you have seen one you have seen them all.

The few large towns are just as distinctive. Anchorage appears quite cosmopolitan; Fairbanks has some big modern buildings; Juneau, the capital, is bursting with politicians. But they all manage to give themselves away: at heart they are still small towns.

Perhaps this has a lot to do with the natural outgoing friendliness of the "natives" (meaning *all* Alaska residents, not just those born there). Or maybe it is the ever-present old-new contrast of log cabins standing in the protective shade of skyscrapers. Perhaps a nostalgic clinging to a colorful past is competing with the inevitable drive toward a most promising future.

At any rate, one feels that the whole land is on the threshold of exciting things to come. It seems to say, "I'm still growing up. I'm not sophisticated like other places. And because I feel unique in this particular place and time in the world, maybe I never *will* become like the others!"

THE PEOPLE

Alaskans are a motley collection: descendants of the original Alaskans, descendants of those who settled for various reasons after Alaska became part of the United States, plus today's evergrowing influx from the "Outside."

The original Alaskans

Though the subject is open to debate, there is evidence to support the theory that people migrated to Alaska from the Asian continent twelve thousand to twenty-five thousand years ago. It is believed that they walked across on ice or land bridges looking for greener pastures at a. time when the going was hard in their homeland. At any rate, approximately one-fifth of Alaska's civilian population stems from these original Alaskans. They are divided into three main groups.

Eskimos are the most numerous. They inhabit the coasts of the

Bering Sea and the Arctic, Little Diomede Island, and the Yukon River and Kuskokwim River deltas. The smallest remaining group are the Aleuts, who were ruthlessly persecuted during Russian rule. There are few full-blooded Aleuts left. Their villages are in the Pribilof Islands, the Alaska Peninsula, and Aleutian Island chain. Southeast Alaska and the Interior are Indian territory. The Tlingits, Haidas, and Tsimshians once lived royally off the land. The Tlingits, especially, were fierce fighters and developed a high artistic culture. The Interior Athapascans were nomads and kept to themselves.

All are Alaskans, and officially citizens since a 1924 act of Congress. More recently, the settling of native land claims and the forming of native corporations for investing newly acquired capital has brightened their future considerably. They are all busy shifting gears, trying to make the transition to modern ways. Many are adjusting well and hold their own as contributing members in a new economy. In other cases, relieving the pangs of transition presents a knotty problem.

Other residents

Regardless of how, why, or when they came, the land begins to shape the residents. And if they don't shape up, they ship out, as the saying goes.

We think we can characterize Alaskans by certain traits we have noticed from our own exposure over the years. High on the list is extreme friendliness—not the nosy kind, but rather a genuine interest in other people. They are inclined to take people at face value; you are a friend until you prove otherwise. If a person needs help, it is given—and questions, if any, are asked afterward. This is probably the outgrowth of living in an undeveloped, sometimes rugged and violent land. They have learned to be very adaptable. So far, the population is still small enough and scattered enough so that people (including visitors) have a chance to know each other as individuals.

This outgoing attitude puzzles their more reserved visitors from "Outside." All we can say is that it is genuine. If someone you know advises you to look up an Alaskan friend, don't hesitate. If, after sharing some convivial hours, you ask your new friend to be sure to look you up when he comes your way, he is likely to do so. Hospitality is a two-way street. The mere fact that you are interested enough to visit the big state and show your admiration is enough to win friends and influence people in Alaska.

One other characteristic we should prepare you for is the boundless energy of Alaskans. Everyone seems to be doing more than one job at a time and has taken a crack at a variety of careers. Maybe it is the invigorating climate, or just the fact that there is so much to be done by so few people, but the pace is fast. In summer, Alaskans seem to regulate their sleeping time by the length of the night, and there is little or no night for almost three months. Fortunately, the Alaskan drive appears to be contagious. We are not the only visitors who discover that we are keeping Alaskan hours—an almost round-the-clock whirl that would put us in the hospital at home!

Well-known citizen Walter Hickel is only one of many examples of tremendous Alaskan drive leading to success. His story is pure Horatio Alger. He arrived in Alaska in the 1950s with less than 50 cents, nurtured it to a fortune, and capped it by being elected governor for 1968. As he was buckling down to the complexities of governing our largest state and stewarding its abundant resources, President Nixon tapped him for the cabinet. Secretary of the Interior Hickel was too Alaskan for the regime. He chafed at waiting six months for an appointment to air his views to the boss, and so he aired them publicly to the point of being fired. Meanwhile, back in Alaska, conservation leader Hickel aspires to state office again—or perhaps higher—as he monitors his growing assets, now estimated at many millions, in deluxe Anchorage and Fairbanks hotels.

We'll put in a word for some special fliers, too. Old bush pilots, like soldiers, never die, they say. Instead they become airline executives. Among the noteworthy, some now retired, are: Art Woodley of Pacific Northern, which merged with Western Airlines; the Wien brothers; Ray Petersen of Northern Consolidated, merged with Wien Air Alaska; and Merle "Mudhole" Smith of Cordova Airlines; and Shell Simmons and Bob Ellis of Alaska Coastal, both airlines merging with Alaska Airlines. The years 1967-68 saw the urge-to-merge strike most Alaska airlines.

There is one maverick, Bob Reeve, still running his own operation, unmerged, out the Aleutian Island chain. His summer tour, from Anchorage to St. Paul village in the Pribilof Islands for the annual homecoming of the fur seals, is spectacular.

Tourists

The word "tourism" usually smacks of dollars and cents and commercialism. Though it is a rapidly growing industry in Alaska and, of course, important to the state's economy, we feel that tourism in Alaska is still on a very personal basis.

There is no way of measuring the losses a primitive people suffers in making a rapid transition to modern ways. In Alaska, tourism may prove to be a most valuable tool for preserving worthwhile elements of native culture and therefore minimizing these losses. Invariably, visitors exposed to both Eskimo and Indian life are genuinely interested, and the native people respond to this. The dancing, singing, carving, beluga hunting, fishing, games, and blanket tossing—an old practice described in the chapter on the Arctic—are still authentic. Many natives are willing to maintain their customs, for tourism's sake, and base their living on them. However, how long the past will be perpetuated for this reason is anybody's guess. Perhaps only for the next few years will one be able to observe both the past and this transition period. Though it is possible, with the help of big companies, that the natives themselves might want to continue some of the old ways, you can't blame them for wanting what appears to be the "better life" as it advances upon them. Unless arts and crafts are passed down to each generation, together with a healthy respect for skills that may no longer actually be needed, a culture will die.

Allied Alaskans

There are others who should be mentioned before we leave the subject of people. They may not live there full-time now, but they commute often. They are concerned about everything that happens in Alaska and they have contributed enough to be entitled to some kind of honorary label—so we will call them "allied Alaskans."

Two favorite "allied Alaskans" are Bob and Lori Giersdorf. He is president of the new and rapidly expanding Alaska Tour and Marketing Services. Lori is vice president. They are innovators, perpetually scouting, sampling, and adding worthwhile destinations, tours, and sightseeing features to the all-over Alaska travel scene.

We first met Bob when he was vice president, traffic and sales, for Alaska Airlines' special projects. These were usually offbeat, like Arctic winter tours and the series of summer charter flights from Anchorage to Siberia, when the "iron curtain" parted briefly to allow the far west gateways to the U.S.S.R. That's how we became aware that he is jet-propelled and as competitive as a whole team of racing huskies. His positive approach is contagious, as he manages to keep "can't" and "impossible" eliminated from the vocabulary by not expecting anyone else to do anything he couldn't or wouldn't do himself.

Over the years, my Bob considers Lori's Bob the best photographer's assistant he has had, from wild animal stalking in Mount McKinley Park to chasing a herd of reindeer in the Arctic to just the right spot for pictures, in spite of a driving rainstorm. Bob S. says there are many times he wishes that he had turned his camera slightly and included Bob G. in the setup. There was a time, for example, when he waded happily out in the Bering Sea in shiny shoes and snappy suit just to steady the model, an oomiak, bobbing around in the brisk wind. Of such stuff are Alaska travel executives made.

Another allied Alaskan is Norman Kneisel, affectionately known as Mr. K. He is based in Portland, Oregon, and is especially noted for his Green Carpet Tours. Mr. K knew by the time he was twelve years old that there was a future in using buses for recreational travel. It came to him when he used to stand on a soda-pop crate to reach the counter to help the agent sell bus tickets. He kept his dream, tested and promoted his theories, and in 1959 launched the first escorted bus tour to Alaska. This was his proving ground. His carefully planned, well-guided, luxury-coach tours all over the forty-ninth state have kept happy customers coming back for more and have revolutionized the bus-travel industry. Mr. K's buses are hard to overlook. They are the ones with the colorful totem poles painted horizontally on the sides.

And there are many other allied Alaskans. You'll find a lot of them mentioned throughout this book, as well as listed in the Travel and Information Round-Up section.

TRAVEL IN ALASKA

Early travelers

In the early part of the eighteenth century, Russia became interested in exploring its neighbor to the east. The motivation was mostly curiosity. Czar Peter the Great was interested in geography and wondered if the two continents might still be joined far to the north. He also wanted to find out whether there was really a huge mass of unknown territory to explore to the east. He hired a Danish sea captain, Vitus Bering, to find out.

Bering's interest in his assignment turned lukewarm when he sailed far enough to satisfy himself there was a sea between the continents, and a series of incidents prevented him from locating much unknown territory to the east. On his return he announced that there was no good reason for further exploration. However, much interest had been generated by this first expedition and several armchair geographers had been at work with their maps. They discredited Bering's report and plans were started for a massive expedition.

This second expedition, which took place before the middle of the eighteenth century, might be considered the first ship cruise to Alaska. Bering was the tour leader and he was forced to take along some tourists. They were men interested in making scientific studies, if the new land was found. Among them was Georg W. Steller, a German biologist.

The land was found, but disaster overtook the ship and all surviving hands were forced to spend the winter on a treeless island off the Siberian coast. Bering and many others died. However, Steller's knowledge of edible vegetation and sea life enabled some of the crew to survive, to rebuild their boat, and eventually to return to Russia. Steller made a complete survey of the flora and fauna of the region, notes that are used to this day. A native bird is named for him—the Steller jay. No doubt Steller's adventure travel story, plus a cargo of furs, including beautiful sea-otter skins, helped Russia decide that the great land to the east, which they named Russian America, was ready for further travel—and colonization.

During the next century, visitors did not exactly pour into the north country, but those who did left their mark. They called it exploring, but it was really only another name for tourism, an excuse to see the country, often on an expense account provided by the country they represented. Ambitious governments were looking for toeholds for settlement, or a chance to extract some wealth in the form of items of trade. The Russians sailed and sold and colonized as far south as California, but the warmer-blooded Spaniards had little interest in heading north. However, they appreciated the ice that Russia exported in quantity from Alaska's plentiful supply, and the fine bells cast in Russian-American foundries which they used in their California missions.

The English, including the well-known Captain Cook, plied the northern inlets and seas. England had visions of profitable colonies. The Americans and Scandinavians were intrigued by the whaling. Indians from the south traveled up into Southeast Alaska to Tlingit country and vice versa. The souvenirs they brought back were quite often people, for slaves.

In the hundred years since William Seward negotiated the purchase of Alaska from Russia, more and more tourists visited the huge land that was at first described as Seward's Folly, or Seward's Icebox. Most of them appear to have been about the same type as those who wandered there through the ages, eager and ready for adventure.

And so they still are. The biggest changes are in styles of travel—tremendous improvements in transportation. The choice as well as the price varies to accommodate almost any vacation budget. You can travel by jet, by car, or by boat. You can motorcycle or walk, if you wish; it's been done. For our general comments we will divide modern transportation facilities into three main categories: land, sea, and air.

Land travel

People who plan to travel mostly by land often want to make use of Alaska's camping facilities. They are excellent, perhaps not as numerous or as elaborate as you may be used to. Few trailer hookups and water systems are available except in private facilities. But this fact is offset, we think, because the campsites have some of the grandest camping scenery you will ever see. Camping in Alaska is not just for people with youngsters. You will see many senior citizens happily purring along in their campers. To many, Alaska is a place where, after retirement, they can head on their own for adventure. (See Roundup section at the end of the book for specific travel information sources.)

An important thing to remember when traveling in Alaska is to keep your cool when the unexpected comes up. As Alaskans will tell you, if something *can* happen, it usually does. Bear in mind that it is risky to estimate travel time according to mileage in Alaska. Allow extra time, so you won't get nervous about reaching your destination if the going is slower than anticipated. Perhaps a slight delay here and there will allow you to see something you might otherwise have missed.

Many travelers prefer to avoid driving responsibilities and go by one of the very fine Scenicruiser tours. Trips are well planned and can be as extensive as you wish, even including the Arctic, though, of course, the whole busload has to take to the air from either Anchorage or Fairbanks to go farther north.

Sea travel

Alaska has everything from small private boats to state ferries and luxurious cruise ships. Alaska state ferries are not to be confused with little river hoppers or island commuters carrying only a few vehicles. Most of the nine-ship fleet have names of mighty glaciers: the *Matanuska, Malaspina, Tustumena, Taku, LeConte, Columbia*—and they come Alaska-sized. Some can carry up to 200 vehicles and 1,000 passengers. They are well-equipped with bar, good food at reasonable prices in the dining salon, and informal snack bars. Cost, for example in 1978, Seattle to Skagway was $103 for one adult one way; $351 for the car. So far, bicycles ride free, and winter rates are lower all around. Staterooms are extra and limited (reserve ahead!).

However, everything is very informal. Ferry overnighters may

Alaska State Ferry in fjord-like Inside Passage, south of Haines-Port Chilkoot, on way to the state capital, Juneau.

sleep in reclining chairs or roll out sleeping bags on deck. There are public showers for those who do not have staterooms with those facilities. Our family has had many a cleanup on a ferry between ports-of-call on the Inside Passage, when we have camped our way through Southeast Alaska. It takes about thirty hours from Prince Rupert, B.C., to Skagway, Alaska. Many campers like to stop over and explore the towns along the way. By planning your itinerary ahead, you can arrange to be unloaded from the ferry, stay as long as you like, and then hop on a ferry another day.

The year-round Marine Highway gets very busy in summer during June, July, and August. Whether traveling the Southeast or

Southcentral system, make reservations, or allow extra waiting time at port cities.

It was forecast months ahead of the season that cruise ships would bring almost 23,000 visitors to Alaska during the summer of 1969. Eight luxuriously appointed cruise liners sailed from California, Washington, and Oregon north to Alaska in a record number of departures. In 1978, eleven ships with a mind-boggling range of prices and sailings, including some from Vancouver, B.C., approached triple the number of passengers. We were surprised to learn that history is again repeating itself. In an old brochure we noted that 1890 was also a phenomenal year for Alaska cruises. At that time, the main luxury advertised therein for the eleven-day and twenty-two-day cruises was "handsome staterooms including the new electric light bulb"!

Air travel

Development of air transportation since World War II has had a great deal to do with the development of Alaska. In tourism the impact has been particularly felt in the last few years. From the East Coast visitors may fly direct to the Anchorage or Fairbanks gateway from main terminals. By transferring to Alaska-bound planes at Seattle, they can have a wider choice of gateways—Sitka, Anchorage, Fairbanks, Ketchikan, or Juneau.

Anchorage is also a gateway for visitors arriving from Europe. Planes fly direct from leading European cities—Paris, Amsterdam, Copenhagen, Frankfurt, Hamburg, London, and Brussels. When Scandinavian Airlines introduced the first over-the-Pole flights via Alaska a little over fifteen years ago, it shortened the distance from this country to Europe, with an extra aesthetic bonus thrown in. Flying from Frankfurt to Anchorage in the fall, we were treated to two sunsets in one day, as well as a brilliant display of the northern lights.

In many cities, owning a private plane is the equivalent of having a second car in the garage anywhere else. A traveler starting from "Outside" is impressed by the variety of planes in which you can travel in just one day in Alaska. We have started with a jet from Seattle and before bedtime worked our way down through a

Constellation, a Convair, a PBY, a Grumman Goose, and finally a little five-passenger Cessna 185 float plane, from which you can really get on intimate terms with mountain goats and glaciers.

Our family's favorite plane is the Grumman Goose, partly because it has such a funny appearance. It is a small, stocky-looking amphibian holding eight people. It has a solid feel, and you can see the pilot up front, or maybe get to ride in the co-pilot's seat. It looks like a goose, and acts like one when it lands on the water with floats, then waddles up the ramp on wheels and appears to shake itself on dry land. Bob finds the Goose good for photography because it is steady and has good visibility. And I am reassured by this craft's ability to land on either land or water in a state where there are such wide expanses of both.

WEATHER AND CLOTHING

"Be sure to warn people about the weather," remarked one visitor busily panning for gold in the Arctic in the rain. It wasn't a complaint; all she had on her mind was that slacks and warm knitwear felt good in the brisker northern climate and on cool evenings. She is absolutely right, and to the items she recommends we would add easily-packed plastic rainwear you can keep handy. As a photographer, Bob is apt to be more aware of weather than most people. Weather can be frustrating if you are working on a picture assignment. That is exactly why the whole family likes to take plenty of time when we travel in Alaska. During weather waits we can always find something interesting to do, outdoors or in. No one pays much attention to Southeast Alaska's wetter-than-most weather. You just dress for it.

Alaska is no Hawaii, weather-wise, but its oppositeness is much of its charm. Actually, summers are very mild and pleasant, neither too hot nor too cold, and most of Alaska is suitable for year-round visiting. As for sunshine, there's lots of it. We are all living proof that you can get a tan in Alaska. And when weather is fair up there, it's breathtaking. The sky is bright-blue, the water sparkles, and the air is unbelievably unadulterated and fresh. People from congested, industrial "South 48" areas aren't geared for such atmospheric purity. As a Los Angeles travel agent remarked, taking a deep but cautious whiff, "This stuff is great, but you can't blame me for being suspicious of breathing air I can't *see!*"

Our advice on type of clothing and how much to take is: *travel light.* In many places you may be toting your own bags. Since we are always loaded down with Bob's camera equipment, we really keep clothing to a minimum, relying on the one-day dry cleaning and laundry services, or the self-service kind found all over Alaska now. Dress is strictly informal with the accent on comfort. The most you might need for dress-up occasions in larger cities would be a sport jacket or suit for men and a dressy dress for women. Slacks are perfectly in order, comfortable walking shoes are a necessity, and sweaters feel cozy in the evening. If you go up to the Arctic, the airlines will lend you a parka while you are there, so there is no need to pack extra coats.

ACCOMMODATIONS AND PRICES

Which comes first, the tourist or the facilities? At this particular stage in Alaska's development, the subject of accommodations generates some lively discussions. Some of them take place in the very early morning hours, between sleepy innkeepers and exhausted travelers. The distance on the map that could have been covered in six or seven hours on "South 48" highways took twelve or fourteen. The reserved room that the traveler thought would be waiting is now occupied by someone else. It has happened to us, but so far we have never had to sleep in the street.

By all means try to make reservations ahead—and verify them as you approach your destination and the day wears on. If you are with a tour group all this is taken care of. The hotel manager gets word that instead of a full house he has a hundred rooms to spare—the large group he was expecting is not going to make it. He has his problems as well as you.

Alaskans, especially those interested in the tourist industry, really *want* to provide adequate accommodations for their visitors and will go all out to do so. With this in mind, don't hesitate to ask for help. You may not get your first choice, or stay in the newest and fanciest. You may be passed around a bit. But sooner or later someone will come up with a place for you to lay your weary head. Sometimes the solution to the housing problem during busy seasons is informal, such as renting a room in a private home. Actually, visitors have found this experience enjoyable, and often learn about the area faster and better through association with a friendly family.

Inflation and the oil-rush-triggered population explosion affected prices and availability of tourist creature comforts. But now there's a breather between oil and gas pipeline construction that may last into the 1980s. New hotels, motels, parks, and campgrounds built and expanded to accommodate the mid-1970s workers influx are now welcoming visitors. Moreover, the spread between "South 48" and Alaska prices is shrinking. Some U.S. and many foreign travelers we encountered recently, such as Australians, Germans, and Japanese, considered Alaska a travel bargain now, compared to Europe. When we travel in Alaska we budget a least a fourth again as much for food as we would if we were traveling around our own state. We may come back with some money or may have to send for more, depending on how close we stick to our planned itinerary.

Prices we quote in various places in this book are the amounts we have paid. We can't guarantee you will find them the same, but they should give you a general idea of the cost of food and lodging. One reliable "rule of thumb" we *will* vouch for. When traveling in Alaska, never pass up food, drink, or "facilities" when proffered. It may sometimes be many hours before the next opportunity.

THE BEST TIME TO GO

To the question "When is the best time to visit Alaska?" we answer, "As soon as possible," while you can see it in transition. It is still primitive and pioneer, friendly, fascinating, and unspoiled, as it moves toward its destiny among more worldly neighbors.

The travel season is year-round. To people used to heading south for a winter vacation, the idea of heading north is a brand-new idea. Arctic winter travel had to wait until the logistics of transportation, supply and comfort, of utmost importance to visitors, were ironed out. Bob has long called the Bering Sea coast at Nome his Arctic Riviera; in the last few years many visitors are discovering that a frozen seashore under the midday sun provides the *new* travel experience they seek.

The happiest travelers in Alaska are those geared to expect and accept the unexpected—with gusto. It helps to have an adaptable nature and a touch of the pioneer spirit. We overheard an interesting exchange among three passengers, all in their upper seventies, during a PBY flight. Two of them were Bob's parents, enthralled with their first trip north; the other, former Alaska senator and governor Ernest Gruening. "Why didn't we come up here when we were *younger?*" Allena and E. B. Spring were saying. The senator's classic and loyal reply: "If a person came up here too young, he'd never go anywhere else—he'd think there was no other place in the world worth going to!"

2 Sitka, the Historic Gateway, and Southern Towns of the Panhandle

THE four-hundred-mile-long section of Alaska known as the Southeast Panhandle embraces all sizes and shapes of islands and a deep fjord-dented coastline. The islands are the tops of a submerged mountain range that make up the Alexander Archipelago. They form a network of navigable waterways that are a challenge to adventuresome sailors. They also protect the well-traveled Inside Passage, the main sea route to Alaska. Its scenery is little changed since Indians and traders plied the waters over a hundred years ago.

This Southeast Panhandle is so labeled because of its panhandle shape which is obvious when you look at a map of Alaska. This area's transition from backwater to mainstream dates from the start of the State Ferry System in 1963. Now, with regular ferry and plane service, cruise ships, and a great deal of good and justified publicity describing the recreational charms available throughout the Southeast, it is rapidly becoming an important visitor destination, even in winter. The climate is mild the year round, and though there may be more snow on the mountains, and the islands may be outlined with a winter snow necklace marking high tide, a visit in winter can be fun.

The economy, described aptly as "fish 'n' chips," is forging ahead, too. The chips in this case are wood chips, a by-product of the flourishing timber industry. They are used by two busy pulp mills, one built by Japanese interests.

Anyone who has an ice-snow-Eskimo concept of Alaska will think he is in the wrong state if he starts with the Panhandle. He'll see plenty of snow and ice the year round on spectacularly high mountains, but they are just the backdrop for beautiful marine views, forests, and fast-growing towns with industries geared to water and forests.

The original natives are Indian, culturally still more or less in transition. The other residents seem for the most part to come from almost everywhere except Alaska.

GETTING THERE

Access to Southeast Alaska is likely to depend only on sea and air transportation for a long time. The high, scenic coastal mountain barrier rules out land routes, though there is some talk of an island-hopping highway. Meanwhile, the Marine Highway, as the Inside Passage water route is named, is served by ferries and cruise ships, and it suffices. Main air access points are at Ketchikan, Sitka, and Juneau, with the takeoff point at Seattle. East Coast travelers will change planes there.

Overland travelers from the East Coast and points between can go by car or rail to Prince Rupert, B.C., where the Alaska State Ferry System begins. West Coast travelers can drive up through Canadian Cariboo country, heading west at Prince George for Prince Rupert. Alaskan ferries also depart from Seattle on a limited schedule. The regularly scheduled Canadian ferry *Queen of Prince Rupert* departs farther north from Vancouver Island, British Columbia. It is a twenty-hour journey to Prince Rupert, where passengers change to the Alaska ferries. Changes in ferry scheduling make it advisable to check current timetables and departure points when you plan your itinerary. The increasing number of cruise-ship sailings leave mainly from Vancouver, B.C., and some depart from Los Angeles and San Francisco.

Whether you travel by airplane, boat, or a happy combination, you'll be impressed by the size of this section of Alaska, and you will get the full impact of the way the rugged mountains cut the coast off from the interior. Looking in the other direction, you'll see peaks almost as formidable crowning the larger islands. These protective sentinels help explain the Southeast's mild, wet climate. The basin between catches and holds the record rainfalls that keep everything looking so fresh, lush, and green.

In the Southeast Panhandle are the towns ranking third, fourth, and fifth in size in Alaska. Number three is Juneau, the state capital. Number four, Ketchikan, is both an air and sea gateway. Sitka, bursting with history, is the newest jet air gateway. Geographically, Sitka is not a "southern" Panhandle town. However, we include it here because we feel its beautiful setting and historic background make Sitka a perfect introduction not only to the Southeast, but to all of Alaska.

SITKA

Glancing through a history of Sitka, it appears that every fifty years, give or take a few, something happens to shake up the residents, whoever they are at the time. Even its beginning was shaky. Early in the nineteenth century the barely settled Russians lost their scalps to the Indians. A couple of years later the Indians were repaid when they ran out of ammunition before the Russians did. For the next fifty years or so the town grew and thrived, a hub of commerce, social life, and even fashions.

Just as everything was going well, the residents heard the startling news that their town had been sold out from under them. The buyer of "Russian America" was the United States. Six months later, on October 18, 1867, the formal transfer ceremonies took place at Sitka, before the moist eyes of the mostly Russian townspeople.

The next fifty years were again shaky, troubled, and difficult. Sitka became the capital of Alaska (as the Americans renamed their purchase) but declined, and soon after the turn of the century, the seat of government was moved northeast to the young town of Juneau.

Another fifty years passed—a full century since the Purchase—and the residents were again shaken up, this time with joy and enthusiasm. Alaska Airlines' Golden Nugget jet service from Seattle to Sitka was inaugurated on a daily basis, effecting a modern renaissance and transforming the city into an air gateway to Alaska. After almost a century of being off the beaten track, it is heady stuff to find yourself a gateway and a member of the jet set.

Actually, Sitka is a logical choice for a historical gateway. Less than two hundred years of age, it is young as cities of the world are rated, but old for Alaska. It is fitting in another way that Sitka was chosen to inaugurate the jet gateway. Only about a century after Bering's first exploration of Alaska, a steam vessel was launched from Sitka's busy shipyards. No doubt it caused as much excitement as the first jet landing, which had the town jumping.

Approaching Sitka by air, it may occur to you to wonder where there is enough space to make an airport to accommodate a jet. That is a good question. As you fly over the myriad small islands, the fact that this portion of Southeast Alaska is an archipelago is apparent. You can see that the small, timbered, offshore islands protruding from the surface are really the tops of a sizable submerged mountain chain. Some slope off gradually, the shelves giving a varicolored tint to the water; others plunge steeply in deep underwater precipices. There are magnificent snow-covered ranges on the mainland side, and respectable-sized peaks, also snowy, rear up on the islands.

Sitka solved the airport problem by whittling out a field on Japonski, the closest neighboring island with enough level area to accommodate the Boeing 727 jet. Fortunately, Japonski is just across a narrow channel from town. That inaugural 727 jet flight made history, too, by being the first FAA-authorized landing with passengers on a gravel runway, now paved.

The first terminal building was a shock to seasoned world travelers, but it takes time and money to add the finer touches. There was a homey feeling of belonging as you rubbed shoulders in the bustling little waiting room, sharing the lack of facilities. The next terminal building, larger and upgraded with the addition of regular plumbing and vending machines, was obviously a temporary stopgap until today's new, fine facility.

Mount Edgecumbe, a Fujiyama-shaped extinct volcano, is the snowcapped landmark you see as you land at Sitka, and it dominates the scene from many of the town's choice viewpoints. The Mount Edgecumbe native school and hospital, serving a large part of Alaska, are on Japonski with the airfield.

The antiquated ferry that took passengers and the amphibious World War II "duck" that took their luggage to Sitka, just across

Sitka airview. Mount Edgecumbe, with snow streaks, is on the horizon. Sitka was capital of Alaska after Kodiak, under the Russians. The town is enjoying a renaissance as today's historic air gateway to Alaska.

the waterway on Baranof Island, are gone now. They have been replaced by the long-anticipated John O'Connell Bridge, named for a former mayor of Sitka and member of the Alaska House of Representatives.

Personally we were happy with the quaint ferry system. After a fast jet flight there is nothing like a ferryboat ride to slow you down to the more relaxed Sitka pace. During the short ride we admired the good view of the town's waterfront. The newer rock wall at the town landing is the same style as the original Russian-built wall to the right, beneath the oil company dock. There were always townspeople going back and forth, visiting someone in the hospital or at school, or going to work. Sitka residents are friendly people. We'd get to talking, and when we ran into them later they would smile and say hello, making it hard to feel like a stranger in town during even a short visit.

Regarding "progress," we have a feeling of kinship with a longtime resident who was asked to make a few remarks at the Inaugural Flight luncheon. He had arrived at Sitka before the turn of the century, by schooner from Liverpool. Memories of that youthful, leisurely, beautiful journey among the island passageways were still fond and fresh. He commented that it took him eight months, compared to our two hours by jet. "But," he ended nostalgically, "I'm still not saying it's an *improvement....*"

Sitka's Russian and Indian Past

The word "Sitka" in the Tlingit Indian language means "in this place." The Russians first settled the site as Fort Archangel Michael in 1799. It is on a sheltered harbor on the outside edge of the archipelago protecting the well-known and well-used Inland Passage trade route. Shortly thereafter an Indian uprising wiped out the new fort. Alexander Baranof (for whom Sitka's island and archipelago were named) was the strong-willed and heavy-handed governor of Russian America. He wasted little time taking back the scenic spot he had picked for his capital. The fort was rebuilt a few miles away and called New Archangel, but it soon reverted back to the Indian name, and the original Russian site is called Old Sitka. When you know the translation, the name is very appropriate. A great deal occurred "in this place."

Sitka National Historical Park

People "doing" Sitka on their own would do well to head first for the Sitka National Historical Park, not far from the main part of town. At the fine new Visitors' Center there are people, pamphlets, and excellent exhibits to give you background for getting the most out of your Sitka visit.

Sitka's National Historical Park is both accessible and small, about fifty-four acres. It was proclaimed a public park in 1890 and a

Totem at Sitka National Historical Park.

national monument a couple of decades later, to commemorate the last stand of the Sitka Indians and to protect and preserve all remnants of their culture. Some of these remnants are displayed outdoors: authentic totem poles like those that originally stood in old Indian villages in various parts of Southeast Alaska, and some of them are almost sixty feet tall. All that is left of the last Indian fort are marks of the foundations. Footpaths lead among the fine carved poles in a dense stand of typical Alaska forest, mainly hemlock and spruce, with alders along the Indian River. Though it is towering timber, it is second growth; the first growth was cut by Russians and later by Americans. Underfoot, mosses and ferns grow lushly, and everywhere berries and devil's club fill in the rest of the space.

Visitors' Center

Inside the Visitors' Center guides are geared to answer questions about history and totemic art. One attractive Indian high-school girl on summer vacation duty confessed she had to bone up on the subject to keep from being stumped by visitors who expected her to know all the answers because of her ancestry. "It has given me a new appreciation for my people," she stated proudly.

The building is constructed in Indian longhouse style, and makes use of house poles of former potlatches. A potlatch was a social get-together that usually lasted several days, where wealth changed hands and important events were celebrated with song and dance. Today, the Visitors' Center houses old as well as present-day art works. There is an arts-and-crafts center in one section where you can watch Alaskan native artists at work. Another exhibit room features the history and growth of Sitka.

The first Sitka National Historical Park superintendent, Ellen Lang, was the first woman and the first Alaska native to manage a National Park Service-administered area in the Pacific Northwest.

Sheldon Jackson Museum and College

Adjacent to the National Historical Park, toward town, is the Sheldon Jackson College and Museum. Jackson founded the school under the auspices of the Presbyterian church long before 1800. He was a typical Alaskan, if there really is such: stubborn, full of drive and energy, persevering, personable, and individualistic. His almost superhuman efforts in behalf of education helped set the guidelines for today's schools, generally considered excellent. An interesting aspect of the school that bears his name is that it spans all the types of educational effort: it was first a boys' school, later coeducational, then a high school, and is now a two-year college. About three-fourths of the students are natives, but the college lures students from the "South 48" for a variety of reasons. Young people, intrigued with Alaska and its history, and those interested in bridging cultural gaps as well as learning about other cultures, could do worse than wend their way to Sitka, and then continue their studies at the University of Alaska near Fairbanks, or Alaska Methodist University at Anchorage.

Castle Hill

One place, Castle Hill, has figured in Sitka's history for many decades. A marker just off the main street (to your right as you walk through Totem Square) directs you up the promontory to a panoramic view of the harbor and offshore islands. It is plain to see why the Indians made this their home and lookout when the Russians came to take back "their" settlement. They may have appreciated the view, too. They were surely aware of its strategic importance. The Indians held off the enemy, but retreated to a fort with stronger walls to withstand the barrage of Russian cannon fire. After several days under siege, the Indians ran out of ammunition and quietly fled to the other side of the island, leaving Sitka to the Russians.

Baranof naturally chose the best view for himself and his officers. His home was his castle; the others lived in substantial and well-fortified residences. Nothing remains of Baranof's Castle or any of the three mansions that followed on this rocky hill. However, if you happen to be a history buff you will be thrilled to examine the old cannon now guarding that bare, windswept landmark. Some say the cannon, marked with the Czarist Russian double eagle, were cast in Sitka's foundries.

Seward's Folly?

On this same hill, just over a century ago, the ceremonies transferring ownership of Russian America to the United States took place. It was a sorrowful occasion on both sides, at the time. Many residents knew they would be pulling up roots and they hated to leave the live capital. From a Russian outpost it had grown to a flourishing center of trade and culture in the new and sparsely populated land. The social whirl was breathtakingly magnificent—and perpetual. Americans were annoyed because they thought their government was paying a fantastic price for a worthless, difficult-to-reach piece of property. Even William H. Seward, who did the bargaining, thought $5 million was plenty, but agreed to the Russian holdout for over $7 million and talked Congress into the deal.

The investment has been repaid many times, and new resources are constantly being discovered and probed. The price of 2 cents an acre sounds cheap enough but think of it in terms of a head tax on the present population. Today, if each resident were asked to pay his share of the original cost, it would be about $18.

If you happen to visit Sitka on October 18—any year—you will be able to see a reenactment of the transfer ceremonies atop Castle Hill. History comes alive as the townspeople dress in costumes of that day, complete with bonnets and beards, and the Imperial Russian double eagle flag flies again, briefly, before being lowered and replaced by the Stars and Stripes and the Alaska state flag.

The Centennial (1967) ceremonies were special. The color guard came from Fort Wainwright, near Fairbanks, and was composed of members of the United States Army's 9th Infantry, the same unit that did the honors generations ago. Some actual descendants of the principals were also present: a grandson of the last Russian governor and a cousin of Secretary of State William Seward. The roll call of states took longer—there were only thirty-seven states in 1867—and when number forty-nine was called, the Alaska state flag rose to the top of the second pole. The first forty-nine-star flag was hoisted in 1959 when Alaska celebrated its graduation from territory to state. A surprise touch (which may be repeated) was a blast from the whistle of that first steamboat launched in Sitka from Russian shipyards, a few years before the Purchase.

It is hard to tear oneself away from the view from Castle Hill, especially on a sparkling day, but Sitka has much to see of historical interest within walking distance.

St. Michael's Cathedral

The original of one of the most charming old landmarks in all of Alaska was destroyed by fire the year before the Centennial. Russian Orthodox St. Michael's Cathedral, placed in the middle of the main street like a traffic divider, was completed in 1844. It was cherished by Alaskans and visitors, who came to see its treasures and to talk with the bishop. Though a replica can never be the same as the original, St. Michael's has been rebuilt exactly as before, in the shape of a cross, and with characteristic Russian "onion dome

Famous and priceless icons from Russian America days are in Sitka's restored St. Michael's Cathedral, a Russian Orthodox church.

and carrot spire." Fortunately, a few years ago the National Park Service compiled exact details of this historic church from which blueprints were made. The replica is exactly the same except for fireproofing, down to the moldings, grain in the planking, bells, and the iron clock, which was forged by the first bishop of Alaska.

The whole town of Sitka did a masterly job at the fire, rescuing the precious old icons and relics. Most of the holy paintings were saved. The rescued Russian cross with its two crosspieces, the lower one slanted, was placed in the still-warm ashes to await its place in the rebuilt church. The valuable art pieces were housed in a building that predated the cathedral by a couple of years, protected only by prayer. Regular Sunday services were held in the small private chapel during the rebuilding, with other Sitka denominations ecumenically sharing facilities for special seasonal celebrations. Now the art has been returned to the rebuilt cathedral, and this 1842 building, a former mission school, is closed pending restoration as a National Historic Site.

Last trip we found the interior close to completion, the precious, beautiful icons back in their places, and Bishop Gregory caught up in plans for the upcoming dedication of the altar. A prelude enthusiastically played by a young bellringer on the newly hung bells enticed us to stay on for the service, candlelit and beautifully sung in the Russian way by a choir of townspeople.

Some of the irreplaceable items that Orthodox seminarians show with pride to touring guests include work of Russian artists of the early era. There is a two-hundred-year-old gold and jeweled chalice still used for special services, a large elaborate silver-covered New Testament printed a century and a half ago, and a smaller one only a few years younger. Some items are kept under glass—embroidered altar cloths done by Princess Maksoutoff, wife of the last Russian governor, and the miter worn by Bishop Veniaminov, the great missionary who translated the gospel into native languages. The oil paintings, which are inlaid with silver and gold, are displayed on the walls. The Sitka Madonna icon was given to the cathedral soon after it was built, by laborers of the Russian-American Company. Offers to purchase it have ranged from $35,000 to $250,000, according to legend. A present estimate of its worth is thought to be at least $100,000. But it is not for sale; mere money cannot match its value to the parish.

Eventually, according to Alice Harrigan, long active in the Sitka Visitors Bureau, the church will own almost all of the priceless collection of a longtime resident, Martha Cushing. "Last summer she made a gift of twenty of her icons to the church," continues Alice. "And she plans to present another twenty. Martha feels that the collection should remain in Sitka—bless her!"

Totem Square

Right on the busy waterfront in downtown Sitka is Totem Square, where Tlingit Indians carved a fifty-foot war canoe from a giant red cedar log as a Centennial project. It is on display outside the Centennial Building.

In the square across the street is the Pioneer Home, enclosed by a hedge of Sitka roses. These roses are a single-petal, bright-pink variety, similar to wild roses in the "South 48," but Alaska-sized. They measure about an inch and a half across. The rose hips, or fruit, high in vitamin C, were often consumed by Indians, ship's crews, settlers, and pioneers in the past. Today's Alaskans use them for tasty jellies and jams. The Pioneer Home is a state-operated haven for "sourdough" gold rush miners and others from that era. A tall statue, symbolizing the rugged pioneer with pack and gold pan, dominates the yard. Old-timers who can talk about those hectic days are getting fewer, but occasionally you can find someone sitting in the sun on the steps or inside, happy to relive his past for a willing ear.

Old Cemeteries

Old cemeteries are fascinating places to visit anywhere, but especially in Sitka. One is on a little hill behind the Pioneer Home and has a replica of an old Russian blockhouse in the background. Weeding and trimming the lush vegetation around some of the older graves is a never-ending job in moisture-laden Southeast Alaska island and coastal areas. Old names and dates are in Russian, including that of Russian Princess Maksoutoff, buried farther on in the old Lutheran cemetery. The blockhouse (reconstructed) was used to guard the stockade walls protecting Sitka from the warlike Tlingit Indians.

The Waterfront

Tourists and townspeople all find plenty of interest along Sitka's busy waterfront. Commercial fishing is an important part of Sitka's economy, and the docks accommodate all kinds of boats: seiners, trawlers and trollers, halibut boats as well as all sizes for private fishing. *Everyone* fishes, and the last two weekends of June are reserved for the town's salmon derby. Visitors are invited to join in the contest, though renting a boat may be a problem.

Even those used to being around such places will be awed at the size of some of the salmon being unloaded for processing and storage. No one minds if you wander in and watch, if you keep out of the way. It is, of course, somewhat wet and slippery underfoot, and has some messy phases.

If you are doing your own cooking, ask about buying fresh seafood. You may have to invite several guests to help use up a couple of dollars' worth of salmon or halibut.

If you're not cooking, you may be able to buy delicious fish and chips to go, and have your own picnic on the beach. Look around or ask where to get cooked crab when it is in season. Pick up a loaf of crusty French bread from Sitka's excellent bakery on the main street, add something to drink, and anything else to round out a meal, and fall to it. This is for the "do-it-yourself" traveler. There are some very good eating places in and around Sitka, all of them specializing in fresh seafood.

Centennial Building

The very impressive Centennial Building contrasts mightily with the old weather-worn Russian mission building nearby. It was built on a landfill and overlooks the harbor and islands. In fact, the view from auditorium seats across the stage and through large glass windows would give stiff competition if the drapes weren't pulled while Russian dances and other performances are given. Any community would be proud to claim this project, from the fine mural of the Alaska Purchase ceremony carved in wood at the entrance to the various fine exhibits, both historic and modern. Neat, polite, enthusiastic young people serve as guides, and an information center is manned by volunteers. The atmosphere is always friendly and the coffeepot hot.

On display here is a scale model of the way Sitka looked a century ago, painstakingly researched and constructed by a dedicated historian-ranger. The stockade wall, sawmill, flour mill, tanneries, foundry, shipyards and docks, and even a bowling alley show what a busy place it was in those days. You note that some geographic contours have changed. For example, where the new Centennial Building now stands there was a bay before. But Swan Lake where reputedly ice was gathered for shipment to San Francisco, is in the same place, near town. Today's residents claim that the lake rarely freezes solid enough in winter these days to provide much of an ice supply.

The historical exhibit is an antique scavenger's delight. Some furniture from Baranof's original castle, old mining tools and the like are tenderly tended by the Double O Club (for "Older Ones"). "These are the folks who made history in Alaska," Alice Harrigan asserts proudly. "We have a former big game guide, a miner, a banker.... Manning the exhibit serves as therapy for these oldsters. They love every minute of it."

Sightseeing by car

If you have a car, you can go farther afield, but not much, for the roads are limited on the island. Rental cars are available, but they may all be rented out to visiting Japanese, who need them to carry on their pulp-mill business, which is not within walking distance. There are also taxis, but for other than short hauls they would be costly. It is better to investigate the bus tours offered by Sitka Buslines. A short tour meets and leaves from the ferries. Daily longer tours depart from the hotels.

Harbor Mountain

A favorite picture-taking spot of Bob's is most of the way up the Harbor Mountain road, which takes off from the ferry highway a short distance out of Old Sitka. This narrow dirt road is quite precipitous. The thrill you get out of it will depend on where you are accustomed to driving. It winds upward about five miles, but we stop before the end. Almost at the top, a wide part of the road overlooks a spectacular marine view of the islands and Mount Edgecumbe, including the route the ferry takes as it picks its way among the narrow waterways. Over the years it has been our favorite picnic spot—and even camp spot, when Bob's pictures required a wait for the right weather, cloud effect, lighting, or some other whim. The road is usually rough, in spite of efforts to keep it graded, but there are adequate turnouts for car passing. None of the turns requires backing up in order to negotiate them—our criterion for rating the difficulty of mountain roads, wherever we find them.

The view is well worth the drive, whether the day is misty or sunny. If you have ever yearned to have an island of your own you'll drool over the seemingly unlimited spread and the multitude of sizes. In fact, some people in Sitka *do* live on their own little islands, and think nothing of commuting by small boat at all hours and in all kinds of weather.

Seeing Sitka on tour

Sitka, like many other Southeast Alaska towns, is small enough so that people can walk to most points of interest with no strain for those accustomed to using their legs. However, there are good tours available with guides who know the background and history of Sitka. We think tours are great timesavers if your stay is short. Even if you have unlimited time, it is a fine way to learn where things are. Then you can go back on your own to browse in museums or take more pictures of things that appeal especially to you.

We can't guarantee prices will be the same as we have found them, but the tours should vary little. For $7.50 visitors hit the high spots of Sitka while the ferry is in port (about two hours). Buses pick up and deliver passengers at the terminal, a few miles out of town near the site of Old Sitka.

Of course those staying overnight or longer have more choice. We have learned and seen much on a three- or four-hour guided tour for $17.50. Ask for information on tours, salmon bakes, and performances of the New Archangel Dancers at the Sitka Visitors Bureau in the Centennial Building. Bob feels that sightseeing and picture taking in beautiful areas like Sitka from small planes chartered from local air services are worth every cent. We've flown with Channel Flying on past trips, and most recently tried a new perspective via helicopter with Eagle Air, hovering over islands, Sitka Harbor, and the mountains behind, plus a close view of Mount Edgecumbe. Based on four passengers, you should budget about $50 for a 45-minute-plus excursion. Plane costs are less, perhaps $35 or $40 a head.

If you prefer sea level sightseeing, you can check in at Crescent Boat Harbor near the Centennial Building and take an evening turn around nearby islands of the archipelago. Captain Bob Allen pilots his 150-passenger *St. Aquilina* 18 miles down Silver Bay for wildlife watching and a glimpse of the Japanese-owned pulp mill so important to the town's economy. You may see Japanese freighters loading lumber and pulp for Japanese production of rayon and cellophane.

In Russian days, Sitka was amazingly well supplied with both necessities and luxuries, especially for the more affluent members of her population. Called the Paris of the Pacific, the town had shops displaying the latest fashions. Stores stocked fruits, vegetables, and meat from Hawaii and from settlements south to Puget Sound and California. Trading was lively for the products Sitka had to offer in exchange: boats built from readily available timber, tanned leather, furs, flour ground from grain brought from the south, boat engines, bells, even spades and plowshares made in a flourishing brass and iron foundry.

Sitka is no longer a sophisticated center in a new land, but it is fifth among Alaska cities and showing fine economic growth. The town's fascinating tie-in with past history is the key to the development of another fast-growing industry, tourism. Thanks to ever-improving jet freight service, the town is well supplied with anything and everything, and if it is not on hand at the moment, it can be ordered. This happy state is so recent that it still surprises us to find such well-stocked food, clothing, and drug stores, at prices little more than we would pay on our West Coast. Besides air freight, the amounts of goods moved by increased shipping has been a big factor in supplying Sitka's demands. Perhaps the impact has been even greater on other, more convenient ports-of-call along the whole length of the Inside Passage.

Sitka also has service-type shops: beauty parlors (a boon in the often dampish atmosphere—shampoo and set was still only $7.50 at Winnie's Vanity, upstairs from the main street), boat and marine supply shops, and book and souvenir stores. Some take their theme from Sitka's past. The Russian American Company across from the cathedral is operated by the bishop's secretary. It is strictly Russian and deals in samovars, dolls, icons, china, lacquer boxes, and all types of genuine Russian items. The Sitkakwan, just beyond the Pioneer Home, handles both Russian and a wide variety of native items. The owner designed the "Little Drook" emblem on the button you should be wearing. *Drook* in Russian means "friend," and entitles visitors to special friendly treatment in Sitka.

Lodging

Sitka has come a long way in just the last two years in expanding lodging in order to keep up with its image as a choice convention center and visitor destination. The eighty-room Sheffield House was built on the dock site of a cold storage plant that burned a few years ago. The plush Native Corporation-built Shee Atika Lodge uptown has over a hundred rooms.

We recall when we needed two adjacent rooms to accommodate our family of five and provide privacy for the assorted ages and sexes. The $56 per night charged at the then newest hotel, the Potlatch House, almost interfered with our getting a good night's sleep. A double room there now is about $35, but you can count on paying at least $45 for a double in the new hotels.

The Sitka Hotel is less fancy, but strategically located on the main street opposite the Pioneer Home and near all the main sights. It is clean, comfortable, and hospitable, doubles under $35.

Food and drink

The Potlatch House is far enough out of the center of town to require transportation, provided by your own car, their "courtesy car," or taxis. However, there is a good restaurant, bar, and coffee shop in the building. In fact, it's a real family bar. We noted a couple of swinging parents with their five youngsters still going strong at 10:00 P.M. Though bartenders are conscientious about not serving drinks to minors, and our twenty-two-year-old model was constantly having to show her I.D. card, Alaskans do not necessarily consider the local bar in a small town a den of iniquity. Children with their parents are admitted. However, coming from a community where women were not allowed to sit at the bar and where drinks on Sunday were illegal until recently, we will have to admit the presence of small fry sipping away at their drinks (soft) at a genuine bar took some getting used to.

The in-town restaurants evidently have a pact on hours, possibly to prevent interference with local fishing and other summer recreational pursuits. At any rate, it took time to learn who was serving which meal when. We suspect it might even vary periodically. No real problem is presented, though. There are excellent restaurants in the two new hotels, and most others are within walking distance. It pays to ask around. We've eaten well and reasonably, and at odd hours due to picture taking, at Moy's Cafe on Lincoln beyond Cathedral Circle. Residents recommend Revard's and Staton's Steak House, on Harbor Drive. The Kiksadi is out of town a few miles on the pulp mill road overlooking a quiet bay. Overhanging the waterfront, the restaurant in the Sheffield House is tiered, so everyone can watch marine activity.

With plenty of marine views to contemplate, thoughts turn toward seafood. Main courses include delicacies of the area—salmon, halibut, king and Dungeness crab, for about $10. A house specialty, Surf 'n' Turf, combining steak and imported lobster or, more often, king crab, is $15 or $18. The Nugget Saloon in the airport terminal serves abalone, crab, salmon and do-it-yourself steaks.

Seafood cuisine is adequately supplied in Sitka. Our personal opinion is that anyone brave enough to start a Russian restaurant—with atmosphere—will have it made.

Camping

Travelers arriving by ferry with camp gear can pitch their tents or find camper space in two Forest Service campgrounds, one next to the ferry terminal, about seven miles from town. These are part of the Tongass National Forest, largest in the United States and noted not only for timber, but for opportunities offered vacationers to hike, fish, watch wildlife, hunt in season, and go boating and swimming. No luxuries exist here like hot showers and electric hookups. The living is primitive with bare essentials of water and toilets. But, as is the case with most unimproved camp spots throughout Alaska, what is lacking in facilities is more than compensated for in scenery and the chance to breathe pure fresh air.

After Sitka

If a jet flight to Sitka is your first introduction to Alaska, you'll have laid a solid historic groundwork. You'll recognize Russian remnants—a church, people's names, old sea walls, cannon, and Indian graveyards with Russian crosses guarding tiny spirit houses—wherever you see them. You'll have a bird's-eye view of part of the geography of the Southeast Panhandle, and a feel for the nature of this distinctive area of Alaska.

The where-to-go-next choices are many, but there are only two ways out of Sitka, by air or by sea. By plane, it means flying to main airports at Juneau, Anchorage, or Fairbanks, where connections can be made for visiting other parts of the state. If you are driving, you will have to find access to the Alaska Highway, or ride back down the ferry route. If you "drove" the Marine Highway, you probably noted the exits at Haines and Skagway.

Whichever you choose, you may be sure that the next face of Alaska—Interior, South Central, Arctic, or that way-out Aleutian Island chain—will be entirely different from the Southeast Panhandle.

KETCHIKAN

Ketchikan calls itself "First City in Alaska," referring to the fact that it is Alaska's sea gateway not far from the entrance to the Inside Passage. It is fourth in size, with a greater population of eighteen thousand; the third is Juneau with twenty thousand. Jets from Seattle used to land on Annette Island, passengers transferred to an amphibian plane, and in about twenty minutes they landed in the water right at the dock in downtown Ketchikan. After the jet, this PBY air ferry seemed even more antiquated than Sitka's boat ferry. On one trip we found that some wag had placed a small sign up front stating: "The Wright Brothers learned to fly here." A new jet airport on an island just to the north of Ketchikan (also on an island, Revillagigedo) is now in use. From the air, you can see the narrow spot in the channel where a bridge may be located eventually. Until then a small ferry bridges the half-mile gap.

This sea gateway and on up the Inside Passage is the same route used for centuries. The scenery has hardly changed. The only new things are the people and their travel conveyances. The start of the

Alaska State Ferry System in 1963 was the end of the frustration felt by the Panhandle cities. They are still pinching themselves to be sure they are at last a part of the rest of Alaska—and of the world. Ready or not, they are getting a large share of visitors, who consider the convenient ferry, with stop-over privileges at all ports-of-call, the ideal "do-it-yourself" way to travel in Southeast Alaska.

Ketchikan was founded on fish a little over sixty years ago. But Indians had been living nearby for centuries. The fishing was good. The hunting was good, too, which may have had something to do with how the town got its name.

There is a Tlingit phrase that means "wings of a spread eagle." Possibly some hunters climbed the mountains in search of deer, and as they gazed down on their settlement spread out on the narrow shelf between mountains and water, they saw a resemblance. At any rate, the words "kach-kanna" caught the fancy of the tribe, and when white people started sharing the town, they pronounced it and put it on maps as "Ketchikan."

It requires little imagination today to believe in that Indian derivation. From the air, the town definitely has a spread-eagle look. Green forested foothills rise so suddenly and steeply behind the waterfront that though several homes make a brave assault and have a fine view, the practical way for town expansion has been along the shoreline. This is evident from the water approach, also. The body of the eagle appears to be formed by the large buildings of the main part of town; the wings are the populated shelf on both sides.

There is not much room for a town between the mountains and waterfront. A rocky foothill almost joins the water in one place. To allow for two-way traffic, engineers had to tunnel through for one lane, and traffic traveling in the other direction has just room to scoot around this natural barrier.

Another of Ketchikan's nicknames, "Salmon Capital of the World," accounts for a large influx of visitors bent on making the natives live up to the name. The protected island waters attract huge fish runs, including salmon, halibut, rock and ling cod, sea bass, and red snapper. Fast streams encourage a lively fall and spring steelhead run, and all kinds of trout are found in nearby lakes and streams.

Townspeople jokingly call Ketchikan the "Rain Capital." They measure the downpours on a huge rain gauge, make bets how high it will go for the year (precipitation has reached over 200 inches), and even try to convince visitors that they don't need a boat to catch salmon but can just put out a hand and catch them as they swim by. Since all of Southeast Alaska owes its lush green look and its growing timber and pulp industries to the large amount of rain, the residents (if not always the visitors) are convinced it's a blessing.

As far as we can tell, rain stops no one. Everyone puts on rain clothes and boots for the duration, which can be non-stop for as long as a week, we have noted, being photographers and especially sensitive to weather. Sometimes it seems to clear almost instantly. The sun comes out, a light breeze wafts through the streets, and everything dries out in short order, and cleaner, fresher "champagne" air you've never breathed. You feel that somehow that rain wasn't very wet, after all. And the water you use for dishes, shampoos, and drinking is soft and lovely to use—only a little bit of chlorine added, say the natives.

Main intersection of Ketchikan, with mountain backdrop.

Lodging

Ketchikan offers a good choice of places to stay, from camp-grounds to modern hotels and motels. The only question is whether there will be enough space to go around at times. People on regular tours, or those who make and then confirm their reservations, can generally be sure of accommodations. Travelers who have their own campers, trailers, tents, and so on, have no worries either. Free souls (like us) who resist being tied down to schedules and reservations take our chances.

As you drive off the ferry, a sign tells you that the road extends about nineteen miles north (left), ending at Settlers Cove camper and picnic sites. A closer camp for trailers, campers, and tents is maintained at Ward Lake, about seven miles from the ferry terminal, with water and sanitation provided. There is usually a small public camper site south toward town just a mile from the terminal. From the ferry, there is a regular city bus service, plus taxis.

The *Ketchikan News* puts out a current, fat, and free "Guide to Ketchikan" for visitors, available at the News Building, 5th and Dock streets, or the Visitors Center on the downtown dock. Handiest to the ferry terminal is the Hilltop Motel. Also in Ketchikan's burgeoning west end is the Marine View Hotel, rightly named, you'll learn, if you eat at the restaurant at the top. The Helm has a magnificent overall view of Tongass Narrows. Downtown are the Gilmore and the Ingersoll, popular with business transients, who like to be in the heart of Ketchikan, so reservations ahead are advisable.

Fishermen are likely to head fifteen miles north to Clover Pass Resort, where there are complete facilities and a marina. Residents say you can rent a genuine "cannery row" cabin that sleeps four (bring your sleeping bag) for $20 a night. The resort is the former historic Waterfall Cannery, sixty-three miles by air on the west coast of Prince of Wales Island, between two small Indian villages, Craig and Hydaburg. Good fishing, they say, and you can cook your own, bringing supplies or buying from the "company store." Or, a four-day package for about $200 includes room, meals, and other amenities. Air taxi to get there is extra.

Food and drink

None of our family (except the cook) is especially enthusiastic about eating out, unless it's a picnic or cooking over an open beach fire—which is smart as well as fun, because when you travel with a family you are bound to save money when you cook your own meals. But we bravely sample the restaurants, each sticking to his specialty. One of us always tries the steaks, another the seafood, a couple live on hamburgers and milkshakes, and there is one experimental soul who samples around. Here are our conclusions: You can't go wrong on seafood, especially if you ask for whatever is fresh and local. It's reasonable, too. Halibut and salmon dinners cost around $12. At Clover Pass, the king salmon highlight of my $11.75 dinner had been swimming only a few hours earlier. At Mattle's Drive In and the Dairy Queen, the hamburgers were still under a dollar for the small size, about $2 for deluxe.

In early travels we considered Ketchikan's Elks Club a most convivial place for dining and drinking. This was often true elsewhere in Alaska, too; Elks clubs flourish there. We happen to be more familiar with the one in Ketchikan. We especially recall attending a Hawaiian luau there, complete with flown-in poi, Hawaiian dancers, and musicians. This particular occasion turned out to be a magnificent study in contrasts. The flower-decked interior, filled with tropical-garbed Ketchikanites, was vivid and lively while outside everything was being drenched by a week-long cloudburst. We have also observed the Elks Club hosting a visiting press group, and it is the-first time we have seen martinis and Manhattans served in buckets!

If you are an Elk or a friend of an Elk, you can still enjoy the very modern facilities which have moved upstairs in the same location, near town center, but you will have to dine elsewhere. The new Fireside Lounge is most convenient, having expanded its scope to 300 capacity plus room to dance, by moving to the old Elks location. The Narrows and Kay's Kitchen, tourist- and towns-people-tested, and popular, are located in interesting settings. The Narrows is just outside of town to the south, overhanging the Tongass Narrows. Dinner features local seafood, and offers a courtesy car to and from town. For lunches, it's Kay's Kitchen.

"Real home cooking" oversees the considerable boat traffic at the entrance to Bar Harbor.

We have also enjoyed the "family-style" Diaz Cafe, a tiny place across from the Salvation Army on the narrow waterfront street south of the main part of town. We probably never would have tried it if we hadn't been with friends from town, Bob Pickrell, editor of the *New Alaskan*, and his family. Ordinarily, we would have been tempted to "potlatch" out at a campground with that many kids, but it was a special occasion. Bob ordered a "family-style mixture" of all the specialties of Filipino and Chinese food, and Mama Diaz, who supervises the preparation, came and chatted with us while we stuffed ourselves on shrimp and beef-fried rice, plain rice, sweet and sour spareribs, pork and shrimp chow mein, egg foo young, and prawns fried and dipped in a special hot sauce, all at a very nominal cost. Liquor is not served here, but you don't have to look far for a bar for a pre-dinner cocktail in almost any town in Alaska.

Stores

If you are shopping for supplies and cooking your own meals, you will be happier with the total bill if you head for the nearest supermarket, and if you hit the food "specials" day. Take tomatoes, for example. As we were checking out, a clerk once remarked, "Did you see the tomatoes—39¢ a pound today; yesterday they were 69¢!" Apparently the reason she was pushing the tomatoes was that a new supply was coming in that day. Except for some items like milk and perishables, prices (though higher in general than those paid in Seattle, for example) are probably the lowest in Southeast Alaska at Ketchikan.

Part of the fun of shopping in Alaska towns is the contrast of old and new. Mixed in with remnants of the "old" Alaska are modern department stores, supermarkets, new hospitals, protected boat moorages, and paved streets. But it is easy to ferret out wooden sidewalks, bars with sawdust on the floors, and totem poles, while rubbing shoulders with fishermen, loggers, and businessmen.

Fishing

Without a doubt salmon fishing is the biggest drawing card in the Ketchikan area, and there are all degrees of it. We confess we are *not* avid fishermen or hunters—we are more the birdwatcher type. Though Bob does a lot of shooting, it is only with his camera. Advice is free and frequent, though, in a place like Ketchikan where practically *everyone* fishes. Just ask anyone.

Fishing is so good here because migrating salmon move in masses when they have to go around points of land by way of narrow waterways. A map showing Ketchikan's location on Revillagigedo Island shows how the salmon run. Salmon crowd through narrow Clover Pass (named for a navy lieutenant who discovered and surveyed it, not the vegetation) and around a point, and then squeeze down Tongass Narrows to round Mountain Point. Fishing is great for king salmon in late spring; cohoes, or silvers run in July or August and continue through September. Boat and gear rentals are available at points near the run.

Dedicated fisherman often go all out on equipment, guides, and boats. On the other hand, people also fish off city docks and floats. A state fishing license is a must. A ten-day visitor's permit costs $15; one for the season is $30; and a one-day is $5. They are readily available at resorts, sporting-goods stores, and Forest Service offices. Luck and skill pay off in valuable prizes offered winners of fishing derbies which run consecutively from April through July. Official rules are updated each year and are distributed widely.

Not only the fish get hooked. Many a visitor only casually interested in fishing takes the plunge at Ketchikan, the Salmon Capital. His beginner's luck may yield a forty pounder in a couple of hours, and, inspired by success, he finds himself fishing his way through Alaska from the Southeast to the Arctic Coast.

Tours

The ground is well-covered by Ketchikan Sightseeing (Northern Bus Company) and the sea by Ketchikan Marine Charters. For literature and current information on these and air tours available, we head for the Chamber of Commerce on Mission Street, or the Visitors Center.

Totem poles

In the old days, an Indian's life and recreation depended on the bounty of the land and sea. The native society was totemic. A tribe was grouped according to the animal or plant it adopted as its symbol, and the members carved and painted their trademark on poles abundantly available in the surrounding woods.

About eleven miles to the north on a small open bay called Totem Bight is a good outdoor display of poles. There are some more just a few miles south of town at Saxman Indian Village. None of these poles are very old; in fact all are well-done replicas. Any originals would be in museums by now, except for some that might be fallen and rotting in out-of-the-way places. Wood deteriorates and colors fade fast, buffeted by the elements in the moist salt air. This didn't bother the Indians, of course. All they had to do was carve another, using traditional patterns, from the unending supply of fine cedar and spruce.

Historic-art fans discuss among themselves whether authentic Indian totem-pole art is dead or dying and whether it is now an art or craft, without arriving at any definite conclusion. One age giveaway is the size. The Indians were not likely to carve the tall poles you see today until they learned to use white man's tools, as well as his more convenient and more durable paints. That places these poles within the last couple of hundred years, though the traditional designs, of course, have been handed down for centuries.

You can see some original totem poles, well-lighted centerpieces, inside the new Totem Heritage Center. Outside, an artist-carver may be at work on a reproduction. The Forest Service Civilian Conservation Corps Indian Division project started gathering together, carving, and preserving the poles a few years before World War II. Workers searched out poles from places rarely visited except by Indian canoe, brought them back, and set them up in communities where descendants of carvers might be interested in carrying on the craft.

Our family is resigned to waiting around while Bob painstakingly sets up his pictures. Sometimes the sun disappears temporarily, and we continue to wait, and sometimes we have come back the next day—or the next. That's how we found out that Saxman Indian village with its park of stately totems isn't a ghost town. Though we didn't meet the grownups eyeing us from windows, the children and dogs soon decided we would be around awhile. The kids resumed their baseball game, using the towering totems as bases. Short-handed in the field, they invited our three to join in, while other smaller children followed Bob and me around. There is no language barrier, and though they are politely shy, if given time to size you up they will warm to you. One small, black-eyed, raven-haired charmer knew little about totem poles, but a lot about community life. Art Linkletter would have loved to interview her.

We asked about the totem that had, unmistakably, a statue of Abraham Lincoln at the top, tall hat and all. Lincoln's likeness started from the knees up, just below his frock coat, about twenty-five feet from the ground. We learned the story when we saw the original in a glass case in the State Museum at Juneau. Lincoln was highly thought of by the Indians because he freed Indian slaves as well as Negro. The Civil War had ended just a couple of years before the purchase of Alaska. The good news that Indians were no longer slaves of other more powerful tribes inspired the Lincoln totem. The reason he was chopped off at the knees was because that was where the picture they were using for a model ended. The museum original shows what effect the elements have on poles; it's hard to believe it is related to the dapper reproduction at Saxman. Though preservatives may have been added to the wood, no attempt has been made to repaint the original. The most recognizable features are the tall hat and beard atop the weathered-wood torso.

Totems had nothing to do with religion or worship. As Edward Keithahn, a former long-time curator of the Territorial, then State, Museum explained, they were "monuments in cedar." In his book of that name he describes and illustrates many of the poles you see in the various collections. To "read" a totem you need background in the mythology, politics, art, and social life of the family or tribe it represents. Poles were made for various purposes: to keep track of happenings, to honor a chief or other outstanding person (dead or alive), to indicate wealth and power, and to pass on legends and stories. There were also mortuary poles outside the house with hollows to contain cremated remains. Other poles were carved wood shells that could be removed from an old house and then wrapped around the plain posts inside the new home. Used indoors, these house poles are well preserved today. If you are lucky enough to see inside an Indian house you may see some house poles a hundred years old or so. Perhaps someone will even "read" them for you.

At Totem Bight, which, as we have mentioned, is eleven miles from Ketchikan, besides a number of poles there is also a reproduction of a tribal house, where tribal counciling, trading, socializing, and merrymaking took place. It is sturdily built, with an entrance that accommodates only one person at a time, to prevent any infiltration by the enemy. A stranger and a possible spy didn't stand a chance. His off-balance entry, necessitated by stepping over a raised threshold under a low arch, made him a vulnerable target.

The park is reached after a short woodsy walk that breaks out into the open for a view of the Tongass Narrows. It is isolated. You are likely to see only visitors as you walk around the clearing and look at the poles, unless a crew (usually Indian) is repainting the symbols, or someone is carving a replacement. Because of deterioration this restoration is necessary, but Bob always hates to get there for pictures after a fresh paint job and just after the reedy grass is newly cropped. He prefers his totems a little on the weathered side.

The view from a boat, seeing the totems and tribal house across the small bight, is almost like catching a glimpse of the way they stood in isolated Indian villages in the past. It is next best to exploring farther afield and perhaps discovering a deserted Indian village with an overlooked remnant, still standing or even fallen, of this fascinating Indian art.

On foot in Ketchikan

There is always activity on Ketchikan's waterfront. Sometimes a big cruise ship turns its passengers loose to shop and explore. Small fishing or pleasure boats continuously pop in and out, and canneries are sometimes open to visitors. You may want to see the totem poles in downtown Ketchikan, the city ball park, and the nearby fish hatchery.

Ketchikan's community Centennial project was a fine new museum. It stands in a choice location close to downtown, overlooking the famous salmon spawning stream. Large windows give a perfect viewing point for salmon-watching as the fish fight their way up the swift-flowing water to spawn. Over a thousand items of Alaskana are on display in the free museum. We noticed a favorite item was missing, but found it again in the new airport waiting room. An intriguing replica of the *Ketchikan Queen*, a seine-fishing vessel, has a mechanism for setting the purse-type nets used in commercial salmon fishing, and it really works.

On the way to a picnic in the ball park, we discovered how to reach the replica of old Fort Tongass, which stands high on a hillside. Walk away from the center of town, up Bawden Street, to the old green hospital building where the street branches, then turn right and follow the stream. In case there is still no sign giving directions, take the first long wooden stairway. Though it looks private, it is a public walkway. You climb at least a hundred steps, plus a ramp, and you are at the fort, with a spectacular view of the town, waterfront, and Narrows.

Pulp mill

The pulp industry has been steadily assuming an important place in Alaska's economy. Cellophane and rayon are made from low-grade logs, formerly considered waste after the better ones were sorted out for saw timber. With a growing export market, and the consequent effect on Ketchikan's prosperity, you can see why the pulp mill is included among the attractions.

The tour we took stands out in our memories, but the reason has nothing to do with the industry, except indirectly. We were traveling with the Ralph Johnson family, which was seeing Alaska for the first time. The parents and three youngsters had a cozily outfitted Volkswagen; we had a detachable tent trailer and our station wagon, full of the usual camera equipment, camp gear, three children, and our dog, Alyeska. It had been raining for days, it seemed. A tour of the pulp mill would occupy us all in an educational manner and we would be warm and dry for a while. To save packing up, all ten of us piled into our station wagon, the dog, too, for the drive to Ward Cove, near the campground.

After the tour we noticed a car wash outside the mill, with a reminder that it was a good idea to run your car through because of the fumes. Bob is a thorough person. With his ten passengers he ran through once, then backed slowly through. As the water poured in an open air vent, "low man on the totem pole"—the dog—headed for higher ground, on top of the passengers. As we fled the flood it must have looked like a rehearsal for that circus act where all the clowns pile out of one car. If you take the pulp-mill tour, *don't* back your car through the car wash!

TRIPS FROM KETCHIKAN

There are over forty rustic cabins within a ninety-mile radius of Ketchikan, all built and maintained by the Forest Service. They are accessible by float plane or boat, and most of them cost $5 per night per party. Fly-ins on a small mountain lake might require about fifteen minutes to get there. Pilots charge for time in the air, generally pro-rating the hourly air rate (around $120 per hour) among the number of passengers. These independent air services, as well as the Forest Service, can help you pick your private lake, depending on your recreational desires and the ages of children in your family.

Cabins are partially equipped, with a boat available, too. It is an old Alaskan custom to take food for two nights if you plan to stay one. Weather can sometimes prevent an expected pickup. Fishing is fabulous in these small mountain lakes, so the chance of going hungry is remote. It is a kingly feeling to have a whole lake to yourself.

New Alaskan editor Bob Pickrell is an authority on enjoyable recreation spots in Southeast Alaska. In fact, this is what his rather offbeat monthly publication is all about. A person could spend a lot of time exploring by small boat such fascinating areas as Rudyerd Bay and Walker Cove. He gave us the latest on Humpback Lake, long a favorite nearby fly-in fishing spot. Besides the original Forest Service cabin, now there is a completely equipped chalet lodge accommodating six, for those who like to rough it in style.

"Things are getting more crowded all the time." sighs Bob. "Better tell your readers not to count on getting a cabin—anywhere—on a moment's notice. Put in your reservation!"

Write ahead to or inquire at the Forest Service Office for the South Tongass area at Ketchikan. You'll find the office on the main waterfront road at Ketchikan.

The nature of the state of Alaska hardly places it as yet in the category of a fashionable resort area. Those resorts that survive usually have something special going for them. There are two neighboring ones about fifty miles from Ketchikan. Bell Island is the oldest resort, and is fondly referred to as a "fish camp," but there is more to it than the fishing. Yes Bay has had a long, fishy history, but the lodge and resort are a new development. These resorts are only 12 miles apart, and each in its own way is very Alaskan and delightful.

BELL ISLAND

In a sequestered cove, less than thirty minutes by sea plane from Ketchikan, lies a Southeast island paradise: Bell Island Hot Springs Fishing Resort. The only way to get there is by plane or by private or charter boat. The sea route winds to the north and west and takes four or five hours, depending on the weather and if you pick the right passages. Everyone in the vicinity has known about the springs for years; the resort is a new discovery for visitors from farther away.

Hot springs in Alaska, even in the Arctic regions, are not exactly news. A "U.S. Geological Survey of the Mineral Springs of Alaska" was compiled by Gerald A. Waring. Patti Garvin of Anchorage, who works for the Division of Lands under the Department of Natural Resources, ran across it and shared it with us. It describes about seventy-five springs, not all as warm as Bell Island. The surprise, though, is the date of publication—more than fifty years ago. And so, if the nature of the land seems violent at times, it's small wonder—it's still boiling underneath in some places.

For ages, Indians believed in the curative powers of warm, smelly waters bubbling out of the earth. They thought nothing of traveling a couple hundred miles for a good soak. An early explorer claimed they would spend hours, submerged to the neck, eating, drinking, and even sleeping in the bath, till their aches were better.

Later, traders and fishermen appreciated hot springs, too. A good bath with plenty of hot water was hard to find in the early days, even in "civilization."

That noted name-dropper Captain Vancouver found his way to Bell Island. His original discovery-claim plaque was found on one of the island's beaches. The captain named the place Bell for a Canadian explorer in his party.

Waring's bulletin says Bell Island was homesteaded in 1902 and developed as a spa to cure the ills often attributed to living in a damp climate. By 1904 it was having a heyday; by 1907 its waters were analyzed and "patented." Apparently the resort looked much as it does today. Attractive new cabins have joined the quaint older ones lining the rushing cold stream. A boardwalk leads to the boat docks and the float-plane landing past typically mossy-green rain forest on one side and the trout-and-salmon-populated stream on the other. It's almost a quarter-mile walk, but pleasant and level, except at the ramp, where steepness sometimes varies greatly with the tide.

The bathhouse tubs and steam room are still popular, but many visitors now prefer to soak in their private oversized cabin tub, or play sociably in the large warm outdoor swimming pool. By the time the 162° water leaves its source, courses through cabins to provide heat, and ends up in the pool, the temperature has dropped to a bearable 84°. An interesting fact to ponder is how two extremes in temperature can exist almost side by side. The end of the boardwalk where the springs erupt and are caught in concrete cisterns is almost within arm's length of the icy fish stream.

Some visitors still come for medicinal purposes. A legend has grown up about two little old ladies in their eighties who used to come and soak and drink the water by the quart for a month every year. Then they would go home so rejuvenated that they would dance a mean polka till the wee hours.

Bell Island's main attraction today is a double feature: swimming and fishing, which most of the time is superb. You don't have to take our word for it. Nearby Behm Canal is rated by those who know (like the sport-fish division of Alaska's Department of Fish and Game) as *the* hot spot for salmon, especially kings, almost year-round. The best time, which varies before and after, is probably June and July. Fighting, flashy silvers peak toward September. Halibut and other game fish are caught, too. The stream that runs by the resort cabins has humpback salmon and also fine steelhead in season. When salmon come up the stream to spawn you might see a four-legged fisher—a mother bear teaching her cub the art.

Sometimes the steelheading is fine when there is a lull in salmon fishing out in the canal. The steelhead is a real fighter. One mid-May, we saw many a fisherman come in soaked to the waist and glowingly describe his battle with a big one upstream. When they head for the deep pools, in order to lick 'em, you sometimes have to join 'em.

But let us tell you *our* fish story. We tested the fishing at Bell Island one July with Myra Waldo, internationally known writer on food and travel subjects, and her husband, Bob. We had assorted designs on the fish: one just wanted to shoot (with camera) what we caught; Myra had plans to cook them; and we all droolingly promised to eat them. Myra caught the first one, a King salmon, as she was letting out her herring-baited hook. In this first short session, we accumulated an assortment of King, silver, and trout and even an ugly bottom fish, which we tossed back. One was especially lively and eager and leaped almost ten feet to land right smack in the net! When we had docked, Myra immediately routed our fish to the chowder pot and a delicious Swedish-style baked salmon dish.

Braver people than we can try to predict when fishing is really best in this vicinity. We have been lucky enough to catch a sixteen-pound King salmon in the second week of August when everyone warned us the run of big ones was over. It was a respectable fish, though dockside spoilsports were quick to point out that forty-pounders and over are the prizes. The rumors then were that fighting silvers were being caught that weighed in at ten or twelve pounds, while peaking up for fall, and the bigger ones weighed up to twenty pounds. "I like the suspense here," said one visitor. "You never know whether the next one will be a monster—regardless of season."

Looking at Bell Island from the family standpoint, we can see much more than just fishing there. It's a place where the fishermen can desert the rest of the family and know they are likely to keep occupied happily. Besides the very popular swimming pool, there is a mossy, woodsy trail up a short distance to a couple of small lakes. You don't have to go out in a boat to fish, either. Our youngsters enjoy dropping a line off the dock, and if you are really lazy, step down from the boardwalk and put a line in the stream that rushes by the cabins.

If you strike a lull in the fishing, there are compensations. Holding a rod gives an excuse to do nothing but sit and watch the sea and land life. We consider the time well spent if our birdwatching includes soaring bald eagles along with assorted ducks. We are easily amused at the antics of a family of otters playfully using a large rock for a slide, and seals sporting in the water.

Getting to Bell Island

The twenty-minute amphibian plane flight from Ketchikan is a typical, interesting example of flying in Southeast Alaska in almost any kind of weather. On clear, sunny days, the pilot takes the high route and swoops over snowy mountains. Such days make one aware of the color variety in this part of Alaska. You look down on light and dark greens, aqua, jade, shades of blue, mountain whites, muted rock colors. Bright colors like red are lacking, unless you count souvenirs of man's temporary stay. You spot rust-red remains of machinery, pipelines, and oil barrels as you pass over deserted fish canneries and logging camps.

Then there is the medium-high route, when there is just enough sun to cast a shadow on the greenery below. Scattered, wispy clouds form and disintegrate before your eyes, and bigger ones hover over and hide the mountain tops.

Some days the pilot has to fly the low route because of the overcast, and you get a closeup view of what's going on below in the boat channel. There may be a pod of sporting killer whales or a floating logging community being moved to a new location.

Accommodations

It is not easy to evaluate the accommodations at Bell Island; it depends on what you are used to. Some might consider this wilderness fishing camp more primitive than we do. Space is limited, so rates are based on sharing a room, with modern plumbing. The main lodge, with open lounge, bar, and meals served buffet and family style at specified hours, is attractive, rustic, and homey. Because it is small, reservations should be made ahead, and operations are geared mainly to fly-in visitors. Rates can vary. In 1979, a three-night package, based on two to a cabin, will cost $590. This rate covers lodging, meals, boat, motor, fuel, fishing gear, bait, cleaning and packing fish, plus pool and mineral-bath privileges. Guides, if available, are extra at an hourly charge. The only other extra is a fishing license. The air fare between Ketchikan and Bell Island is about $70 round trip.

Prices for swimming, meals, baths, boat rentals, etc., are quoted upon request for drop-in visitors not planning to occupy cabins. A drop-in may stay overnight if a cabin is available. Don't count on finding space without a reservation, however, especially when the fishing is good. Write ahead: 131 Third Ave. No., Edmonds, Washington 98020.

YES BAY

The nearest neighbor (about twelve miles) to Bell Island is Yes Bay Resort, accessible by private or charter boat or float planes from Ketchikan. Approaching by boat, you see what appears to be a large lodge when you turn into a bay off the main channel. Standing miragelike in the midst of wilderness, it just keeps looming larger and larger in its open yet sheltered bay bordered by tall, heavily timbered slopes. The land around it has the look of having been cleared and used before, maybe even landscaped. It has been—and the aura of history that surrounds the land on which this modern lodge stands is part of the attraction.

The lodge didn't open for business for more than ten years after it was first started. It was originally planned as a casinolike resort to be ready for operation when, certain factions hoped, statehood for Alaska would legalize gambling. Statehood was achieved in 1959, but the gamblers were out of luck. There are signs in the massive beamed lobby of the original intent, but the only part of the floor plan that materialized was the bar in the corner. The floor plugs for the machines, the roulette-wheel design, and the cardroom insignia are only decorations. It is a spectacular lobby, with a huge, circular raised fireplace at the bar end, and a panorama out of every view window.

Yes Bay Resort, reached only by boat or float plane, has excellent fishing and fascinating history.

The friendly, enthusiastic young couple who first attempted to make this beautiful piece of real estate both respectable and serviceable after what might be considered shady beginnings were Susan and Roger Lohrer. We visited Yes Bay during their first season of operation. History buffs, they were busily exploring the surrounding area for things that might be of interest to visitors, in addition to the fine stream, lake, and fishing. From them we learned how the place got its unusual name. It was derived from the Tlingit word "yaas" or "yas," meaning "mussel."

This lovely, peaceful setting was considered a hunting and fishing paradise by the Indians, but before 1880 white men were moving in. By 1900 a solid commercial fishing and canning industry was well under way. The town had almost a hundred permanent residents and over a dozen houses. The transients were an unusual assortment. There were seasonal fishermen, paid $40 a month from the day they arrived to the day they departed, plus their transportation and full board. There were native Indian men and women who drifted in and out to work in the cannery or bring in fish to be processed. There were even tourists who came by excursion boats on tours originating in San Francisco, lured by the list of such intriguing ports-of-call as Wrangell, Juneau, Glacier Bay, Sitka—and Yes Bay.

Then there were sixty or so Chinese, who kept to themselves and worked for a pittance under contract. They were preferred for the monotonous but exacting cannery work because they were skillful and exact and would work as long as there were fish to be packed to supplement their 38 cents per day wage with the small bonus based on the number of extra cans filled. Down the beach, where they took baths, some interesting items are still found: tiny opium vials indicating that they used to soak and smoke, probably to make bearable what must have been pretty grim living conditions.

The Hack family, present lodge hosts, are quick to point out other points of interest in the vicinity such as an old cemetery, and to see that you get there if you are interested. There is plenty of stream and lake fishing, clamming, and exploring to be done.

We hiked up the trail along the waterpipe line behind the power house in back of the lodge while Bob and Terry took off for fishing pictures. There are signs of the previous town's existence—a fireplace or chimney or foundation here and there. Beyond is a very beautiful, woodsy walk reminiscent of Washington's Olympic rain forest, but with smaller trees. Feathery green moss decorates the long fallen trees as well as the living ones. Even the stones, big and small, are softened by green vegetation. The shades of green are subtle and varied. Along the trail are natural sofas and chairs, all thickly upholstered with the same soft moss padding. It's a wonderful place to sit and ponder how, in hardly any time at all, signs of previous civilizations can be covered over by the lush forest.

Prices at Yes Bay

Current rates can be obtained by writing to Yes Bay Lodge, Ketchikan, Alaska 99901. Reservations in advance are essential. The four-day, three-night per person rate in 1978 was $585 (based on two in a room). In the package rate are room and board, boat, motor, fuel, tackle, bait, rain gear, fish care: cleaning, packing, icing, or smoking; guide if desired, and round-trip air fare from Ketchikan.

NORTH ALONG THE INSIDE PASSAGE

The next two ports-of-call along the Inside Passage are Wrangell and Petersburg. The distance is about ninety miles or six hours from Ketchikan to Wrangell by ferry, and another three hours from there to Petersburg. If you are flying, the time is cut considerably, unless you detour inland (on charter) as we did, to inspect and photograph the mighty glaciers and rugged mountains that form a natural barrier between Canada and the United States.

The small towns of Wrangell and Petersburg have less than three thousand inhabitants. The two towns are entirely different in character, though they also have many similarities. For one thing, neither is a "cliff-hanger" like Ketchikan or Juneau. Though mainland mountains are still an important part of the scenery, Wrangell and Petersburg, both on islands in the narrow sea passage, have room to spread out. Both towns are dependent on seafood and timber products to keep the payrolls active. Wrangell leans more heavily toward lumber export, and though a pulp mill has yet to materialize, they were first to realize the importance of the Japanese market. Petersburg harvests and processes all kinds of seafood, and a tiny, tasty shrimp found in surrounding waters is a Petersburg specialty.

Another similarity of the two towns in this day of developing tourism is not a detriment at all. Both are just beginning to realize that what they have taken for granted is just what visitors are seeking, namely hospitality and friendliness. Hospitality is still on a very personal basis in Wrangell and Petersburg.

Facilities so far are adequate and good. Before long they will be expanded, brochured, advertised, and organized. We hope somehow the towns manage to keep their informal charm and extremely friendly attitude toward the increasing number of visitors drawn to their area.

The LeConte Glacier

The LeConte Glacier is the southernmost active tidewater glacier on the North American continent, and is said to be the fastest-moving glacier in the world. This rapid movement causes almost continuous "calving." Huge chunks break off and head down the bay. The noise they make caused natives to name the glacier Hutli ("Thunderer") after their mythical Thunderbird, who is often seen in Indian designs, and who makes thunder just by beating his wings. The glacier lies in a deep canyon at the head of LeConte Bay, to the east of Petersburg, and quite close. The town has had reason to wish their glacier would be a little less active at times. Though the chunks of ice are doomed as soon as they break off the face of the glacier, some of them are immense. They travel toward Petersburg, melting all the way, but they are still large enough to be hazardous. A recent news item carried the headline "Iceberg Hits Petersburg Ferry Pier," and went on to describe damage estimated at several thousand dollars caused by an iceberg "as big as a house." It grounded on the beach as the tide went out. Residents sighed with relief to learn they had been bombarded by a "little one." A short distance to the north another one, three times as large, was beached. A combination of spring tides and offshore winds sometimes triggers a discharge of the varisized icebergs seen in the waters of the Inside Passage.

Out of Petersburg, a cruise ship, the *Blue Star,* takes passengers far into the bay, through the ice, and approaches LeConte Glacier. The slow pace gives passengers a closeup look at hundreds of harbor seal on ice floes, as well as Steller sea lions and killer whales, sporting in the water. Mountain goats make their home in surrounding lofty cliffs. Often a dozen or more are spotted.

Cruises are scheduled three times a week during summer. Anytime eight or more passengers want to make the trip, an extra cruise is scheduled. The price, which includes dinner, was $32.50 a person, with children half price. For time of departure and other current information, look up Captain Roland Burrows in the Petersburg phone book. Like all Alaskans, you'll note that he wears many hats, with Blue Star Plumbing & Heating listed along with the Blue Star Cruises.

It's a tossup which is the most rewarding view of the LeConte Glacier, from sea level or from the air. We think everyone should see these mighty spectacles *both* ways. Our fond memories of our airview of the LeConte are probably colored by the fact that we saw it under ideal conditions. It was a perfect day, which to a photographer means sunshine, blue skies, and sparkling water in Alaska's smog-free atmosphere. We were flying in my favorite craft, a Grumman Goose, piloted by Bill Stedman of Petersburg, who knows and appreciates every glacier, bay, and peak in the vicinity.

We took a turn over Petersburg, which is located at the northern end of Wrangell Narrows. From the air, it is evident how narrow the Narrows are, especially if a fair-sized ship happens to be passing through. Often things seen in miniature from above look better than they actually are. Neat Petersburg doesn't need this advantage, but it looked even more like a model town, its boats and houses reflected in the glassy-still harbor.

When you're flying you have a new awareness of subtle color variations not so readily noted from ground level. Consider the greens, for example, a basic land color due to the amount of precipitation, and also much evident in surrounding water. Logging scars on some lower slopes were turning green with regrowth, contrasting with the darker evergreen of untouched upper reaches. The milky tan silt of glaciers flows down bays, turns jade-green, and is finally precipitated. The blues are of infinite variety, too: sky, water, and that hard-to-describe frosty aquamarine in glacial ice, seen on surface pinnacles, glacier faces, or on floating icebergs making their journey to oblivion.

Some rocks are surprisingly colorful. Sheer, glacier-scoured cliffs may have dark criss-cross streaks or appear quite red. You wonder how the vegetation finds enough nourishment to survive on steep soil-starved cliffs. Here and there are rockslides, contrasting with avalanched snow slopes, a reminder of constant change in the mountains.

Petersburg, at the north end of Wrangell Narrows on the Inside Passage, is known as Little Norway.

"See one and you've seen them all" is no more true of glaciers than it is of towns in Alaska. There are too many to name. They vary in size and type from hanging glaciers that come to an abrupt end at the edge of a high cliff to glaciers that look like smooth, broad superhighways (from the air, at least). There are even lanes marked by moraines, piles of rocks and gravel debris placed neatly by the moving river of ice. The Sawyer Glacier has heavenly blue, waterfilled pits in its crumpled-up surface. There are also seracs, pinnacles of ice poking up. It is hard to judge how tall they really are with no familiar measuring gauge to use for perspective.

"This is a dirty glacier," remarked Bill Stedman, referring to the large amount of dark moraine dirt. "The LeConte is my idea of a good clean glacier, and it's the most spectacular." We went over to take a look, by way of the Dawes Glacier and Devil's Thumb, which

Bill wanted to show us "up close." It was an impressive landmark, all right. The almost perpendicular shaft, rising above the crest of the mountain range, appears more jagged up close than when viewed from below.

Bill is right about the LeConte. We felt on intimate terms by the time Bob had his fill of shooting its magnificent beauty. Its crevasses are deep and blue-hued, and so are its seracs. Its clean face, nearly a mile wide with a sheer ice wall 300 to 350 feet high, calves almost constantly. The seals and sea lions dwelling on the never-ending supply of icebergs and floes paid no attention to the bombardment nor to our airplane when we "buzzed" them for a closer look.

Bill is now with Alaska Island Air in Petersburg. Though the Grumman Goose has been disappearing from the Southeast scene, he proudly pointed out the one active Goose in his fleet, smartly painted in AIA colors and sporting their totem pole insignia. If you ever feel the need to rid yourself of "earthbound" feelings, our prescription is to try glacier flight-seeing. Even a short flight is exhilarating.

WRANGELL

Wrangell's past is fraught with political confusion. Its residents in a little over a hundred years underwent three flag-raisings: Russian, British, and finally the United States. The Russians established a settlement at Wrangell in Southeast Alaska as well as at Kodiak and Sitka, mainly because they were concerned over British encroachment on the fur trade. By building a fort at the mouth of the strategic Stikine River that pierces the mountain barrier into Canada, the Russians intended to control the supply route. Their fort, Redoubt St. Dionysius, effectively curbed the infiltration, and the Hudson's Bay Company was forced to negotiate a lease. In exchange for two thousand otter skins per year, the British were allowed access to the Southeast Alaska mainland coast. They happily replaced the Russian flag over Fort Dionysius and changed its name to Fort Stikine. When the British lease was up and Russia decided to sell out, the United States bought all existing forts lock, stock, and barrel along with the rest of Russian America.

Under the Americans, the third flag was hoisted and the fort's name changed to Wrangell (pronounced "wrangle"). They were not naming it for the type of public relations existing among the three fur-hungry countries—it was in honor of a Baron von Wrangel, a Russian governor of Alaska.

The town thrived as an important supply point for fur traders and goldseekers, and trade on the Stikine River was brisk. Prospectors swarmed to the area in three separate gold rushes in the last half of the nineteenth century: the Stikine, the Cassiar, and the Klondike. The influx of hordes of goldseekers played havoc with law and order at times. Meanwhile the town was settling down to its present comfortable role as lumber exporter and processor of products of the sea.

Food and lodging

Wrangell is having the same awakening as the other small towns of Southeast Alaska. The State Ferry System, daily jet planes, and one or two cruise ships a week are breaking the isolation barrier and bringing in more visitors. So far, the Stikine Inn overlooking the docks, Thunderbird Hotel downtown, and the Roadhouse four miles out of town, all completely modern, even with TV, have been adequate. The hotels also dispense hunting, fishing, and sightseeing information. Campers can stay at a very pleasant campground about ten miles south of town.

"Aunt Winnie's" Restaurant housed in the Stikine Inn serves good food, and you can usually count on some kind of fresh seafood. Some of us usually order a Shrimp Louie, made from the tiny local shrimp, which are sweet and delicious.

Sightseeing

There is little evidence left of the Russian or British occupation, though a sign marks the site of old Fort Dionysius. However, one of Wrangell's chief attractions is a collection of Indian totem poles and a tribal house standing on its own little island, which is reached by a footbridge near the main part of town. The Bear Tribal House is a reproduction of one belonging to Chief Shakes, leader of the once warlike Stikine Indians. This is no lonely, deserted display of the ancient craft. Townspeople make good use of this centrally located park on Shakes Island. Under the watchful eye of totemic faces, parents picnic and visit while youngsters swim in the reasonably warm, sheltered water, cleansed twice daily by the tide. Though not originals, the totem poles are faithful reproductions of many of the best historic designs.

Some original Indian art work can also be seen. It is scattered along the beach both to the north and south in the form of petroglyphs, carvings pecked into rocks, the sign of a very old civilization long predating the totem era. The petroglyphs are believed to be a form of "doodling," to pass the time during boring guard duty or waits for fish and game. Guessing at the significance of the crude drawings is a favorite game of visitors, as well as ethnologists.

Stikine River trips

Riverboating enthusiasts are unanimous in recommending a trip on the Stikine River for condensing a lot of spectacular Alaska scenery intermixed with lively history into about four days. It was a popular trip even before 1900, and during peak periods like a gold rush the river was so crowded that signalmen had to be stationed to direct traffic at one narrow canyon.

The Stikine, described as the fastest-flowing navigable river in America, slices through a mountain range as it drops 560 feet in about 150 miles. It flows past historic landmarks, including a gold ghost town and Boundary House, which now marks the U.S.-Canada boundary. It used to be a customs and weighing station during gold rush days. The venerable geology of the mountain range is exposed and there are countless glaciers, along with infinite stories to match the highlights. The Great Glacier near the Scud River, for example, has a bloody history. The Stikine used to flow under this glacier, trapped in its narrow valley, and wily warriors massacred invaders by throwing rocks on their canoes as they emerged from under the ice tunnel.

Float trips are becoming popular, with bird and animal watching a favorite pastime. In the flats are cranes, ducks, geese (even snow

Chief Shakes Island with totems and tribal house, Wrangell.

geese), and swans. Bear, deer, wolf, and moose roam frequently along the river, or swim in it. At night boats can tie up at a convenient beach or sandbar.

The starting point, Telegraph Creek, 150 miles from Wrangell, dates from before 1900. It is the kind of town that is fun to poke around in, isolated except for the river and a dubious "road" that eventually wends its way over 100 miles to connect with the Alcan Highway, as the Canadian portion of the Alaska Highway is labeled. Its graveyard has dates that go back to the town's beginning, with inscriptions that tell how some of the deceased met their ends.

It is hoped that a riverboat will again take passengers on its four-day working trip up and back the Stikine River. For years, the

Margaret Rose carried needed supplies to areas along the historic river highway, and included up to twenty-four lucky "river rats" who paid an all-inclusive tour rate to go along. She was the lifeline for miners' camps and for an isolated ranch. Sixty-four feet long, she looks as a riverboat should: broad of beam and shallow of draw, the better to inch her flat bottom over sandbars, or line through rapids with rocks inches away. Though the trip up, loaded with freight and going against the current took three days, the trip back took about twelve hours—a fast review of the same awesome scenery with a whole new perspective.

The guest book of the *Margaret Rose* contains names of millionaires, dukes and duchesses, and world travelers, and their comments. The one we like best that sums up the whole trip came from a writer friend. He wrote: "Mark Twain woulda loved it!"

PETERSBURG

"Is this *Alaska?*" we wondered when we first saw Petersburg, several years ago. It looked more like pictures we had seen of fishing villages among the fjords of Norway. A large, freshly painted fishing fleet lay at anchor. Neat white houses, backed by snowcapped mountains, lined tidy streets. There was no jerry-built look of a quickly chosen site, a hastily assembled gold rush or seasonal fishing town. Petersburg has a solid look. The folk attracted here came with the idea of staying. They built homes to last and in the style preferred by seafaring people: square and compact, a sturdy foundation, short flights of steps to porch and first floor, and an attic-type second story topped by a peaked roof.

Hardy Norwegians founded Petersburg. It was named for one of them, Peter Buschmann. The early settlers carved the town from the wilds shortly before 1900, approximately the time that Wrangell was being shaken up by its third gold rush. The thrifty Petersburg settlers could not have cared less about gold; they were interested only in fish. Besides, they were busy building those permanent homes and putting their town in order. Once settled, the towns-people preferred to concentrate on the job they knew best: harvesting the bounty of the sea. Today, some third-generation descendants of the pioneers work in logging camps. The main occupation, though, is processing and gathering about twenty million pounds of seafood annually, including their own speciality, tiny Petersburg shrimp.

The best way for a visitor to appreciate a town like Petersburg is to see it through the eyes of someone who knows it well. A good time is over the Fourth of July, or May 17, our favorite Petersburg holiday. This is Norwegian Independence Day, dating from 1814, when Norwegians declared themselves separate from Sweden, though they did not get their own king until 1905. It is still a good excuse for a celebration in Petersburg, starting on the nearest Friday and lasting the whole weekend.

Our "guide" was Ken Thynes, whom we had first met in Ketchikan. He grew up in Petersburg, and his parents and some brothers still live there. Ken goes back to visit at the sligtest excuse, usually for festivals and always for the herring season. He knows everyone in town and we could swear that most of the kids called him Uncle Kenny.

As the weekend progressed we felt absorbed by the community, beginning with the earliest commencement exercises we have ever attended. Ken remarked that it was a big class, about thirty, and the reason for the early school dismissal was because the fishing season was under way. All but one senior, who was out in a fishing boat, made it back for his diploma. By coincidence, the speaker was the one who addressed Ken's class, Senator Ernest Gruening, whose Petersburg ties included a daughter-in-law. Afterward, out in the pure spring air and still-light Alaskan evening, the graduates lined the school walk and the whole town filed by to shake their hands and offer congratulations. Then the kids headed for their graduation dance at the Elks Club hall. The rest of the town headed for the groaning smorgasbord at the Beachcomber ($3, all we could eat!). It is a few miles out of town to the south, on a dock overlooking the channel; costs $7.50 now.

Town highlights

Petersburg's waterfront is a busy one. Even in festival time, if a boatload of fish comes in, there is work to do. We watched a crew unload halibut, huge to our eyes, though the workers swore these weren't the big ones yet. The feed that night was fish, served in a big warehouse nearby at Petersburg Fisheries. We had a preview of one of the main delicacies as we watched women fileting the fresh-caught halibut, cutting out the cheeks, and slicing some choice sections into inch-sized chunks. Naturally, we asked about the chunks and learned from a worker they were to be served at the dinner, after being dipped in a batter made from Krusteaz and *beer* and then deep-fried.

"The beer in the batter makes them puff up and keeps the halibut extra moist—it's good for shrimp, crab legs, or any deep-fried seafood," she claimed. Later we met her serving at the fish dinner. She came down the line of hungry waiting customers and passed out samples. She was right; those cubes, supplementing all the other delicious fresh-caught seafood spread out, were the best we've ever tasted.

We asked Ken if camping visitors could get seafood and how. He said anything in season would be available at the stores or from the processing plants.

"In fact," he continued, "if you happen to be down on the docks when they are unloading and ask if you can buy some fish, someone is likely to *give* you a ten- or twelve-pound 'chicken'"—that is, a small halibut.

Continuing his downtown tour, Ken pointed out Sing Lee Alley (labeled Indian Street now), a most picturesque remainder from the past, with false-fronted old buildings lining the short winding street that ends in a wharf. Lee was an ill-fated Chinaman, done in by foul play in the early days. We walked the length of the waterfront, in which Ken had a personal interest. He had worked on the crew that dredged out the harbor, built the bulkhead, and filled in the area of the business district.

"Never underestimate the logging skills of these Norwegians," Ken said. "They solved the problem of a bulkhead for the engineers by picking out the right-sized trees down the channel a ways, and then cut and hauled them by water and put them in place. Saved a chunk of money—the town got a rebate thanks to all the enthusiasm of these hardy souls who don't like to wait around on jobs that need to be done."

The automatic drydocks next to the bulkhead are run by the tide. At high tide the fishermen park their boats on skids, and wait to do the necessary work when the bottoms are left high and dry at low tide. When finished, they are prepared to take off on the next high tide.

Petersburg's Centennial dividend is a small, interesting museum, the pride of the townspeople, who, as in all community projects, met the matching funds provided by state and federal governments. They thriftily stretched them to the utmost by pitching in with labor, skills, and materials.

In front of the museum is an unusual and charming fountain called the Fiske Memorial. It's not a people memorial; it's for "fiske" (fish), and all in the area are remembered: halibut, all kinds of salmon, and a school of important herring, most artistically fashioned in copper. Carson Boysen, the artist, was a temporary member of the community, a high school art teacher who left his mark before going on to further studies. The town is proud of its fountain, and the creator, they are sure, is headed for fame.

Inside the neat building is a continuously growing collection of items representing Petersburg's Norwegian and Indian cultures. They have been wheedled and garnered from pioneer families. We noted a lovely old pump organ and also an old crank-turned type that was used in an early skating rink. Along with lace and cut-out work, for which Norwegian women from various sections of the old country were noted, and assorted heirloom costumes, were Indian artifacts found in the vicinity. The pestles and mortars were more elaborate than most, which probably indicates that the Indians had leisure to work them in this area abounding in fish and game. Here is the final resting place of a 126½-pound record salmon, stuffed and mounted. It's hard to realize what a giant fish it is till you see it! (Petersburg's "World Champion Salmon Derby" runs all year.) There are old pictures of Petersburg, and the name rosters read like an Oslo telephone directory—Clausens, Enges, Trones, Mathisens, Thynes, Hagermans, Thompson. Of interest to writers is a very early model of a portable typewriter.

Visiting Petersburg during the Independence Day Festival points up the Alaskan-Norwegian character of the town. Your ear catches

English spoken with an accent and toe-tapping music of the schottische and the polka. Eyes are dazzled by bright old-country dress and mouths water at smorgasbords and typical Alaskan delicacies.

The only part of the festivities that could be called formal was held at the gym, complete with horseplay by Vikings who met planes and ferries, and a group of Indians in authentic costumes. Charming dances by the Little Norway Dancers (a children's group decked in real Norwegian costumes), an exhibition by a crack, healthy-looking girls' drill team, a square dance demonstration, and a minimum of speeches rounded out the program.

Afterward we went up to Ken's sister-in-law's house and had some schnapps, snacking heavily on "rulapulsa," made from venison, "gaffelbitter," a pickled-herring confection, and salmon, cold-smoked for twelve days. Tora Thynes, like everyone in town, holds down several community jobs. She had taken in other stray visitors whom she happened to discover, among them a mostly Norwegian-speaking TV crew who were photographing the town and festivities for an Oslo program. Language was no barrier—"skol!" was sufficient.

Petersburg was not through celebrating until after the Saturday-night Elks Club Dance, and a salmon bake with more dancing at nearby Sandy Beach picnic wayside on Sunday.

Ken had already driven us around most of the island's forty miles of roads, pointing out that there are campgrounds to the south of town. At Sandy Beach, he showed us the Horn Cliffs rising across the water—good goat-hunting territory—and we watched icebergs that had broken off the LeConte Glacier float along the steep far shore, obviously bound for Petersburg.

Transportation and information

Alaska Airlines delivers 727 jet service to both Petersburg and Wrangell. In fact, what may be the shortest jet flight in the world joins the two towns. The air schedule allows for twenty minutes, but the day we flew we clocked the time we were actually airborne at only eight minutes. It was flightseeing all the way at about 500 to 700 feet above the channel. The two towns are included in ferry schedules and some cruise ship itineraries. Anyone traveling there in their own boat will meet a lot of kindred souls.

Visitor information is dispensed in the towns' museums, or just ask any of the friendly residents about the hunting, fishing, and sightseeing. They will be happy to point you in the right direction— or maybe even go along with you.

Food and lodging

In Petersburg, besides the campgrounds there are at least three hotels. We stayed at the Tides Inn ($38 double), which overlooks downtown Petersburg and the fishing fleet. There are a few restaurants downtown, besides the before-mentioned Beachcomber, which now has some rooms ($33 double).

3 Northern Towns of the Panhandle

JUNEAU

JUNEAU, generally speaking, can be summed up in three words: gold, government, and a glacier. The gold is not all gone by any means, but it was temporarily forgotten as a source of income as long as the fixed price was $35 an ounce. Much government business is conducted in Juneau, both federal and state—it is Alaska's capital. Juneau's biggest attraction for both residents and visitors is a huge glacier, the Mendenhall, so accessible that you drive right up to it. Juneau has profitable fishing and forest industries, of interest to tourists mainly as they relate to recreational possibilities.

Though Juneau, unlike previously mentioned Southeast Alaska cities, is on the mainland, it might just as well be on an island. A formidable mountain barrier effectively isolates it, and the only approaches are by water and air. People converge on the capital by cruise ship, state ferry, private boat, and plane. Jets land at the airport. Small planes may land at the city dock Seadrome if their craft is equipped with floats. In the latter case, airplanes and boats have to keep an eye out for each other. Whichever way you arrive, you'll have had ample views of the area's trademarks: islands, water, mountains, and trees.

As you fly in you'll begin to realize how few signs of civilization exist in the vast expanse between Alaska's cities.

From the air, extensive ranges of mountains can be seen off in the distance, and from this seagull's view it is easier to spot occasional logging scars reflected in quiet inlets. Sometimes there'll be a fishing boat and small cannery. Or a small jewel-green lake, trapped in a high mountain hollow, may sport a tiny cabin and boat, signs that the Forest Service has been there. But the evidence of human encroachment seems infinitesimal to anyone seeing such a quantity of real wilderness for the first time.

No doubt about it, Juneau is another cliff-hanger. A newly modernized skyline stands out against a bulky mountain backdrop, its large office buildings, hotels, and stores confined between the mountains and the Gastineau Channel. The streets are narrow and hilly, mostly one-way, and homebuilders have had to scale the slopes or hop the channel by bridge to Douglas Island, across the way. The other choice is to expand to the suburbs where attractive new homes with a view are springing up on land leveled by the still-retreating Mendenhall Glacier. Up and beyond the town proper stretches the Juneau Ice Field, source of massive glaciers, for years the site of much scientific research, and an awesome spectacle to flightseeing visitors.

The reason for starting any Alaskan town in the late 1800s was never based on whether it was a convenient location, or whether there was enough room for a town. All that mattered was its closeness to a source of wealth. In the case of Juneau it was gold, and the discovery site on Gold Creek is not far from the center of town. A geologist who was poking around the mountains and glaciers in the vicinity passed on the information that he noted the same type of rocks around Juneau that appeared in other places where rich gold discoveries were made. Teams from mining companies were assigned to check the rumor out. Joe Juneau and Dick Harris made the strike. Such news is as hard to hoard as gold, and the town grew rapidly. It was first called Harrisburg in honor of Dick, and then changed to Juneau in honor of Joe. Large mining operations tunneled through the mountains behind Juneau and dug holes across the way at Douglas.

Juneau was founded after the United States purchased Alaska from Russia and after Sitka had started to decline. It wasn't long before residents of the new boom town started agitating to have the territorial capital moved from Sitka to where the action as well as the larger population was. Among historians there seems to be disagreement about exactly when, in the first dozen years after 1900, the transfer was actually made. But they do agree that buildings had been erected, records were in place, and all was in order in time for the first meeting of the first territorial legislature in 1913.

Alaska's capital history may be repeated. After agitation, and for the same reasons, state citizens voted to relocate. They picked a site (Willow) between Anchorage and Fairbanks, but they are having second thoughts about the high cost of building and moving.

At first glance, Juneau appears very modern because of the new skyscrapers on the horizon, but as soon as you wander around downtown and along the waterfront, drive the narrow streets, and take a second look at the buildings, it is easy to see that much of the old flavor remains. But don't judge Juneau on its face value. Delving under almost any rough exterior reveals that all the latest comforts and conveniences are there, and functioning. As you travel out from the center of town the buildings are new and attractive, and large well-stocked shopping centers serve new residential areas in the best contemporary style.

As the capital and third-largest city in Alaska, Juneau is a busy place, especially downtown. During business hours there are many people milling around, hardly any of them native Alaskans. You could tap shoulders till your arm is tired before finding someone born in the state. (One hitch is that Alaska did not graduate from territory to state until 1959, which limits the prospects, technically speaking, to those under twenty years old.) A large number of the people doing business in Juneau are the comelatelies, and if they are in politics, there is a suspicious tendency to look on them as carpetbaggers, no matter how long they have been there. Any Eskimos or Indians you see are likely to be born-in-Alaska citizens; moreover, they might be legislators from Barrow or other outlying political districts.

Confined as the downtown area is, you are likely to see almost anyone you are looking for breeze by, including the governor, perhaps headed for lunch at the executive mansion from the Capitol Building. Former Governor William A. Egan and his wife, Neva, were especially friendly sorts. We watched his progress as he strode briskly up the street at noon one fine Juneau day greeting people right and left. When he got to our station wagon, parked while we were waiting for Bob and loaded with the usual gear, three kids and our Alaskan husky, he gave us a special nod, though we were tourists, non-voters, and it was an off-election year.

Another well-known face was that of the late Senator Ernest Gruening. For fourteen years he served as territorial governor, probably longer than anyone except the best-known Russian governor, Alexander Baranof.

We first met him in 1952 when we interviewed him. We had our three-year-old Terry with us, and he played in a corner of the governor's office with his tinkertoys while we "worked." Bob took photographs, and I held flashbulbs, while Governor Gruening talked about his favorite subject—Alaska. We especially remember his story of how the simple but attractive state flag on a standard by his chair was created. The American Legion held a contest in the Alaska public schools in 1926, for the purpose of designing a flag which would be typical of the territory. The winner was a thirteen-year-old Indian boy, Benny Benson, living in the Jesse Lee Mission Home, then located in Seward. The idea was simple: eight gold stars on a field of deep blue, arranged to form the Big Dipper and the North Star. And so was the concise explanation of its symbolism: "The blue field is for the Alaska sky and the forget-me-not, an Alaskan flower. The North Star is for the future State of Alaska, the most northerly of the Union. The Dipper is for the Great Bear— symbolizing strength."

Juneau is a proper place to mention some of the other Alaskan symbols, instigated by enthusiastic sessions of the legislature over the years. They all seem appropriate and abundant: State Flower, forget-me-not; State Tree, Sitka spruce; State Fish, King salmon; Official Bird, willow ptarmigan. We would have nominated the Alaskan husky for State Dog, but the way things are going, it appears that the snowmobile may be taking over.

Sightseeing

There is considerable evidence of the old days and culture in the general vicinity of the Capitol Building. Out of doors, representing

Impressive face of Juneau's most accessible "neighborhood" glacier, Mendenhall, and its ice-strewn lake is visitor highlight.

the Indians, are two fine totems, one in the square next to the library, the other dressing up the Governor's Mansion, which, except for the totem, looks very un-Alaskan—more like a southern plantation home. Hemmed in, and almost hidden by new buildings, a short distance from the Capitol and up the hill stands a Russian Orthodox church. Its cross, mosquelike dome, and colorful circular architecture are unmistakable—and charming. But practically everything of interest along historic lines is displayed in the State Museum. After being shunted around, the museum now has its own building, a Centennial project, within walking distance from the main waterfront. Crates of historical residue had been in storage because of lack of space. With room at last to spread out, the curator and staff, paid and volunteer, spent months unpacking and evaluating. They have done a fine job of displaying all to best advantage.

Pick up a downtown shop guide and a good walking-tour map free for the asking at most shops and the Information Center at 2nd and Franklin, or ride the newest mode of transportation for conquering those steep streets, a tram. In summer the Gold City Trolley winds up, down, and around Juneau's downtown on daily scheduled tours ($4.25).

House of Wickersham

High on the slopes behind Juneau, overlooking the town and Gastineau Channel, stands the House of Wickersham. It is called the "house of living history." Along with the history lesson, the hostess, Ruth Allman, serves up a dash of botany and a touch of culinary art. Hospitality is the catalyst. Don't let the formal-sounding name cause you to avoid the place as you might a wax museum. Everything within is pure, authentic Alaskana.

Judge James H. Wickersham, who made his home there until his death in 1939, was not a native Alaskan. He was born in Illinois and moved to Tacoma, Washington, near Seattle. He left his mark in Washington. He explored the wild Olympic Peninsula jutting into the Pacific Ocean and named and urged setting aside the large wilderness area now known as Olympic National Park. He was well acquainted with and sympathetic to Washington's native Indians.

His profession was law, which he used to bring order out of chaos wherever he saw it. After straightening things out at home in Tacoma, he traded his mansion for a log cabin in Eagle, Alaska, in 1900. He set about bringing law and order to Alaska for the next thirty-nine years, leaving an indelible imprint on the Great Land's development. As a territorial judge, his beat was a broad one, and it took physical stamina to fulfill the duties of office. He had it, and his record of achievements is a long one.

"Wick" was a dynamo. After cleaning up Nome's gold scandal, he went on to serve Alaska well. As Congressional delegate he hammered away until Alaska got its territorial legislature and home rule. He had a finger in the building of the Alaska Railroad, helped establish the University of Alaska and Mount McKinley National Park, named Fairbanks, and was the first to plead statehood for the Territory of Alaska way back in 1916. He was interested in everything Alaskan. He kept in marvelous physical shape, leading the first attempt to climb Mount McKinley in 1903. This was when you had to do it the hard way—on foot. There were no planes or helicopters to plant you part way up the 20,320-foot peak, and no airdrop supplies, in those days.

But the most remarkable thing about this energetic judge was the fact that he kept an amazing daily diary record of what was happening in Alaska during his thirty-nine-year span. It's all there in his neat, readable handwriting, in the original small notebooks—forty-seven of them.

In an entry on June 7, 1923, the judge describes finding the Lincoln Totem, under glass now in Juneau's State Museum. Already fifty years old, it had been carved by slaves of Chief Shakes. It stood on the shore fifty miles from Ketchikan at Alaska's southern boundary, watching the steamers go by till it was salvaged for posterity.

Judge Wickersham's good works are well known throughout Alaska. Like Kilroy of World War II fame, name the place and he was there. Ruth Allman, who grew up in the House of Wickersham, is his late wife's niece and might be called the "keeper of the flame." Fortunately, she is a saver. Along with the diaries, she has saved the judge's lawbooks, history books, artifacts, letters, documents, and treasures dating back to Russian-America days.

Daily, Ruth Allman serves flaming sourdough waffles to guests at Judge
Wickersham's long family table. Behind her is a portrait of the judge with
some of his many books, diaries, and Alaskana.

Ruth is a cheery soul, widow of Jack Allman, newspaper man and
sourdough prospector. The fascinating hour-and-a-half tour spent
among the mementos of the past, gleaning a perspective of that not-
so-long-ago era, is based on Ruth's personal memories and
experiences. Her culinary triumph is her own concoction, Flaming
Sourdough. She tells you all about sourdough as she gives you a
generous sample made from "starter" from her sixty-year-old pot.
Buy her homey handwritten and illustrated cookbook *Alaska
Sourdough* and you can try your own at home. "Sourdough" was a
prospector's best friend, his daily bread and pancakes. He had to
beg, borrow, or steal a "starter" (leavening agent like liquid yeast)
and then keep it alive, active, and available for whenever he set up
his lonely camp. Each time he used it he held back a little pure
starter for the next time. Then he added more flour, water, and a
little soda, to sweeten and lighten the sourdough before baking it.
He carried the reserved starter in a little pouch next to his skin, to be

sure it didn't die from the cold. The rather sour odor came to be identified with these old prospectors, so they, too, were called sourdoughs.

The botany lesson is in connection with what goes with the sourdough, delicious rose-hip syrup and butter. Alaskans like Ruth had to find out what native plants and fruits might be used to supply vitamin C and other nutrients in a land lacking ordinary fresh fruits and vegetables.

This tour is given twice a day May to September and costs $7 for adults; children $5. For more information, check with the Baranof Hotel, or at the Chamber of Commerce on the corner of Second and Franklin. They can tell you how and when to get there, and assure you that your name will be in the sourdough pot.

We could lose ourselves for weeks browsing and photographing that unequaled collection (as long as Ruth Allman would feed us her high-protein, B-vitamin, nonfattening sourdoughs, nutritionally balanced by that delicious rose-hip confection). We worry that everything might be wiped out in that vulnerable old frame house before plans materialize to protect the priceless items which even the Smithsonian Institution is interested in cataloging and preserving. Meanwhile, there is a great deal of charm in seeing them in their natural setting, lovingly cared for by someone who knows them intimately. We always come away with a *privileged* feeling—like kids allowed to play in the attic.

Visiting a gold mine

Approaching Juneau by water or air from the south, visitors are bound to notice a prominent scar high on the steep slope of Mount Roberts, rising behind the city. Its deteriorating rusty-red framework is not unattractive against the perpetually green mountainside, and as long as it lasts it will no doubt be a conversation piece. It is the Alaska-Juneau Gold Mine, which produced low-grade ore until World War II focused attention on more essential industries than gold mining. Continued inflation caused production costs to overtake the selling price of gold, forcing the final shutdown.

The closest visitors can get to the mine now is the old messhall at Last Chance Basin, where local melodramas such as "Delilah's

Dilemma" are the main course now. There is also an exhibit of goldrush Alaskana to browse through. Dinner is served nearby, though, an Alaska-style outdoor salmon bake (with big plastic dome shelter, if it rains). It's a neat little package with a free bus to and from nightly. All you can eat for $9, then across to the play site, admission $4. Children are half price for both.

Before the decaying old mine fell down to the point of being too hazardous, it was possible to ride in one of the ore cars attached to an old engine. It burrowed into a tunnel in the gold mountain and came out at a viewpoint overlooking Juneau, Gastineau Channel, and Douglas. The noisy, tooth-jarring ride, fortunately short, was the real thing. In constructing trunk lines and trains, comfort was never considered. Chunks of ore don't care, and miners had to expect a certain number of hazards and discomforts. Kids adored the ride, and adults not easily unhinged by clatter considered it worth it for the view, but it's not for dogs—not even the husky. Since it was a small group and no one objected, Alyeska came along. All sixty-five pounds of her was reduced to a mass of quivering, terror-stricken dogflesh—she was a lap dog all the way.

The Mendenhall Glacier

Juneau and vicinity has the most road miles among the Southeast Panhandle cities, and a fine paved loop road leads to her major attraction, Mendenhall Glacier. "This is probably the only drive-in glacier in existence," quipped our Juneau friend Jim Johnson.

An editor once crushed Bob, who finds glaciers perpetually entrancing as photo subject matter, by calling the Mendenhall a "dirty old mass of ice." It is true that glaciers in their travels are inclined to expose areas of crushed rock, boulders, and dirt. A black-and-white photo hardly does the subject justice; a color picture, especially taken on a dull day, points up the magnificent blue hues.

The way to get the full blow of this mighty and ancient river of ice is to drive right up to it, then get out of your car and walk even closer, to the edge of its lake. From your puny height and ground-level view, walking up and looking a glacier in the face is an impressive experience.

If you are lucky, a large chunk *might* break off right in front of your eyes with a thundering crash, setting off its own small tidal wave. It's bound to happen eventually; where else would those sizable icebergs in the lake come from?

The Mendenhall is retreating (approximately ninety feet a year), but hardly anyone except scientists can notice it. However, the rocks on which the Visitor Center stands were exposed beginning about 1936. If the glacier had not continued to recede, that 1½-mile-wide, 100- to 200-foot-high face would be staring in the window. Someone remarked that all it would take for the Mendenhall to start advancing again is a slight but continuing drop in the temperature, predicted by the year 2000. No one appears very worried about this possibility, least of all those who have homes in the new suburb, developed on choice view property, nor the picnickers and campers enjoying their stay almost in the shadow of the glacier. Everything has a look of permanence with schools and handy well-stocked shopping centers nearby. Perhaps, if the recession continues, roads and houses may eventually follow the Mendenhall on up to its source in the Juneau Ice Field.

Meanwhile, since it is probably the easiest-to-reach glacier most visitors will encounter, it is well to take advantage of all the interesting displays, walks, and talks offered through the Visitor Center. The surrounding terrain is a study in contrasts, varying from lichens just getting a toehold after the glacier has relinquished its grip on the land to neighboring valleys and mountain slopes lush with forests and dense vegetation. Scientific minds consider such an area an on-the-spot laboratory. Visitors are more likely to be awed by the unusual pure scenic grandeur and the fact that they can now stand on glacier-scoured rocks or hover over the Mendenhall's crevasses in a helicopter or fly over the Ice Field.

Having your own car in Juneau can be an advantage, because of the good roads leading to interesting recreation areas, as well as to the glacier. However, there is scheduled bus service, a variety of tours, taxis, and rental car services for those in need of transportation. Information is available at hotel desks, airline offices, the Juneau Chamber of Commerce, the Alaska Division of Tourism, and the local travel agencies.

Nearby recreation possibilities

People lucky enough to live in areas where infinite opportunities for outdoor recreation abound are naturally in the best position to make full use of them. Alaskans not only do this, but are most generous and friendly in sharing with visitors who show kindred inclinations. Next best to having relatives to visit is making friends quickly. We feel that we helped "plant" some special friends in Juneau—Violet and Bill Morrice. Bill retired young from one career in the state of Washington, and when another was offered in Alaska, our enthusiasm for the state over the years probably had something to do with their settling up there. Through their viewpoint as relative newcomers, combined with our experience as rather independent and chronic visitors, perhaps we can point out best some things that visitors might be able to enjoy within vacationtime limits.

The Morrices were easily hooked on Juneau and vicinity, because it is quite similar to Puget Sound country and their favorite stomping grounds, the San Juan Islands. "It is still undeveloped up here," they wrote enthusiastically. Vi admitted that for the first several months she was too busy for her painting hobby, though there was no lack of subject matter. There were too many fish to be caught and frozen or canned, and too many local edible berries to pick and try out for jellies and jams. "Besides," continued Vi, "there is a lot of social life going on in this town!"

Since fishing had been one of their favorite sports, they found that they had settled in a choice spot in Juneau. One of their first purchases was a small boat, and they set about testing the rumors that there is some of the world's best salmon fishing in neighboring waters. They had lots of company. Juneau's salmon fishing attracts visitors all summer, with the greatest influx during the annual Golden North Salmon Derby, held toward mid-August.

"There must have been thirty-six hundred fishermen in about fourteen hundred boats out at peak times," marveled Bill. "People were using anything that would float!"

He was talking about the 1967 Derby, the twenty-first to be held. Though no one managed to top the record set ten years ago (a fifty-nine-pound, three-ounce beauty), a lot of fine fish hit the scales in competition for the worthwhile prizes. First prize was $2,500 cash and there were ninety-nine others worth $100 or more, plus special prizes.

These figures have now inflated to eight thousand fishermen competing for a $5,000 first prize. And there are many other prizes, adding up to a total of over $40,000.

The King salmon fishing is so good that people forget to mention that coho salmon and halibut are also excellent saltwater sport fish. Freshwater anglers are happy with the abundance of cutthroat, Dolly Varden, eastern brook, rainbow trout, and steelhead. Hunters find no shortage of birds or game to test their shooting skill during the hunting season. There are fly-in trips and hikes of varying difficulty to nearby viewpoints, as well as Forest Service cabins. If berrypicking expeditions are your forte, keep in mind that you may be competing with the bears for the succulent fruit.

Food and lodging

In Juneau we have rarely been overwhelmed by either lodging or food. We consider the campground at Mendenhall Glacier to be the most spectacular place to stay. A close second is the campground at Auke Bay. Otherwise, the "in" place is the Baranof Hotel in the center of town. Don't be chalked up as a "cheechako" by giving it the Russian accent. In Juneau, it's *Bar*-an-of, with accent on the first syllable. We have also enjoyed the Prospector near the new museum, and the Breakwater Inn, out of town a short distance and overlooking Gastineau Channel and the small boat harbor. A $3 million, 100-room Juneau Hilton—the first in Alaska—is the newest. All the above have good restaurants.

Residents readily recommend some favorites: Yancey Derringer's on Merchants' Wharf; the City Cafe and Sally's Kitchen; the Latchstring in the Baranof, Mike's Place across the bridge in Douglas; Bullwinkle's Pizza; and the Hideaway, up steeps stairs and hidden in the basement of the Bergman Hotel, now a National Landmark. We'll put in a good word for the Red Dog Saloon's "poor boy" sandwich and beer for lunch. It's also a noted night spot, with sawdust-sprinkled floor.

At times, such as during the legislature, Juneau can be bursting at the seams. However, if you need help in finding space in a pinch, you'll get it by asking—anyone.

GLACIER BAY

Like many other worthwhile Alaskan destinations, Glacier Bay is reached only by air or sea. Small charter excursions from Juneau and many cruise ships include the sidetrip up the bay to the glaciers in their itineraries. Plane charters are available from Juneau, Skagway, and Haines. Float planes land on the water in front of the lodge and tie up at the dock. In summer, daily scheduled jet flights land at Gustavus Airport, only thirty minutes from Juneau. There, guests transfer to a bus for the quiet, mossy, ten-mile ride through cool rainforest to the lodge.

Because Bob finds glaciers so intriguing, it is not surprising that we particularly enjoy Glacier Bay National Monument. Our family's first visit was the eye-level one, an expedition by small boat with enough time for us to explore up into the farthest reaches, camping and taking pictures. We felt especially lucky to travel with Bob Howe, newly appointed superintendent of the monument, his wife, Doris, and one of his sons, teen-aged Greg. They were every bit as enthusiastic about this survey and get-acquainted trip into their new territory as Bob was to photograph new places. We parked our trailer in the Howes' back yard beyond Tee Harbor outside of Juneau, and traveled by small boat the approximately one hundred miles to their headquarters at Bartlett Cove, at the northwest end of the Alexander Archipelago.

We readily understood Bob Howe's eagerness to know as fast as possible Glacier Bay's peculiarities, possibilities, hazards, beauties, wild life, and vegetation, which change at the whim of more than twenty massive glaciers, most of which are retreating up their private inlets. Both Bob and Doris are true outdoor lovers and naturalists. They put our advance research to shame in the amount of boning up they had already done on their 4,400-square-mile "kingdom." Although we all agreed at the end of the trip that it was an experience we could never forget, it wasn't till we took a charter flight the following summer that we realized what lasting impressions and memories we were able to pool and recall as we retraced our itinerary.

"Someone is camping at our Goose Cove," pointed out Tracy. Sure enough, there were a couple of small tents. Our pilot, Pete

Goodwin, dropped in low enough with his small float plane so we could see that the tide had deposited the usual ration of icebergs on the beach. That brought back memories: "Do you remember how Tracy and I put the buckets under the drips to collect our water till Mrs. Howe happened to find that little stream over there?" reminisced Jackie. Bob and I had our own memories. We were recalling what lovely ice cubes those blue-hued bergs provided for our predinner cocktails. Bob Howe claimed the reason it was so crystal-clear and long-lasting in our cups was because it was centuries-old and highly compressed by glacier weight.

Landmarks looked familiar from the air, and there was a story or more with each. Sealers Island, taken over by the birds, was where everyone watched the miracle of eggs hatching and moist baby seagulls take their first steps. The black swatch across the mountain separating the Muir and Riggs glaciers was scoured by the glaciers where they used to come together. The lovely marble cove at the mouth of Tidal Inlet was where the helicopter appeared from nowhere, almost catching the girls in the altogether as they bathed in a tide pool.

The most impressive aspect of the monument, the opportunity to observe life zones from sea level to alpine and above, and the constant retreat or advance of life forms depending on how recently the glacier occupied the territory, is even more evident from the air. This is partly because you see a wider expanse. The same life processes repeat themselves over and over again throughout vast expanses of wilderness. By boat, as we traveled up individual inlets to glacier faces, we were aware of the vegetation becoming less and less to the point of nothing near the ice. We observed the opposite as we returned to our camp spots at night, about ten miles behind the glaciers, and by then flowering profusely.

Going back two hundred years or even one hundred years in the history of this prehistoric area, there are such marked changes in character that it is hard to believe that old books were referring to the same place. They were, though, and the difference was that glaciers once filled the area, with ice a few thousand feet deep in many places. Before 1800, when Captain George Vancouver was in Icy Strait, there was no Glacier Bay, just another dent in the shoreline. But because of a warming trend in the next hundred years, plus some earthquakes, the present trend began, and, according to scientists, it is continuing. The retreating glaciers are followed at a respectful distance in time as well as space by forests, wildlife, and people bent on wilderness vacations.

We were surprised to learn that cruise boats have been touring the area for a couple of generations. They were unable to steam blithely up inlets as we did, however. Even forty years ago much of our itinerary would have been under several hundred feet of ice. The remains of naturalist John Muir's cabin points up this fact. Only about seventy years ago he was living and doing research at the snout of the glacier that now bears his name. Now Muir Glacier has retreated a good twenty miles away. It was probably John Muir, with his knowledge of gold-bearing rocks, who mentioned the similarity of geology around Juneau and started the search for gold there.

Certain things we had noted from boat level were even more impressive from the air, especially in Pete's low-flying, float-equipped Cessna. For example, we could readily see why mariners are suspicious of kelp beds. They really are jagged reefs under the tangle of long tails and bulbous masses. Islands, all shapes and sizes of them, many with sandy or gravel beaches surrounding them, looked all the more enticing from the air, and we played "choose your island." Jackie won with her choice, a charmer with a separate little leash, a sandy spit we felt would be perfect for clamming. We understood why Bob Howe considered the icebergs, especially the larger ones, worthy of caution. Maneuvering among small ones, gently prodding them out of the way, is no great hazard. But from our vantage point we could detect how gigantic a portion was under the surface compared to the amount on top. Before our eyes we saw more than one iceberg turn over without warning, causing a flurry of fair-sized breakers.

At sea level we had the advantage of viewing seals, including babies on ice cakes, whale and porpoise, and the prolific bird life: scoters, orange-beaked puffins, sea gulls, and guillemots. For photographing goats, one of Bob's objectives, the plane was ideal. Eagle-eyed Pete spotted some beauties on the upper reaches of Mount Wright, and dropped down for a closer look. We had barely been able to make out goats on the ledges during our previous boat

Tour boat from Glacier Bay Lodge picks way among floating ice in Glacier Bay National Monument. Seals are not perturbed.

tour. Now we could almost count their whiskers. We made several passes until Bob was satisfied and, we hoped, out of film. The trouble with having a photographer along is that (if he is like Bob) he won't take pictures *through* the window. He has to open it, and the icy blast at that altitude frosts the rest of the passengers in a hurry, to say nothing of what it does to coiffures. He quit just in time—the children passed him a note requesting him to please step outside for the next shot.

We lunched at the National Park Service accommodations at Bartlett Cove, near the entrance to Glacier Bay. The facilities come as a surprise, if you have never been there. Among the trees is a large, luxurious chalet-type lodge, new and modern, with rooms, meals, and bar. It seems impossible that the glaciers are at least forty miles away, but that only two hundred years ago the land was smothered in ice.

Though it is possible to visit Glacier Bay in one day from Juneau, we feel the least time a person should take to see the Monument is two days. We have met people who have been exploring it for many years and feel they have barely begun. In two days you can fly in on a scheduled flight, stay overnight at the lodge and take the seven-hour tour to the glaciers.

The lodge boat, a sort of round-trip "time machine," takes passengers from lush vegetation to stark ice-age cliffs. At times, the feeling of traveling back to an earlier era is overwhelming. On the way, the small ship eases through icebergs, from imagination-provoking statuettes to house size. The climax is being at the right spot at the right time to watch a glacier "calve." The relentless, slow-motion river of ice causes the abrupt glacier faces to slough off into the sea to start the last leg of their journey (perhaps to end up in the Glacier Bay Lodge Bar).

The lodge's season is from mid-May to mid-September. Gustavus Inn, a homey place near the airport and town of the same name, is open year round. The food is wonderful at both places, with the accent on seafood: salmon, halibut, and crab, considered exceptionally fine flavored due to its icy habitat. Both places offer excellent fishing, and have charters, boats, tackles, and guides.

The daytime trip on the lodge's *Thunder Bay* was untoppable, we thought, until Alaska Tour & Marketing Services came up with an overnight tour. It's sensational, and makes the most of the bay's unique audio and visual appeal. Budget about $200 for the whole adventure: flight from Juneau round trip, bus to the lodge, and meals aboard the *Glacier Bay Explorer* (with twin-bedded state-rooms). After lunch at the lodge, sixty-four lucky people can board and head up bay to spend the night within sight and sound of some of the biggest glaciers. A naturalist goes along to interpret, and during the evening people may go ashore and walk on moraine near one of them. Your "money's worth" might not be in sleep (if you are like us)—not for lack of comforts, but because of the exciting setting. In mid-June, the sunset glow was still bright on surrounding mountains. It highlighted the ice, keeping Bob snapping until midnight and after, while curious seals surfaced all around to inspect their overnight "company" moored in their midst.

Bob Howe is retired now, but Superintendent Tom Ritter is equally anxious to provide future visitors with a choice of experiences within the Monument. He is also dedicated to its best use and preservation. Park rangers, alert to hazards of the area, strongly urge people to plan carefully, acquire all information pertinent to their form of travel, and check in and out with the Park Service. Boating guides and brochures are available by writing the Park Superintendent, Box 1089, Juneau, Alaska 99802, or at the Glacier Bay National Monument summer headquarters at Bartlett Cove. The National Park Service also has an information office in the Federal Building in Juneau.

Though there are no trails in the upper reaches, there are many spots designated for primitive camping, and arrangements can be made to drop off campers and then pick them up at a specified time later.

"Campers should be self-sufficient and allow enough food for an extra day or two, in case something unforeseen delays a pickup," Tom advises. "Also they should bring plenty of warm, dry clothes. Never can tell about this place—that's part of its charm!"

Regardless of how you arrive, or in which style you choose to live, everyone is welcome to take part in all the activities, some free, including fine nightly nature talks and films, and daily naturalist-guided trails in the rain forest and along the tidelands.

HAINES AND PORT CHILKOOT

When we start talking about the northeast tip of the Panhandle it's hard to be objective. We'll try not to get carried away, but be forewarned: these are some favorite places! Over many years we have come to know them well. We think the people here are the greatest. To keep ourselves in line we'll consider some pros and cons gleaned from travelers we've met there. They are bound to be less subjective and more critical than we. Many of their criticisms are valid.

On one point we all agree. The setting of these towns in the upper reaches of beautiful Lynn Canal is spectacular. Though the towns are completely different in character, they are all surrounded by similar beautiful scenery—deep, fjordlike Lynn Canal; streams; lakes; high, snow-clad mountains. It's a place to feed the soul. For sure, it's Bob's choice—he never tires of shooting his favorite vistas. The rest of the time he spends photographing the energetic and

Visitors wait, cameras poised, for ice chunks to drop off face of Riggs Glacier on daily cruise in Glacier Bay National Monument.

colorful residents. There are few places we have found where the natives keep busier or seem to have more fun. Their good spirits are contagious.

Getting there

Compared to points to the south, Haines and Port Chilkoot, and also nearby Skagway, are veritable hubs of transportation. They can be reached by land, sea, and air. A variety of modes and operators of transportation is available. Planes, trains, ships all offer adequately frequent schedules, or charters (air). Because of possible timetable changes, a traveler should check at the nearest information center, depending on his mode of travel, to be sure that his schedules are current.

Land travelers can come on their own or by bus by way of the beautiful 159-mile Haines Highway, which takes off from the Alaska Highway one hundred miles to the west of Whitehorse, Yukon Territory, Canada, and ends at Lynn Canal, part of Alaska's Marine Highway. Cruise ships as well as ferries ply the Marine Highway, the latter tying up at the State Ferry System dock on the Lutak Road, a few miles out of Haines. In 1978, lunching at the Lighthouse in Haines which overlooks the small-boat harbor, we watched considerable small-boat traffic, some sizable yachts, and even a hydrofoil making use of the Haines Marina. Alaska Flyers, Inc. has been testing the feasibility of such craft for one-day tours from Juneau to Haines, Skagway, Tracy Arm, Taku Harbor, and Glacier Bay.

"Just like Kennedy Airport!" quipped a New York City friend as we came in for a landing and then had to go back upstairs and circle while a Grumman Goose waddled down the airstrip, got up power, and flew off. Haines Airport, three miles out along the Haines Highway, is small and surfaced. Flight costs, especially charters, do vary; we've found L.A.B. Flying Service very dependable in determining lowest rates.

These three ports—Haines, Port Chilkoot, and Skagway—can be regarded as either gateways to Alaska or escape hatches, depending on which way you are heading. Here we will have to mention one of the growing-pain hazards of transportation plaguing Southeast Alaska, though it is bound to be smoothed out eventually. When planning to hop a ferry south from Haines you may be delayed unless you have reservations for your vehicle. Our best advice is to be prepared for this and wait it out, meanwhile taking the opportunity to explore and enjoy further this beautiful area. If you are delayed long enough, you are likely to find yourself blending into the community.

Another alternative is to catch the ferry to Skagway, only an hour's ride from Haines, and escape via the White Pass & Yukon Route railroad. That way you can ride in comfort over the same pass the gold rushers plodded, piggybacking your car and getting off at Whitehorse. Or you can drive the new Skagway-Carcross

Highway. It also connects with the Alaska Highway near White-horse.

Haines and Port Chilkoot are sometimes referred to as twin cities. They would have to be considered fraternal twins, for other than being located side by side, they are not at all alike. In appearance, Haines, the older of the two, could be almost any small western town. It was founded by Presbyterian missionaries in 1881, who kept things under control even during the gold rush of 1898. An enterprising non-sourdough, Jack Dalton, blazed his Dalton Trail, and made his "poke" by packing supplies to the gold fields for eager miners craving life's necessities. Today's Haines Highway follows this route.

Haines is still the supply source, with well-stocked stores and prices not too bad, considering the supply problem. It is the business center for both towns and a boon to visitors with its laundromat, motels, and most other facilities they might require. The town has no regular drugstore, but there is a health clinic with doctor, dentist, and public health nurse, for treatment and prescriptions if needed.

Industries in Haines

Prevailing industries are lumber and fishing. Japan is a good timber customer. Japanese freighters make regular trips to Haines, and you might see them being loaded at the dock. Canneries may be operating. Bob's favorite is located at Letnikoff Cove, out the Mud Bay Road. Not that he is so fond of fish, but the setting amid calm water, greenery, and mountain peaks of this barn-red structure is photogenic in almost any weather.

Agriculture is not at the top of the list, but one unusual crop is worth noting. In early days, a settler pioneered a fine, large, sweet strawberry that still flourishes in some family gardens. The Strawberry Festival celebrating early days and luscious berries has now grown to a large and lively annual Southeast Alaska State Fair. Held on grounds near the Information Center, Mile One, it grows bigger and better every August.

Henderson's farm is a magnet for the kids of Haines and Port Chilkoot, as well as visitors. A science teacher at the school, Mr. Henderson experiments, and grows and raises all sorts of things, animal and vegetable. We purchased fresh vegetables and goat's milk, which our three youngsters drank with gusto, keeping an eye on the interesting livestock: colts, kids, burros, and even peacocks.

And have you ever seen a tank farm? There is one about three miles north of Haines on Lutak Inlet. It's another blossoming activity, a storage facility for petroleum distribution by pipelines from Haines to Fairbanks. In addition, to brighten the future, there are iron and other important mineral deposits in the vicinity, according to recent explorations.

Historic Port Chilkoot

Port Chilkoot is a real Alaskan museum piece, now designated a National Historical Site. It comes as a startling surprise to visitors to find that the town looks just like an old fort. There are officers' quarters, barracks, a hospital building, a recreation hall—all in the stately architecture of early 1900. At its heyday, Fort William Seward probably was distinguished as the most scenic and isolated, but least militarily active, fort in the United States and its territories. After World War II it was sold off as surplus.

The purchasers were five World War II veterans and their families. After having seen the world collectively, they decided this was the place. They wanted it for the same reason that the nearby Chilkat Indians had guarded it from invaders in the past. It seemed like a good place to establish a home near game-filled forests and sparkling fjords teeming with salmon. Moreover, they saw the possibilities of developing the newly incorporated town, adjacent to older, well-established Haines, as a fine resort area. We first became interested in Port Chilkoot when we visited there and tented in a small campground in 1952.

Typical of Alaska, a few people are doing a tremendous job in the area, now municipally merged. At last word, all five original families are in Port Chilkoot, and actively wearing many hats. Treat the fellow at the hotel desk with respect. Besides being the proprietor he could also be the mayor.

A Port Chilkoot program, which originated as "Alaska Youth" and was later incorporated as "Alaska Indian Arts," has been sparkplugged over the years by retired Army major Carl Heinmiller (also town magistrate). We will discuss it mainly as it relates to tourism, touching briefly on the great good, socially and economically, it has done for both Indian and Eskimo natives, especially the handicapped, and the young people of Port Chilkoot, both white and Indian. It is a training program to perpetuate the arts and crafts of the Tlingits, mainly the Chilkat tribe. Somehow, Carl has kept it going, though funding has been sporadic. Visitors can walk around the parade grounds and buildings and are welcome to observe and ask questions about the various projects going on.

Here we should mention Klukwan, older than the other towns (its name means "always there"), an Indian village about twenty miles

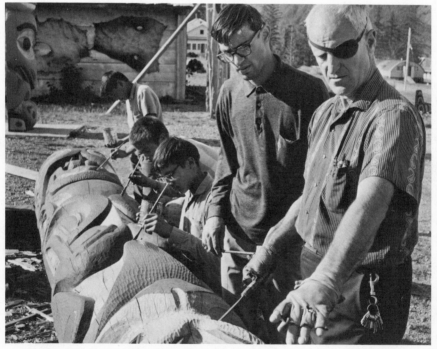

Totem carving at Port Chilkoot. Carl Heinmiller, a founder of Port Chilkoot and director of Alaska Indian Arts, Inc., right. Authentically reconstructed tribal house in background.

from Haines. Through Carl's work and rapport with the Chilkats, he has been able to learn about and reproduce their authentic designs, songs, and dances and interest young people in carrying them on. He is an expert wood carver, and his real breakthrough came when he carved a mask they couldn't distinguish from one carved by their best Indian carver. Over the years Carl has been held in high regard, adopted into the tribe, and honored by being given a high and worthy Indian name of the Raven clan.

No Russians ever had a toehold in these upper reaches of Tlingit Indian country; the tribes were too fierce to conquer. These tribes, only a hundred years ago, were the scourge of pioneers and invading Indians alike. They effectively guarded mountain passes and waterways and clobbered gold-and-fur-seeking invaders at every opportunity. Our theory is that the reason they were so warlike is that they knew a good thing when they saw it. They took a dim view of any outsiders interfering with their affluent, leisurely life and their civilized pursuits like dancing and fine woodcarving.

Port Chilkoot's Chilkat Dancers

The colorful Chilkat Dancers perform often in summer in the Centennial project auditorium, formerly the barracks gymnasium. Before the audience grew so large they danced in an authentic tribal house built, with the help of the Alaska Indian Arts program, on the parade grounds. Most costumes, dance rattles, drums, and other accoutrements were made by the dancers. You may see Chilkat trainees at work; girls sewing pounds of buttons on button-blanket designs, repairing or replacing well-worn moccasins. A new, important project is trying to re-create the famous Chilkat blanket. Original ones which remain are now museum pieces, with some on loan for use in the dances. An Indian lad may be busily scraping off goat hair for making yarn or shredding cedar bark, two of the basic materials for willing learners. Time is short—none remain at Klukwan who know the art of making these dance blankets with their bold yellow, blue, and black designs.

The loud-singing, drum-beating paleface "chief" of the perform-ance is often Carl himself. The Chilkat Dancers originated several years ago as a Boy Scout project. They were so enthusiastic and

Chilkat Dancers at Port Chilkoot. Girl on left wears button blanket and holds dance rattle. Boy wears original Chilkat blanket (now a museum piece) and ermine headdress.

their performance was so authentic that they took first place on their first venture into major competition, the Intertribal Indian Ceremonies at Gallup, New Mexico. Since then they have traveled widely and expanded. Today, it is a well-integrated group, in terms of age as well as race. The colorful dances tell ancient stories, such as the origin of mosquitoes and the tides, and deeds of derring-do.

Besides the maintenance and creative work demanded by the Chilkat Dancers, travelers wandering through the informal classrooms can watch natives teach and work at various crafts: carving Alaska soapstone, ivory, and wood; etching silver; buffing copper. Outside someone may be in the process of carving a fragrant Alaska cedar into a thirty-foot totem pole.

Though the work is usually going full blast, especially in summer, it is possible to visit Port Chilkoot during a "lean" period, when lack of funds curtails activities. The prevalent dream is that somehow someone somewhere will at last recognize the worth of a program that helps native people to make the transition from the old ways to the new, while preserving their pride in their abilities and their culture.

Besides the Indian dances, townspeople periodically put on a Gay Nineties program for visitors, including a melodrama titled *The Smell of the Yukon*. During winter a little-theater group puts on plays, and nothing is too ambitious to attempt. In fact, their lovely renovated auditorium is kept busy the year round, with as many outside artists and concert groups as they can coax to Port Chilkoot.

Nearby sights

Except for heading out the Haines Highway, you won't go far on the other roads. The longest ends at Mud Bay, the others don't go much beyond the ferry landing and campgrounds. But along all of them are spacious, scenic and relaxing beachcombing, fishing, swimming and exploring possibilities.

And it's a great area for birdwatching. Fifteen to twenty miles from the Haines Highway is one of the largest and last nesting grounds of the American bald eagle.

Information

There isn't a person or business in either Haines or Port Chilkoot that won't tell you where to go, or point you in the right direction. Formally, there is an information booth at Mile One before Haines. You'll recognize it by the Welcome Poles carved by Alaskan Indian Arts. Be sure to pick up the Halsingland Hotel's well-drawn city map and the descriptive "Walking Tour of Historic Fort William H.

Seward," published by the Haines Chamber of Commerce. For history of the area, visit the Sheldon Museum, which will be well-established in its new building near the Haines waterfront soon.

There are fine little shops, dealing in crafts, books, and souvenirs, any one of which will also furnish information. You may be able to buy finely crafted items made in the Alaska Indian Arts program depending on availability. Authentically designed totems are commissioned in assorted sizes, priced at over $100 a foot now—at least.

Lodging

Though there are several adequate places to stay in the area, including nearby campgrounds (and they are expanding to meet the growing need), there is one place you shouldn't miss, the Halsingland Hotel in Port Chilkoot, if only to take a look or have a meal. It's part of the compound bordering the parade grounds. Three sides are taken up by the Indian Arts program and private homes, renovated and modernized inside. (One at the end of the row of stately mansions was recently repainted in original style and color, quite a chore with all those shutters.)

The Halsingland, started by Hilma and Clarence Mattson of the original five veterans, forms the fourth side and incorporates three former officers' quarters. You have to appreciate old things to appreciate the Halsingland. The waste space is enough to make an architect go mad. The innkeepers can put up a hundred people coming in on tours and have plenty of space for tourists dropping in. There is room to spread out in the high-ceilinged rooms, and enough confusing corridors, pantries, stairways, and doors to lose people. They have to post arrows showing the way out. And watch those double swinging doors between adjoining rooms sharing the bath! The new look is a cocktail lounge added off its vintage lobby. Otherwise, it's clean, comfortable, if not fancy, and meals are super. All is within walking distance, and overlooking the parade ground. Makes you feel part of the action.

There is camping and trailer space in the trees behind the Halsingland. For a charge, a little more per night than in other states, visitors have showers, coin-operated laundry facilities, and the hotel restaurant nearby.

The Glacier Camper Park is just north of Haines on the highway. It has complete facilities, including gas, carwash, restaurant, and store.

Food and drink

In Haines, several small restaurants serve good food, and the bars, close to the harbor, have seaworthy names, such as The Reef and The Riptide. However: "The Totem Bowl and Bar is no longer as we knew it," sighs Mimi Gregg. "No more bar; soft drinks only." This army original on the lower side of Port Chilkoot's quadrangle housed a convivial bar with Dalton Trail days decor, where nightlife seekers used to congregate. To one side of the bar there was a charcoal grill where you could purchase a thick steak, supervise its cooking, and have it served by the girl in the red velvet swing.

Port Chilkoot "potlatch" near town dock. Ted Gregg planks salmon Indian style before smoke-cooking it by open fire, while young people swim and boat.

Suspended from the ceiling at adjustable levels, the swing was created by Ted Gregg, one of the original Port Chilkoot founding-veterans. You never knew who would wander in, perhaps some notable passing through. One night, to the amusement of all, and some consternation, in came a convivial porcupine. It took exception to being bounced and finally, cornered behind the bar, bit the hand that freed him. That about sums up the formal wining and dining possibilities. However, there is one highly informal but always enjoyable institution, labeled by Ted Gregg "The Port Chilkoot Permanently Established Floating Potlach."

Over the years, the potlatch has been a loosely invitational thing, a sort of spontaneous potluck dinner triggered off by the arrival of relatives or friends. And it is easy to become a friend, or a friend of a friend, in tiny Port Chilkoot. Everyone brings something, and the main course, salmon, is purchased at the cannery. Ted Gregg is the acknowledged chef supreme, and he planks the fileted fish Indian style and sets it next to a green alder open fire until it is deliciously cooked, juicy, and slightly smoked in flavor. With a gimlet before, and Ted's home brew to "keep the digestive juices flowing," there is nothing like it. The potlatch is "floating" because the picnic spot is kept flexible and often determined by the weather. Sometimes we don't know where it will be till almost time, but the word is transmitted quickly once the choice is made. A favorite spot is on the beach between the boat landing and Portage Cove Campground, where parents can keep an eye on all pups, kids, and young people as they swim and paddle around in Lynn Canal. It's not too cold, they say, especially when the tide comes in over the warm sand on a sunny day.

Residents anticipate great things for the future in this beautiful area: continuing renovation and preservation of the historical buildings, and a large state park is under way.

Smoked salmon always reminds us of a story Carl Heinmiller tells of an Indian who used, in the old days, to dry it, then smoke it near Klukwan. Carl had a congressman in tow, very fond of salmon, who was interested in the Indian's method. The only thing that bothered him were the flies lighting on it. The solon finally asked the Indian if he minded all those flies. The Indian cheerfully replied, "Oh no—they don't eat much!"

SKAGWAY

Haines is an example of the proper, "salt of the earth," missionary-founded small town; Klukwan is the old native village, still too shy to receive transient visitors; Port Chilkoot is a living museum piece of early 1900 military construction. Skagway, only about seventeen miles farther up Lynn Canal by boat and only a few minutes away by plane, is different from all of them. It is the epitome of a ghost town, complete with "gunsmoke" history and facade—false-fronted buildings, boardwalks, and unpaved main street.

Skagway had its heyday when thousands of gold-hungry people used the town as a gateway to the Klondike gold fields, just before, during, and after 1900. In all the confusion, law and order disappeared as prospectors tried to accumulate enough supplies to enable them to claw their way over the formidable mountain barrier. Supply ships dumped livestock over the side to swim ashore and left piles of necessities on the beach to be sorted out and claimed, not always by the one who prepaid for it. The situation worsened before it got better, finally leading to a famous duel between a "good guy" and a "bad guy," Frank Reid and Soapy Smith, respectively.

There are some who say that Soapy wasn't all bad. He got the nickname from his style of fleecing unwary "suckers," with the help of a couple of con men. He sold bars of soap for a good price, making a great show of slipping bills under some wrappers. Naturally the soap went like sourdough hotcakes, but the only ones who got the money were Soapy's men. He had many tricky things going as he took over the town with one hand and organized worthwhile charities with the other. But the games got rougher and finally vigilante Frank Reid and Soapy came to a draw—a quick one on the Skagway dock. A "draw" describes the outcome, too. Both men died. You can visit the cemetery and find their graves. Frank's is marked suitably with a tall monument; Soapy was grudgingly granted a small plot on the edge. His real monument is his infamous "parlors" standing down near the water, a small frame building containing appropriate mementos from his lurid past.

Looking at Skagway today, it is hard to believe it was once a rip-roaring takeoff point for the Klondike. And though it looks like a ghost town, the people there are very much alive. Due to their efforts and interest in preserving historic memorabilia the town has kept its atmosphere. The museum, housed in a large stone building, would be hard to overlook. A small admission is charged, which is used to help keep it going. Most of the staff are interested town residents, working on a volunteer basis. When we visit Skagway, we all head to different sections of the museum; some like to decipher old court records and papers preserved under glass; others are drawn to rooms with old-fashioned clothes, furnishings, and dishes or native artifacts.

On the main street, we periodically catch the residents replacing the boardwalks. Like Indian totem poles, boardwalks rot away in the damp atmosphere. We can imagine the discussions pro and con regarding to pave or not to pave that fascinating main street.

Dust can be a trial on Skagway's frequent brisk windy days. In fact, the name "Skagway" comes from a native word meaning "the home of the North Wind." The Indians were superstitious about the wind, and predicted that a chinook (sudden warm wind) would melt the snow on steep mountain slopes, causing avalanches that would bury the white invaders or their land. This actually happened, but it didn't stop the goldseekers. They relocated the route elsewhere.

Speaking of routes, Skagway Air Service has charters (from $20, two persons minimum) that pass over and identify those gold rush passes, along with glaciers and icefield hazards of the Trail of '98.

The town is small enough to walk everywhere on these historic boardwalks, and people are friendly. The stores are good for browsing and buying souvenirs or camp supplies.

Ambitious visitors can hike halfway up a mountain for a good view of the town and harbor. Fishing is good off the dock or in nearby streams.

Night life generally coincides with the tour-boat and ferry schedule. Summer entertainment is in keeping with the days of '98: an evening of variety acts preceded by old-style gambling games with play money, and drama based on Soapy's demise. Though the actors are paid now, we understand profits (if any) go for historical maintenance, such as offsetting the mortality rate of the can-can dancers' long stockings.

If you happen to be in a small town during a celebration, just join in. We hit a Fourth of July holiday a few years ago we'll never forget. They celebrate the way you used to hear about: parade, contest, food, prizes for costumes—all right in the middle of this sleepy-looking ghost town with its unpaved main street, board-walks, and false fronts. Our kids joined in as if they, too, belonged. The little girls put on their hiking pants (lederhosen), tied a cask around our Alaskan husky dog, joined the costume parade, and won a cash prize—50 cents each!

Roads ended in short order at mountain barriers until the completion of the much-wanted Skagway to Carcross Highway. You drove to a few viewpoints, to the real ghost town of Dyea (though little is left now), or toured with a local guide, happy to tell tall tales of Skagway's lusty past and people. The 110-mile highway is expected to become a popular part of a loop route, especially cheering to Whitehorse residents. They've been coveting a shorter do-it-yourself route to saltwater fishing.

White Pass & Yukon Railroad

Long before the new highway, Skagway could boast an unusual escape hatch from Southeast Alaska—the White Pass & Yukon Railroad. A few years ago they say that a salesman, new to Alaska, waited nine or ten days for a plane to fly out of Skagway during a siege of bad weather because he didn't know that this narrow-gauge railroad went through to Whitehorse, Yukon Territory, Canada, whence he could have flown back home. The White Pass & Yukon Railroad is a working train, and an important part of Skagway's economy, as well as a principal supply route for Yukon Territory.

For visitors, the White Pass & Yukon Railroad is an experience that plummets them right back into the turn of the century. The amazing thing about this railroad is that it was built at all. Following hot on the heels of those heavily laden, gold-crazed hiking miners, a Canadian-born Irishman, Michael J. Heney, proved wrong those who considered a railroad impossible. By 1900 it was in use, and gold seekers who could afford it switched to riding the rails to Lake Bennett and later to Whitehorse, where they could then take water transportation to the Klondike.

Today, Skip Burns' Klondike Safaris guide ambitious hikers, including families, on their way along the Chilkoot Trail, watching

Fourth of July parade, Skagway. Historic Golden North Hotel is domed building on right. Unpaved street, boardwalks, and false-fronted buildings give ghost town appearance to this gold rush camp dating from days of '98.

for signs of that great trek along the way. Or you can ride a horse instead, by contacting packer Wes Nelson just out of Skagway on the river road. The adventure ends at Lake Bennett and the summit station, where people can take the train back down, pondering the tunneling and bridging feats of those early construction engineers, seeing the relics of Canyon City, and watching for actual markings of the Trail of '98 while resting up.

The developing Klondike Gold Rush National Historical Park has components along the Trail of '98 that stretches from Seattle to Dawson in the Yukon Territory. Skagway is an important station with several downtown blocks designated as an Historical District and with buildings under restoration. It's too early to predict the effect of the Skagway-Carcross Highway on tourism patterns. Hopefully, the White Pass & Yukon will continue to play its role, transporting tour groups and also individuals who might wish to ship their car to Whitehorse as a more satisfactory alternative to driving or taking the horse or hiking route.

"Please don't call my railroad old-fashioned," begs retired WP & YR executive Roy Minter, who is as dedicated to this fantastic route as the original builders. We have known Roy for many years and invariably run into him whenever we are in "his" territory. He's right—the operation is strictly modern; for practical reasons the old steam engines had to go. But for sentiment or visitors who appreciate atmosphere along with their scenery, some quaintly appointed parlor cars still remain. Seated on plush-upholstered reversible seats near a potbellied stove and watching the kids taking turns at the ancient water cooler supplied with tiny cornucopia paper cups, it's easy to imagine how appreciated this little train was in the old days.

Lodging

Skagway illustrates perfectly the variety you are likely to find in Alaskan accommodations. All in plain view, on or just off the 1900-flavor main street, are three buildings, one very old, one contemporary, and the other very plush and modern, but suggestive of the luxury of the Gay Nineties era.

The Golden North Hotel dates from 1898 and originally faced a different direction. In 1903 two men and a team of horses turned it around to face the main street and built the dome, now a picturesque landmark. If you stay there you may sleep in a bed that came over the Chilkoot Pass in the early 1900s. The rooms have been furnished throughout in keeping with those early days (though

Old church at Lake Bennett built by miners. The White Pass & Yukon Railroad was built to the lake by 1900. Here gold seekers took the water route to the Klondike gold fields and Dawson City.

the plumbing is modern). Townspeople rummaged through attics and collected charming old pieces to carry out the theme.

We thought it was intriguing that many rooms are dedicated to certain pioneer families, with old pictures and a summary of their history. Our girls recognized Jack Kirmse, a Skagway businessman, in a family photo in their room. They were used to seeing him strolling the streets or in his shop wearing his gambler's garb, complete with three-pound gold-nugget watch fob, and thought it remarkable that he looks so much like his small-boy picture.

We slept in the Henry Clark room and found out that not everyone gave their all for gold. Clark tried his luck in the Klondike, but in 1899 gave up and settled in Skagway to make his living "off the land" in, of all things, agriculture. He did amazingly well, sold produce door to door, and expanded his market to the vegetable-hungry towns in Canada. He farmed forty-two years and died at eighty-one, a gardener to the end. His method was to start his vegetables in greenhouses, and some of the results are legendary—rhubarb, for example, with a seven-foot stock from base to leaf tip. Many a perennial in Skagway yards today is a living memorial to Mr. Clark's green thumb. The whole story with pictures is told in a large gilded-frame plaque which hangs on the wall of the hotel room.

All the Golden North rooms have a lived-in feeling. It's a great place to recapture the flavor of the past, if such appeals to you.

"I've got a houseful of antiques," stated one lively older visitor to Skagway. "Give me the Klondike every time. That place is gorgeous—makes me feel like one of those dance-hall girls."

We understood perfectly. The Westours modern Klondike Inn, built to accommodate tour groups, does indeed have the luxury atmosphere of those early days. Not fancy on the outside, they have gone all out on the inside, using rich reds and golds in the decor and adding many an elegant touch for visual pleasure, as well as comfort.

In between in style and price are the Skagway Inn and the Sourdough Inn, a little under and a little over $30 double, respectively. A sign on the Bunkhouse just off Broadway offered a bed and hot shower for under $10 per night.

Camping

The informal transient-living possibilities are summed up on a town map with a directory on the back. Services listed include a camper park and campground in town, and also at "Liarsville," a small pleasant campground a few miles out of town on the Skagway River. Several years ago, before this designated campground, someone directed us to the airport when we asked where to camp. The traffic accepted our presence as if it was customary, and we erected our own small pit teepee facility. Some friendly neighbors, living in houses across the way, furnished our water, presented us with halibut steaks, stopped by to chat, and generally made us feel welcome.

In the peak of the tourist season it's conceivable that you might have to do a little looking if you are on your own rather than with a tour group. It is advisable to make advance reservations.

The Chamber of Commerce Visitors Information Center is in the historic Arctic Brotherhood Hall on Broadway. It is the prickly-looking one with the siding made out of sticks.

DAWSON, A CANADIAN COUNTERPART

Goal of the horde passing through Skagway was the Klondike, Canada's famous gold fields where the Klondike River joins the Yukon. News of the 1896 discovery leaked to the outside by July, 1897, and the rush was on. In 1898 the route choice was via the longer, more gradual White Pass or the steep and infamous Chilkoot Pass. From the Yukon River headwaters, miners paddled almost anything that would float. If they survived the hazards, including the treacherous Whitehorse Rapids, they eventually drifted down the Yukon to Dawson. By 1900 the White Pass & Yukon Route was completed from Skagway to Whitehorse.

You can still go this way by car. After your car is unloaded from the railroad flat car at Whitehorse you start driving the Klondike Loop from Whitehorse to Tetlin Junction, going by way of Dawson City. This side trip is almost 500 miles, but it adds only 121 miles to the distance you would travel if you took the direct Alaska Highway route, on your way north to Alaska. You can also go by bus and plane. A timesaver—and full of action—is an air-charter package that flies from Anchorage and overnights in Dawson. Though there has been talk of reviving the picturesque stern-wheeler trip of yesteryear, so far people have to be content with viewing the beached *Klondike* at Whitehorse, or visiting the *Keno,* now a museum on the banks of the Yukon at Dawson.

We have tried all the access routes. The only conclusion we can make is that however we arrive, we quickly are overcome by the same ghostly feeling of having taken a long step backward in history. After its rather brief heyday at the turn of the century,

Historic White Pass & Yukon Route narrow gauge railroad parallels gold rush Trail of '98, connecting Skagway, on the Inside Passage, and Whitehorse, Canada. Built in 1898-1900.

Dawson seemed to remain much as it was then, almost as if it were preserved in a deep freeze that is not quite cold enough to keep it from slowly disintegrating. Though there were sporadic spurts of self-preservation, usually triggered by a commemorative festival in the offing, we wondered if saving Dawson was a losing battle. It breaks Bob's heart to go back and find a favorite old false-fronted building a step nearer to becoming a heap of rubble.

Then the Canadian Government declared Dawson "an historical complex." The first boost was authentically reproducing the Palace Grand Theatre to its hang-down, unfrosted electric light globes, red velvet curtains, straight-backed chairs, boxes, and planked floors. The *Gaslight Follies* are put on in summer by a professional group of actors and singers. Their material is in the style of vaudeville, as served up in the old days by "Klondike Kate" Rockwell and Douglas Fairbanks, Sr. Many in the audience then, or on the other side of the footlights, became famous later, including writer Jack London, poet Robert Service, and Alexander Pantages, theater-chain tycoon. After the *Follies,* everyone heads for Diamond Tooth Gertie's for the floor show and *real* gambling. Gertie's flashy past and its present historical status allow it to be the only legitimate gambling hall in Canada.

Around town now, Bob is delighted to see buildings being jacked up here and there and *saved:* the hardware and gun shop with a jumble of supplies still on shelves, blacksmith shop, Red Feather saloon, and that one-time center of London and Paris fashion, Madam Tremblay's. Parks Canada has purchased and is in the process of totally restoring many old buildings, among them the post office, Commissioner's Residence, Ruby's Place, and the Bonanza Hotel.

Food and lodging

A few years ago, you had to be genuine gold-ghost town enthusiasts like us to overlook the lack of creature comforts in Dawson. The residents were happy if you had your own sleeping arrangement with you, because hotel rooms were scarce. Some of the old historic hotels had to be condemned. However, the town really tried to make provisions for guests. Someone directed us to the schoolyard in the middle of town and we were comfortable enough in our travel trailer.

Our only problem was that we were out of food and drink. We had come over the scenic but unpopulated high route, starting at the northern end of the Klondike Loop. For pictures we pulled off in our trailer for overnight at a lonely spot. It put us behind in our plans, important only because we were counting on shopping at Dawson before everything shut down for the three-day-weekend Discovery Day celebration. We had forgotten about one formidable barrier—the Yukon River, the last hurdle between us and Dawson.

Gold-panning in front of idle dredge, near Dawson City, Yukon Territory, Canada.

At that time, service was by a tiny three-car ferry without a formal dock. In fact they rebuilt a landing in the soft riverbank each trip. As we wound down the steep mountain road to river level, we were aghast to see all the cars backing down the narrow ramp. Bob hopefully suggested to the ferry operator that we just drive on head first then back *off.* But for reasons beyond our comprehension, it was necessary to back the trailer *on!* This maneuver took Bob just long enough to prevent our arriving until after the stores were closed. There is nothing less commercial-minded than a small town bent on celebrating. We got by on cheese sandwiches, appeared promptly whenever the one restaurant opened its doors for a meal now and then, and patronized the "mooseburger" stand at the ball park where the main events and speeches were taking place.

Hotel rooms are being added and creature comforts are improving, beginning with the ferry. It's free, expects to continue operating on a twenty-four-hour basis and can take at least eight cars at a time. Near the landing, across the river from Dawson, is a Yukon territorial campground. There's another about twelve miles south of Dawson. In town, the Klondike Gold Camp comes with showers and a laundromat.

Everyone's favorite picture-taking view point of the whole vicinity around Dawson is on top of Midnight Dome. From there you can survey the town's situation from all sides. To the right is the Yukon River; to the left, and a different color, is the Klondike, flowing into the Yukon. There is a panoramic view of Dawson, the opposite shores, and the gold fields ridged by heaps of tailings left by the dredges. The last dredge quit work in 1966, but you can still see them floating in their private ponds. There is a road to the top of the dome now. Hardy Canadians used to dash up on foot to view the midnight sun, especially on June 21.

Yukon bard Robert W. Service migrated from Whitehorse to Dawson in 1904. The main gold rush was over, but the atmosphere lingered on. He worked in the bank there during the day, researched his subject matter in the bars, restaurants, and streets at night, and somehow found time to write his ballads and *Trail of '98* novel in the eight years he buckled down at Dawson in his small log cabin up from the center of town. We visited the Gold Room of his bank, which stands by the river next to the dry-docked riverboat *Keno,*

View from Midnight Dome above historic Dawson City, Yukon Territory, Canada. Confluence of Klondike River coming in from left and Yukon River, right.

now a museum. The room is up a flight of stairs and contains mementos of the early days, as well as some ledgers inscribed in Service's neat accountant's script.

A query to Athol Retallack, public relations manager of the Whitehorse WP & YR, who is also a Klondike enthusiast, was answered with all the latest news and plans, plus a phenomenally long list titled "Dawson City, What to See and Do." She suggests that visitors stop by the Yukon territorial government's Information Center. They'll have maps and current suggestions, usually dispensed with hot coffee. The plans sound great for the rejuvenation, through preservation, of this fascinating town. In our opinion, as long as there is a wall standing of a historic spot like this there will be history buffs and people interested in "where the action was" who will come and visit.

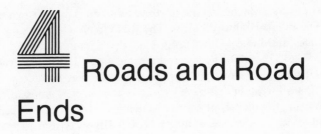

4 Roads and Road Ends

THE South Central and Interior portions of Alaska definitely lend themselves to "do-it-yourself" traveling. Here is the road network, about five thousand miles of it, mostly paved. A visitor can travel in his own style, at his own pace, and be as independent as he likes, especially if he carries his own solution for bed and board along with him. On a map it appears that the present roads cover a relatively small section of this huge state, perhaps less than a fifth. Almost every road ending, however, is also a gateway, a challenge to explore farther by taking to the air, or water.

We find it hard to judge how much time to allow from here to there when traveling by car. We aren't inclined to rush through scenic and recreational areas. Moreover, we have learned that Alaska's terrain makes it difficult to maintain roads, even when they are paved. Road crews and equipment at work are likely to be a perpetual part of Alaskan scenery. We always allow extra time for unexpected delays, almost as inevitable as the yearly Tanana River ice breakup, and just as unpredictable.

The main highway, and the longest, is the Alaska Highway. If you drive all of it, beginning at Mile 0 at Dawson Creek, British Columbia (seven hundred miles north of the United States border), three-fifths of it will pass through Canada. It merges with the historic Richardson Highway at Delta Junction to continue to its official end 1,523 miles later at Fairbanks, Alaska. There the Steese

Highway branches to the northeast and ends at the town of Circle. The Elliott Highway, called "The Road to Nome," gives up after 163 miles at Manley Hot Springs, on the Tanana River.

The 358-mile Anchorage-Fairbanks (or Fairbanks-Anchorage, depending on your politics) Highway #3 was completed in 1971. This all-weather, all-paved route is the shortest, most direct road passing the portals of Mount McKinley Park. It doesn't replace the older, mostly gravel, summer Denali Highway, but it provides an approximately 150-mile shorter northern approach to the park, and shortens the distance between Alaska's two largest cities by eighty miles. It passes through grand and rugged wilderness scenery for which Alaska is noted, with views of the mountain. Highways don't come cheap in Alaska, and this one, twelve years in the building, is to date the most expensive, over $150 million.

The Glenn Highway takes off from the Alaska Highway at Tok (Toke) Junction and terminates at Anchorage. From Anchorage, the Seward Highway follows Turnagain Arm. Fifty-five miles before it ends at Seward it is joined by the Sterling Highway, which veers across the Kenai Peninsula and heads down the opposite side, ending at Homer.

Everyone stops to "shoot" moose feeding in pond by side of Alaska Highway just south of Fairbanks.

The Richardson Highway, terminating at Valdez, is one of the most beautiful as well as the oldest, having evolved from a trail to a wagon road and finally to today's paved highway.

The Denali Highway, branching west off the Richardson at Paxson, is a true wilderness road, unpaved and open only during summer. In fact, it invariably has to be rebuilt in spots as the summer traffic starts. Its destination is famous Mount McKinley National Park. It continues through the park to Camp Denali, just outside the far boundary, plus a few miles farther to Kantishna, a ghost gold-mining camp.

The unorthodox Marine Highway is the only route you can "drive" if you approach Alaska through the Southern Panhandle. Extensions of the State Ferry System from road ends at Valdez, Seward, and Homer lead to Kodiak, on an island in the Gulf of Alaska and Russia's first colony in the new land.

ANCHORAGE

Anchorage claims a three-way title: road end, gateway, and "Air Crossroad of the World." A few years ago it was labeled an "all-American city." For sure, its character is all-Alaskan. It is the biggest and the youngest, vigorous, fast-growing, and modern. Skyscrapers are surrounded by impressive marine and mountain views, topped by majestic Mount McKinley. Yet, with every big-city convenience and comfort, it still locks horns with frontier. They say in winter, moose still have the right of way on suburban roads, golf courses, and occasionally a back yard.

Anchorage, situated at the north end of Cook Inlet, is a hub of activity and an international transportation center. The metropolis-versus-frontier character of Anchorage, plus its cosmopolitan population (200,000 including surrounding area, at last estimate) present a true cross-section of life in the forty-ninth state. That the residents are air-minded is obvious. There are more private planes per capita here than anywhere in the world. You see them near the International Airport lining Hood and Spenard lakes, and stashed on small private landing fields out of town. Moreover, a surprising number of Alaskans, true natives and transplants, pass through the air portals of Anchorage, bent on business and pleasure, just like their visiting counterparts from the "South 48" and other parts of the world.

Destinations are varied. By air, Anchorage serves as the gateway for Europe and the Orient, as well as the roadless Arctic and Aleutian Island chain. It's a takeoff point for Mount McKinley National Park by the Alaska Railroad, and road gateway to the Interior and Kenai Peninsula. Though many visitors merely pass through, a growing number of people recognize the recreational possibilities nearby and make the city their headquarters, or set up camp in nearby campgrounds or trailer parks.

The climate, tempered by its proximity to a large body of water and sheltered by mountains, is moderate. Enough snow falls on the slopes of nearby Mount Alyeska in winter to keep skiers happy. Dog-sledders and snowmobile enthusiasts can count on enough snow for their fun, too. Anchorage is becoming a year-round vacation city with much to offer visitors, whether they are just passing through or choose to stay a while. Besides assorted ski competitions, the Championship Dogsled Races are held here during the annual February Fur Rendezvous.

Downtown Anchorage, Alaska's largest city. Largest buildings at left are modern hotels.

Anchorage's history is short, but action-packed. The town wasn't even thought of until 1914 and it started in typical Alaskan style, with a boom. Not gold, but transportation sparked Anchorage's beginnings. The U.S. government picked the site as a base camp for laborers when Congress voted to construct the Alaska Railroad. Seventy-one miles had already been built, starting from Seward. It seemed practical to extend the railroad north to the Interior following the Susitna River route. An anchorage at Ship Creek at the head of Cook Inlet was selected as the best place to build a wharf for unloading supply ships. The "a" in anchorage was capitalized, and the new, rapidly growing town had a name.

At first a tent city, Anchorage was a neatly planned town by the time the railroad was completed in 1923. Communications were set up, and homesteaders, miners, and trappers in the nearby river valleys were also depending on the community for supplies.

Anchorage's importance to national defense became shockingly apparent with the Japanese invasion of our Aleutian Islands in World War II. Since the war Anchorage has continued her key role in polar defense as headquarters for the combined Alaska Command, the Alaskan Air Command and U.S. Army.

Today, tons of necessities (and luxuries) pour through the city's active port, then fly on to the farthest fringes of the state. Growth keeps pace with getting oil-related supplies in and oil out, from the North Slope and closer. Oil explorations and discoveries boomed the Kenai Peninsula and drilling in Cook Inlet. We've seen gas burnoffs, almost as impressive as Northern Lights, while approaching Anchorage by air in dark of winter.

Information

Anchorage is the largest city in Alaska. To visitors used to bigger ones in the "South 48" and elsewhere, it will hardly seem formidable, in spite of some impressive tall buildings and its spread-out character. It is an easy city to get around in and well laid out. If you study a city map, available at any service station and many other public places, and orient yourself by a few landmarks, you may not even have to ask directions.

Downtown Anchorage skyscrapers contrast with pioneering homestead symbol, highrise "cache" for protecting provisions from hungry wilderness marauders.

The city is big enough to make having your own car a convenience. However, there is public transportation: airporters, taxis, buses, and some excellent sightseeing tours of the city and points both near and far. Rental cars are available, and we find these most practical when there are several of us, besides being necessary for Bob's picture taking.

One of the first places we visit in Anchorage is the attractive log-cabin headquarters of the Greater Anchorage Chamber of Commerce Information Center at 4th and F streets. It is a fount of information and open 9 to 5 Monday through Saturday, during the summer visitor season (which may be extended with the new winter-tour promotion). Inside there are racks of information reading material: brochures of things to do and see in Anchorage and surrounding areas, lists of Alaskan reading material, and current guides—mimeographed lists of hotels, motels, restaurants, travel agencies, camper rentals, and companies with charter or package tours.

The authentically sod-roofed cabin, another symbol of Alaska, intrigued our family lawn cutter, who noted that the grass was over a foot long and needed cutting.

"Wonder how they manage that," Terry mused.

He found out later at the Fairbanks Chamber of Commerce log cabin. A fellow about his age was up on top lopping it off with a power mower.

Food, lodging, and stores

We have always credited Anchorage with having all the comforts of home, even before one could truthfully say there *were* a lot of comforts, for travelers anyway. In contrast to places we had been exploring at the time, Anchorage seemed like a haven of civilization. What it had, we were grateful for.

On our first visit to Anchorage we followed the Sterling Highway, then under construction, on the Kenai Peninsula to its end at Homer, then drove back up to Anchorage. It was a spectacular, unforgettable trip, as we waited while road crews scooped out, then regraveled the thawing dirt. Then the road crew waited as we inched our way through, ready to pull us out if we needed it. Bob would have been chafing at the enforced leisurely pace if it hadn't been for the really spectacular picture possibilities. Three-year-old Terry, of course, was ecstatic with all that heavy equipment to watch.

It was this car trip that taught us the most about Alaska and Alaskans. We were self-sufficient, with plenty of food, as it was the beginning of our trip, and we are experienced campers. But wherever our paths crossed, the few residents—few in comparison to today—cared enough to visit and make *sure* we knew where we were going and were prepared for what lay ahead. If a road wait was near a homesteader's cabin, we and any others were invited in for

Homestead in Matanuska Valley near Anchorage has commuter airplane at the ready in front of pioneer barn.

coffee and a snack, often delicious sourdough bread and rolls, of course.

By the time we reached Anchorage, happiness was a place to catch up on the laundry, stock up on supplies, and sleep as many nights under a roof as our budget would allow. We found a laundry center, with wringer washers, run by gas motors. It was a well-used place, but very friendly. They even lent me an iron to use without charge. Ever since, we have felt that laundromats, at least in Alaska, should be listed with chambers of commerce and other information-dispensing agencies. What you glean in a laundromat is sure to be informal, but usually reliable and based on the experience of someone who has tried it.

How times have changed since that first visit in 1952! Now there are department stores, supermarkets, self-service cleaning and washing establishments, including the one-day service kind, and specialty stores. Many are branches of the same chains already thriving in the "South 48." Offhand, we can't think of any that are missing.

The Captain Cook and Sheffield House (several in Alaska and Yukon) hotels match the finest anywhere. They have been joined by familiar names: Westward Hilton, Holiday Inn, Travelodge, International, Barratt Best Western, to name a few we can vouch for. We noticed that the Roosevelt Hotel where we stayed and showered down the hall on that early trip has had a facelifting, and expanded in size. But though there are now many more places to choose from, there are many more people passing through. At times, tourists may compete with an influx of oil industry, and related, personnel. To be sure of a place to stay when you are ready to call it quits for the day, make advance reservations and verify them if you will be late showing up.

Ask where to eat and stand back for "Clinkerdagger, Biggerstaff and Petts." Anchorage residents not only love its English pub style, but also love proving they can say the name without a falter. The Anchorage panorama spread out below draws people to hotel tower restaurants: the Crow's Nest in the Captain Cook; the Top of the World in the Westward Hilton. Off the latter's lobby is the General Store Coffee Shop, on the actual site of an early-day country store. Nostalgic touches are hard candy sticks and jelly beans behind the counter. And how about dinner with a poet? Larry Beck's "Alaska Show" in the Westward Hilton features a Sourdough Buffet and spellbinding recitations of Robert Service ballads.

We like both food and surroundings at the Nikko Gardens, not far from the International Airport on the main road to Anchorage. Decor is Japanese and so are the food specialties. A plain-steak man, Bob enjoys their thick chunk of choice steak teriyaki-style.

The restaurant has a quiet, peaceful setting whether you eat in one of the private little rooms, Japanese-style (reserve ahead of time), or in the main open dining room with a pretty stream running through. Top prices in these top restaurants, of course.

Thrifty residents and chronic travelers to Anchorage may recommend the Oriental Gardens on the old Spenard Road, the Peanut Farm, where there is ice skating in winter, or the Rice Bowl, downtown. Not for the thrifty is the "experience in dining out" offered at a sporadic eatery with the intriguing name of "Stuck-again Heights."

However, geared to family traveling, our tastes, except for special occasions, are modest. When we choose a restaurant, we consider the cost and try to judge where the food will be clean and tasty. We are happy to find old friends like Colonel Sanders, whose concession to this Alaskan location is offering fish 'n' chips along with his finger lickin' chicken. We also recognize Stuart Anderson's Cattle Company, famous for steaks, and a phenomenal McDonald's. Along with a Big Mac cheeseburger (90 cents) and a shake (45 cents) we learned that Anchorage and Guam vie for the highest volume of McDonald's sales.

To prevent Future Shock, we must warn you that accommodations, food, and drink are not inexpensive in Anchorage. Nevertheless, we have been well satisfied sampling around. Like most places in Alaska, food is likely to be served up with friendly conversation by someone newly transplanted and enthusiastic, or by someone who has been there a while and is equally anxious to tell visitors about the delights of the area.

Sightseeing

Anchorage displayed the epitome of Alaskan spirit and determination after the devastating 1964 earthquake. One of the most impressive reminders is in the downtown area. Several blocks of nothing but paved parking area mark the site where buildings of the original downtown section used to stand. Uptown Anchorage with its many new buildings looks like any growing city.

Another reminder of the 1964 tragedy is Earthquake Park. Here you see no grass, benches, or picnic tables—just a jumbled mass of tortured earth. Clay pinnacles forced up by the grinding mass will erode, and someday vegetation will slowly cover the scars. A simple sign tells the story of what happened.

Turnagain By-the-Sea, one of the fine residential sections, is back to normal. Only a crack in a sidewalk or foundation shows here and there. Some houses on the choicest view lots were swallowed in minutes. Half-wrecked ones have been removed, and all others repaired. It is reassuring to visitors to see these restored places.

The city is convenient to recreation and scenic areas. People not planning to drive the Glenn Highway might enjoy a short drive out of Anchorage to Palmer in the Matanuska Valley. This valley is as close as Alaska has come, so far, to success in agricultural pursuits. It was the scene of a fairly modern pioneer expedition in 1935, when the government encouraged people to come and homestead there. The going was not easy, but thanks to rich soil and long hours of summer sunlight, settlers have proved that certain items can be grown on an Alaskan scale—big. Really giant vegetables are harvested for the annual Labor Day Matanuska Valley Fair. We noted the prize cabbage in 1968 weighed seventy-two pounds, and the runner-up weighed seventy!

We watch, as we drive, for signs of the original barns. Most of the farm homes have been redone, and the barns have been modernized and new materials used. You can identify the old barns by the log foundations.

Another typically Alaskan rural sight that intrigues us: small planes in the fields adjacent to many of the farmhouses and barns. While someone tends the farm, another member of the family may commute to a job in Anchorage, by plane instead of car. Most planes, however, are probably used for weekend fishing trips.

Indian graves

There is a unique little graveyard about twenty-five miles from Anchorage just off this same highway. Take the side road that leads to the almost-ghost town of Eklutna. The cemetery is behind a little old church and school. It's unusual in that the graves are topped by miniature houses and show a mixture of Indian and Russian influence. They look like a settlement of tiny dollhouses, each house bearing the traditional Russian Orthodox cross. Many of the houses are gaily painted in yellow, red, blue, and white, and though old, they used to be well kept. Styles and designs vary. Some have definitely Indian patterns, others ornate Russian. The houses may be one, two or three stories high, possibly depending on the rank or wealth of the departed one. There are glass windows in many, and you can see the treasured belongings of the deceased, placed inside according to Indian custom. We noted clothes, shoes, dishes, and toys (apparently a child's grave) and even a pair of long underwear. The few graves without houses had an Indian blanket covering, and in one case the cover was a Navy pea jacket.

Farther back in the woods are some ancient-looking houses, mostly falling apart. There is a sign on the church door inviting people to look around but asking them not to molest the church or graves. We peeked in the window and would guess that the church is seldom used, but it still contains the sacramental objects of the Russian Orthodox Church. There is a newer church here, too.

Indian graves and Russian church at Eklutna, near Anchorage, off Matanuska Valley (Glenn Highway) road. Combination of cultures are represented by Russian cross and Indian spirit house.

MOUNT ALYESKA

Mount Alyeska, from a skier's point of view, has everything—a Day Lodge and the beautiful new Nugget Inn, excellent food, easy accessibility from Anchorage (forty miles), convivial atmosphere, excellent snow conditions, a fine chair lift, tows, and a variety of runs to suit any degree of ability. Its most endearing feature is the length of the ski season. It never stops. The diehards just shift to higher levels and continue skiing on the numerous glaciers as summer makes its inroads on the lower, conventional ski terrain.

But what if you're not a skier? Don't let that keep you away from Mount Alyeska. You can enjoy the same fresh, pure air, beautiful scenery, good food, convivial company, go glacier tripping, ride horseback or in a horse-drawn sleigh, try a snowmobile or dog team—everything, with a fraction of the effort and expense put out by those crazy skiers. Here's how:

Getting there

Takeoff point is Anchorage, and there are good daily bus tours, well guided and informative. They take several hours and include a visit to Portage Glacier a few miles beyond Alyeska. It is timed so the group gets to Alyeska in time for a very delicious buffet lunch and the scenic chair-lift ride.

If you have your own car you take the paved Anchorage-Seward Highway, or you may want to rent a car. This is the same highway from which the Sterling Highway branches and continues on down the Kenai Peninsula to the state ferry connection through the Gulf of Alaska.

Though we have taken the tours to Alyeska and can vouch for the fact that they are very worthwhile, Bob is frustrated unless he is master of his own transportation and can stop and take his time getting his pictures. The drive is very photogenic, almost any season of the year. More snow covers the mountains in winter, but summer is colorful, with rampant purple fireweed and lots of greenery covering the fairly steep slopes. The highway follows Turnagain Arm, as does the Alaska Railroad, which terminates in Seward at beautiful Resurrection Bay. Beyond Alyeska, at Portage, a trunk of the Alaska Railroad tunnels through the mountains, portaging people and vehicles to the port of Whittier on Prince William Sound and state ferries that cross to Valdez. Turnagain Arm got its name because Captain Cook explored down that way but found that there was no through passage, just a long bay, and he had to turn around and come back.

Turnagain looks like two different places, depending on whether the tide is in or out. The tides are tremendous, considered second only to the Bay of Fundy. The water is sucked out completely and then returns with a mighty rush, forming formidable waves, almost a wall of water. It is unsuitable for boat navigation. Bird Creek is a good place to watch the bore tide of four or five feet.

Also at Bird Creek you might happen to notice an odd little building with a big fake bird poking its head out of its roost. It's called the Bird House and its main claim to fame is that it dates from railroad-construction days. From the outside it is hard to tell that this old-timer is currently a swinging place, with four inches of sawdust on the floor, and stumps to perch on. The bar and floor are so slanty that when things begin to look straight it's time to call it quits and go home—so they say.

Along Turnagain Arm between Mount Alyeska and Anchorage, Seward Highway and Alaska Railroad.

The chair-lift ride

Even though you think you are afraid of heights, don't pass up the chair lift, which rises twenty-two hundred feet in a span of 1¼ miles. You get a faster ride in winter because of those eager skiers; in summer they slow it down to about twenty minutes each way, the better to enjoy the scenery. Two can ride together, if you need moral support, and a bar comes down in front to give you an added feeling of security. Plenty of careful, polite attendants help riders on and off. In fact, we have seen the same little one-legged lady mentioned previously riding the chair summer and winter, with no difficulty. And one of the most reassuring things about riding the lift as a tourist is that you don't have to ski back down. Just relax as you descend in comfort, soaking in the beauty of Turnagain Arm, the mountains and the Girdwood Valley, its varied greens textured in cloud-dappled patterns.

Wear something warm for the lift ride. The rise in altitude is like a change in season. Toward fall there are tinges of red and yellow in the berry bushes and the foliage beneath. The feathery ferns have started to turn yellow and on the steep slopes there will be blueberry pickers, bent over harvesting the crop. People have seen moose from the chair lift. One spring a mother and calf hung around for a couple of weeks, apparently people-watching. When you get above the timber and hit the open meadows, it feels like fall, but wild flowers may still be blooming, for summer arrives later at the higher altitude.

At the top, some visitors follow the trail and hike on up the next foothill. If you walk around the Sundeck though, you'll find plenty of camera fodder. The Sundeck, an attractive octagonal building used as a warming hut and snack shack in winter, is a choice vantage point for viewing several glaciers, the lift, and Turnagain Arm.

Meanwhile, back at the lodge...

"As a professional ski bum, I feel right at home at Alyeska," Chris von Imhof, enthusiastic manager of Mount Alyeska Nugget Inn and Day Lodge, will tell you. "Right here in Alaska we have skiing and scenery that compares with any in Europe."

We'll take his word for it. Tall, young, good-looking Chris was reared in Garmisch, as his delightful accent and courtly manners indicate. Though sometimes temporarily hard to track down in winter, as he can't resist those ski runs, Chris is an avid promoter of his mountain and an expert on conditions, equipment, and competitions as well as anything to do with just plain tourism. He was once director of the Alaska Travel Divisions, and therefore is knowledgeable about all of Alaska.

His beautiful wife, Nina, is a real born-in-Alaskan. Her father is Frank Whaley, long-time bush pilot and airline executive. She has been well grounded in things Alaskan, especially in the Arctic. We've known her since her early teens. A former Miss Alaska, she is now a gracious hostess, and as enthusiastic about Alyeska as her husband is. Her hobby is raising husky dogs, and she is working on a matched team to enter in the Anchorage Dog Sled Races held annually during Fur Rendezvous time. At Alyeska, you are likely to see some beautiful dogs for petting and photographing. Nina is a true example of Alaskan womanhood. And don't let that delicate feminine look fool you! She brought home her own polar bear rug from the Arctic a few years ago.

Three gift shops offer a variety of good Alaskan souvenirs. The Kobuk Valley Jade Company, specializing in jewelry and raw jade from the Kobuk River Valley, is a browser's joy, with rare carvings, paintings, and items like bone-slat armor and prehistoric bone dolls from the Arctic Eskimos. Also in the valley is Alyeska Village, a complex of privately owned chalets, a small historic gold mine, and the town of Girdwood, with post office, library, store, fire station, and free·public tennis courts. The chalets, each individually styled, are picture postcards in the snow. In summer, they are even more colorful, with window boxes, hanging baskets, and yards, lushly green and abounding with flowers.

Bob and I hark back to the days when skiers were lucky to find lodge food hot and filling. Perhaps that is why we are always amazed at the gourmet spreads at Alyeska, whether it is a buffet for a large crowd at the Day Lodge, a full-course dinner in the Nugget Inn restaurant, overlooking the ski slopes or a snack or more at the Skyride Restaurant at the top of the chairlift. Some Alaska

Turnagain Arm from chairlift at year-round Alyeska Resort, forty miles from Anchorage on highway to Kenai.

specialities are sautéed king crab legs and London broil, a tasty combination of lobster and steak, accompanied by superior bread and pastry baked by a former chef, Werner Egloff, now running his Alyeska bakery nearby. We have found the price for a superb meal less than what we would pay in the fanciest city restaurants. There is a bar handy for a predinner cocktail.

Glacier flights from Alyeska

Fortunately, everyone who goes on glacier flights is not required to ski back. Frank Whaley, Jr., Nina von Imhof's brother, then flying with Alyeska Air Service, Girdwood, was our pilot, and he landed with his small ski-equipped plane on a glacier long enough for us to get out, look around, and take a couple of pictures. The snowshoes he had stashed in back were for walking in the deep snow.

Any good bush pilot is always happy to discuss an itinerary with you and then figure out how to get you there. However, there are regular ski-tested jaunts set up, the price depending on the extent of skiing and sightseeing and the number of passengers. The pilot washes his hands of you once you are out of the plane, but makes every effort to determine whether you are qualified for the run down before accepting you as a passenger, or else he recommends that you have an experienced ski guide along with you.

The airport is just a mile from the lodge, and we started out with a pass over Max's Mountain, a three-thousand-three-hundred-foot-high foothill of Mount Alyeska and the backdrop for the Day Lodge. The sundeck looked like a little white-capped mushroom. Max's Mountain has a flat top about three-hundred feet long for ski-plane landings.

"If we don't touch down in the first fifty feet, better skip it till the next time around," advised Frank. We'll buy that. As someone once said, there are old pilots and there are bold pilots, but there are no old bold pilots. Frank isn't old, but he's experienced and learned from his veteran dad. Sitting in his father's lap and being told to "hold that needle straight" is an early memory.

Frank pointed out the myriad glaciers and flew close to be sure anyone nearsighted got the full impact, figuratively speaking. He spent $4,000 to modify his plane and can do some fine maneuvering with confidence. It was a thrilling ride as he practically skied down the long runs in places, close enough to see the crevasses. Unless you are very experienced it's well to follow a guide while skiing in crevasse territory. For some reason I felt as weary, but exhilarated, as if I'd skied the whole route when we came out at Portage Glacier.

We counted eight moose along the river as we circled for a closer look. Frank said that invariably he saw sheep and goats in summer at the high elevations.

Glacier skiing and sightseeing by plane are neither first nor exclusive at Mount Alyeska. At Mount McKinley, Juneau, Petersburg—in fact, anywhere there are ski-and-scenery-minded people, and mountains and perpetual snowfields—you'll find tours. Alyeska is exceptionally convenient, being near a large population center. The slopes so far are still uncrowded. It has been a pleasure to know and explore there in these early undeveloped years.

We have already given high family honor to this beautiful place. We named our husky pup Alyeska, after the mountain—and the state.

VALDEZ (VAL-DEEZ)

Flying over the site of Old Valdez, looking down on nothing but seawater lapping the spot where the dock used to stand, triggered off some old memories. That obliterated dock was one on which our whole family had stood many times, while Bob focused on the busy waterfront and fishing boats passing in and out of the harbor. In 1964, thirty-two residents and visiting workers (including a family of five) were not so lucky as we. The earthquake that wrought devastation around the South Central and Gulf of Alaska area swallowed the docks and everyone on them in a few seconds.

A memorable trip to Valdez was a short charter flight from Anchorage in the winter. It was a sort of goodwill, good-luck greeting to the town now moved to its new site on firm ground about four miles away from the old, destroyed in 1964. It was still winter there, and the snow on the ground and nearby mountains made its nickname the "Switzerland of Alaska" even more appropriate than in summer. We were glad we came to share coffee and talk a while. If ever a town of only 850 to 1,000 population deserves special mention for courage and resiliency in accepting and overcoming tragedy, this one does.

By coincidence, and a fine gift of property from the children of the pioneer Meals and Hazelet families, the new town is built on the site originally chosen for the town in 1897. The reason it wasn't placed there then was that gold seekers and their suppliers felt that this farthest-north ice-free port at Old Valdez was a few steps closer to central Alaska gold fields. The miners were anxious to grab their supplies and get going.

The main route to Valdez is the Richardson Highway, which we, and others, consider a spectacularly beautiful road as well as the oldest and most historic. Though improved from trail to paved highway over a period of seventy years, its route is little changed from the way it was first staked out by Lieutenant Abercrombie. It winds its way through a variety of scenery from low interior terrain to high mountain passes, near waterfalls and beautiful streams. Watch for historic signs like wagon ruts and an incomplete tunnel started by rival railroads. The story of this bloody battle is told in Rex Beach's novel, *The Iron Trail*.

The Richardson Highway replaced the old Valdez Glacier route, a real killer. Many were buried by slides and crevasses. The new road was named for General Wilds Richardson, a pioneer in the construction of the trail. Today's soldiers stationed at both Anchorage and Fairbanks bases know the recreational value of the Valdez area and this is where many of them head during their time off. It is 363 miles from Fairbanks, 305 from Anchorage. In the summer there is regular scheduled bus, ferry, and plane service and charter air taxis for hire. Though the Richardson is an all-weather highway, the main tourist season so far is May-June through September.

Sightseeing

"Though it is hard to pull up roots, especially under such tragic circumstances, we are convinced our new town has everything the old town had, but better planned," pointed out our resident guide, Bill Whitnall, district highway director. "Except history," added his wife, Marie.

Worthington Glacier reflected in roadside alpine pool, near Valdez. The historic gold rush trail that passed here became Richardson Highway.

Chilkat Dancers in assorted sizes perform age-old dance accompanied by song and percussions for visitors at Port Chilkoot.

Beaming salmon fisherman (the author) and her catch at B⟨ Island Resort on Behm Canal, famous Southeast Alaska fishi⟨ grounds.

Dogsledding on the frozen Bering Sea, just an icicle's throw from the cozy Nome Nugget Inn.

Ketchikan, perhaps most active fishing port in the world, and southern sea-air gateway to Alaska.

Totems and tribal house stand guard at Totem Bight, a state park near Ketchikan.

Happy Eskimo mother carrying child in traditional manner, in back of roomy parka.

This is true. Nothing is left at Old Valdez, now a historical site. We shall miss the Morgue, a picturesque waterfront cocktail bar at the time of the quake. It was first built as a stamp mill, but got its name from a later use. Bodies of those who died during the winter were stored there until the ground thawed enough in the spring for burial.

An impressive sign in Valdez says: "No bear shooting within city limits." You are likely to see black bear on the green mountainsides in summer. "Occasionally they may even come closer," averred Bill Whitnall. "We had one wander into our highway office, and quickly out again. We had to shoot one that was determined to join the town after the quake. We figured he had been shaken out of his hibernating cave, and possibly a head injury addled him." Besides bear, there are mountain goats, moose, an occasional deer, and beaver. Many migratory birds in season intrigue birdwatchers, and there are plenty of wild flowers and berries.

New Valdez aimed for a firm footing after losing ground (the whole area sank about six feet) due to the quake. Residents based their plans on tourism as the future major industry. But now that the pipeline is no longer a "pipe dream," Valdez is committed to rising to its potential as a port and permanent base of operations for oil shipping. It appears that the population explosion caused by the famous earlier gold rush will be equaled—and perhaps even surpassed—by the black gold rush. No one knows what effect this will have on lovely Valdez. Perhaps it can never be the same....

Venturing down the Richardson again soon after the pipeline construction period was over, we confess to having some compunctions about the major addition to the scenery—the pipeline itself. Some places it comes into jarring view, a great silver snake hugging ridges and suspended over rivers. Most of the time it is buried out of sight. But not quite out of mind, yet; its green "cover" was still too new to blend in perfectly. We found ourselves preoccupied with following its relentless advance, our eyes alerted to every deviation in the terrain. Our mood was mollified, though, by exceptional views of glaciers, such as the Worthington with tongues of ice reaching almost to the highway. We arrived in Valdez, refreshed by the spectacle of Thompson Pass switching to brilliant fall color, and by the waterfalls of narrow Keystone Canyon.

Keystone Canyon on Alaska's oldest highway, the Richardson, which evolved from a trail that led to interior gold fields seventy years ago.

Aiming to make our early morning ferry reservation, and being self-contained in our RV, we were not too concerned about accommodations. Asking around, it appeared there is no great problem, though this is a popular circle route from Anchorage. Package tours take cars of their own. They switch travelers from bus to ship at Valdez, cruise them across Prince William Sound to Whittier, and railroad them through a mountain tunnel to Portage for their bus pickup back to Anchorage.

The marine life is fantastic in Valdez Bay and nearby Prince William Sound, whether you observe it from aboard the state auto ferry's daily scheduled run from Valdez to Whittier, or from fishing and sightseeing charter boats. The route meanders among islands surrounded by prolific bird and sea life, and always in sight of really magnificent marine and mountain scenery. Both ferries and charters putt audaciously to the face of the mighty Columbia Glacier, about four miles across and three hundred feet high, and very active. Undaunted, they pay their respects with a whistle toot, which is usually sufficient to cause blue and white ice chunks to break away from the disintegrating cliffs with thunder and splash, as the Columbia marches on at a rate of four to ten feet per day.

Where next?

Since its main access is by highway, Valdez fits our road end category. However, because of its location it can be considered a gateway on two counts. The State Ferry System takes off from here to make stops at Kodiak and at points up the Kenai Peninsula, where you strike the highway to Anchorage. One alternative is to get off at Whittier and put your car on the Alaska Railroad, which tunnels over to Portage, and then drive up Turnagain Arm to Anchorage. It makes a fine circle trip, with no duplication of scenery. Or you can reverse the whole itinerary and arrive at Valdez, and thus consider the town a gateway to the Interior.

The Kenai Peninsula with bus, ferry, and air service, is the most easily accessible of three interesting areas which lie south and west of both Valdez and Anchorage. Well-maintained roads lead to the main Peninsula towns, starting from Anchorage. Kodiak town on Kodiak Island is the most out-of-the-way port of call on the State Ferry System. It is reached from take-off points at Homer, Seward, and Valdez. Part of the route is through open ocean waters, and a sturdy pair of sea legs is an advantage at times. Western Airlines has daily flights between Seattle-Tacoma International Airport and Kodiak. Wien Air Alaska flies twice daily between Anchorage and Kodiak.

Before the day of airplanes, getting to the Katmai area was not easy. It had to be by boat, and the Russians used Kodiak as the starting point. The first leg of the journey was a forty-nine-mile boat ride across Shelikof Strait. They then hiked over a native trail, transporting supplies to larger rivers emptying into the Bering Sea, and finally delivered them to their coastal and Aleutian trading posts. It was a lot of work, but safer than swinging around the stormy Aleutian Islands and braving the Bering Sea. No such problems present themselves today. Wien Air Alaska serves the Katmai.

THE KENAI

The Kenai deserves fuller treatment than we can give it here. It is noted for superb hunting and fishing. To inquisitive sightseers, it offers an excellent opportunity for poking around and discovering evidences of former Russian occupation. Many of the names offer a clue: Kenai, Kasilof, Kalifonsky, Soldotna, Ninilchik. To photographers, it is ruggedly beautiful picture-taking country and overrun with moose.

Traffic has picked up considerably on Kenai roads in the last few years. The reason for the big boom and population explosion in small towns and communities is the pursuit of Alaska's newest, most exciting form of wealth—oil. Comparing *The Milepost* descriptions of only a couple of years ago with today's current issue points up just how fast things are developing there. The town of Kenai is the largest on the Kenai Peninsula and it is one of Alaska's oldest permanent settlements. The best way to find out what's new is to consult someone who knows the country. We met Rusty Lancashire the first time we came to Alaska, and have been consulting her on the subject for years.

Bob needed pictures of a homesteading family for a magazine story he was doing. Everyone in the village of Kenai directed us to the Lancashire family, just out of town, in the process of "proving up" on their acreage. Our first memory of Rusty is watching her drive a tractor while keeping an eye on three little girls, baking bread, and giving a hand to her husband, Larry, when he needed help in hoisting logs in place for the new barn he needed to finish before winter.

Rusty was an Alaskan from the day she was born, in the Midwest. It just took a few years to find out where she belonged. She is a perfect example of multi-careered, perpetually busy Alaskan womanhood. Pretty enough for a modeling career, she gave that up when Larry came back from World War II. A flier, he had been cooling his heels in a prison camp after being shot down during a raid on a Rumanian oil field. Rusty had been plying him with literature on Alaska homesteading for the duration of his prison-camp stay.

They started their life in Alaska from absolute scratch, clearing, building, and planting as they "earned" their land. As Rusty says, "It has been a great life to watch." Though we Springs have lost track of the Lancashires for a year or two at a time, we manage to keep up with their adventures and the progress of the daughters, now young women. Throughout the years, besides homesteading and her job as wife and mother, Rusty has found time for politics, an RFD mail route, tending bar for Larry's business enterprise, and taking on a travel agency.

Our latest exchange caught Rusty and Larry headed "outside" for the winter. She answered from their destination, an Alaskan opposite, desert country. Of their drive out the Kenai Spur Road to join the Sterling Highway, then the Seward Highway on to Anchorage, Rusty noted: "You would never recognize the Kenai. It is so grown and there are so many new people in big industry here that even I do not know a lot of them. And they say it is just the beginning...."

A hint tossed in about mid-letter was a dead giveaway that Mesa, Arizona, can only be temporary for the Lancashires: "I miss the old way of life as I felt it was a lot healthier. At home on the Kenai I always just enjoyed shooting the breeze with people, hearing where they were from, and how they were getting along in Alaska. I'll adjust, but the desert isn't green and it's not cool...." On our next trip to the Kenai we expect to find Rusty, a true extrovert and full of Alaska stories, available for "shooting the breeze."

Hearing from Rusty brought back some more memories of that first trip to Alaska, when we continued on to the road end at Homer. In fact, we camped on the Homer Spit, all by ourselves, and had to carry jugs of water from the nearest service station. Homer was a quiet town where people could live off the sea and land. They developed small industries like making jams and jellies out of native

Homesteader at the tip of the Kenai Peninsula. Sand spit extends into Kachemak Bay: boating, beachcombing, fishing, and cruises.

berries, and engaged in satisfying crafts using local materials. Some ventures depended on sea harvests, like king crab. But along with the work, there seemed to be plenty of time to enjoy the particular beauty of Kachemak Bay.

Homer is the same today, only more so. Some visitors consider it an "arty" community. We are pleased that the same kind of industries (some are the original ones) are thriving. For years, the residents have been sharing their bounty with fellow Alaskans, particularly those from Anchorage. Homer is developing rapidly as a resort area with very good creature comforts in hotels, motels, and restaurants. Practically every one of the fifteen hundred residents would be happy to direct people toward the recreational possibilities.

It is a do-it-yourself type of resort community, especially if you have time to stay a while. Otherwise, sign up for some of the excellent sightseeing tours. The Kachemak Bay Tours head out into Kachemak Bay with its whales and porpoises; to Gull Island, alive with all kinds of sea birds; to the isolated fishing community of Seldovia across the waterway; to Halibut Cove and its art galleries; and to the crab and shrimp grounds when the pots are pulled up.

Yes, there is still a campground on the Spit, but you won't be lonely. It is near all the action of the busy boat harbor with full access to fishing, clamdigging, crabbing, beachcombing, and sightseeing. Not only is there water there now, but showers with unlimited *hot* water are advertised. In future years, the price may increase, but we'll wager it will still be a bargain.

KODIAK

Kodiak has seen a lot of changes, too. It is the oldest town in Alaska, excluding native villages, of course. The Russians started their first settlement on Kodiak Island at Three Saints Bay in 1784. Alexander Baranof moved the town to its present site in 1792, and it was the capital of Russian America until he decided to move to Sitka in 1804. As the capital, it was a tremendously busy and successful town with tough, hardworking citizens, who were expected to carry on a profitable fur business, colonize, and somehow manage to carve room and board out of the land at the same time.

The residents gave their all. Flourishing businesses included a grist mill, tannery, brick kiln, and foundry. They built houses and ships and made products for export to California. Mission bells especially were in demand.

From Anchorage, Kodiak is about an hour via Wien Air Alaska's 737 jets. The flight heads over the Kenai Peninsula and features distant vistas of the Alaska Range rimming Cook Inlet on one side and the Kenai Mountains on the other. They include some of North America's highest peaks, and the most rugged. In the often stormy sea between the Kenai Peninsula and Kodiak Island are small, barren exposed mountain tops. The islands get bigger; Afognak, heavily timbered with Sitka spruce, and then Kodiak, amazingly lush and green.

Looking down on the town of Kodiak, ten years after the earthquake, it is hard to imagine the devastation caused by the tidal wave that sucked the fifty-foot-deep harbor dry. Downtown has been rebuilt as before—and improved—and the boat-filled harbor is bustling. The waterfront is lined with marine supply and other fish-oriented, new-looking stores.

Among Kodiak's growing population of about sixty-five hundred are seven hundred native Aleuts, many with Russian and Scandinavian blood and names. About fifteen hundred men and their families live at the nearby coastguard headquarters. Everyone is interested in various phases of the expanding fishing industry. Kodiak king crab, which often attains a six-foot spread and thirty-pound weight, is famous. It rates its own celebration the first weekend each May. The King Crab Festival kicks off Kodiak's summer season with a parade, ball, and contests, including king crab "shaking" (shelling) competition, of course. Shrimp and tasty small scallops are part of the sea harvest. Just off the island are some of the world's best halibut grounds, and the waters also produce codfish, black cod, and fine salmon. Streams and lakes are well supplied with trout.

Kodiak is noted for another giant too. Kodiak bears are a prized hunter's trophy, with the reputation of being the largest carnivorous animal in the world. These bears were tough enough to survive the eruption of Mount Katmai, though most other animal and plant life on the island was smothered by a layer of powdered volcanic ash several inches deep in 1912.

Hunters and fishermen have long been attracted to Kodiak. Many visitors now come for the day or longer to sightsee in this friendly, lusty fishing town, and at the same time take a refresher course in Russian American history—where it all began.

There is much evidence left here of the Russian occupation. The jewel is the Russian Orthodox Holy Resurrection Church, established in 1794 by Russian priests who came to Kodiak by a small hand-hewn wooden ship. The present church dates from 1945, the third rebuilding, but always in the same style. The priest or his wife (Orthodox priests may marry) conducts the tour of the church.

We talked with Father Kreta, formerly from New York, about one of the founders, Father Herman. This saintly man was revered for his dedication, certain miracles, and good deeds, such as establishing a school and educating and caring for orphans, especially Aleuts, on nearby Spruce Island. Father Kreta was present at the canonization ceremonies held in this church in 1970, elevating Father Herman to Alaska's—and America's—first Russian Orthodox saint. Saint Herman's relics, along with his cross and other items and memorable icons are here and in his chapel on Spruce Island. Both churches are religious shrines to which the devout make pilgrimages every year.

We flew over the island in a small plane later that day and could see Saint Herman's small chapel, reminding me of some of the predictions attributed to him. Though he died long before the 1867 Purchase, he prophesied that Russia would not keep Alaska. Father Kreta had related the story of Icon Bay. Father Herman himself had placed an icon on the beach and warned that the church must be built no closer to the sea. Where the icon stood was as far as the 1964 tidal wave came.

Along the waterfront in Kodiak the earthquake uncovered a really choice Russian remainder, a portion of the original sea wall. It was probably the foundation of an old log warehouse, laboriously hand-built of stone, some blocks imbedded with large mooring rings. The sturdy walls survived and were exposed, though more modern wharves and dock buildings in current use collapsed and were swept out to sea. To the consternation of active Kodiak historians, it was covered over again by new buildings. They would like it uncovered again (but not by an earthquake!).

The 1793 headquarters of Baranof, first Russian governor, still stands. This museum is said to be the oldest wooden building on the west coast of the United States. It has a fine collection of Aleut baskets and other native Russian mementos. Exposed inside is a portion of the original log wall, chinked with moss. On the lawn outside is a millstone used by the early Russians at Mill Bay.

You can drive on your own or take a well-guided tour around the vicinity. The view from the summit of fourteen hundred-foot Pillar Mountain is sensational. The ten feet of soil covering the well-drained (steep) slopes of this high point supports a lot of verdure: wildflowers, berries, brush and some sizable trees. The Shelikof Straits and the archipelago-like patchwork of islands including the far out Sea Lion Rocks, Near, Woody, and Spruce islands, marine activity, and the town of Kodiak can be seen and photographed from various vantage points.

Fort Abercrombie State Historical Park has leftover bunkers from World War II. Canneries are open to visitors in season. We learned that old Puget Sound ferries don't die either. We recognized the "streamlined" loaf-shaped metallic *Kalakala* that used to run between Seattle and Bremerton. She's drydocked and serving as a cannery, a short distance out of town.

With all the boats around, there are bound to be some for charter. We went looking for the sea lions on their rocky islets. Saint Herman, described by Father Kreta as the "seaman's comfortable saint to pray to" came to mind as we encountered some open-water waves that appeared formidable to a landlubber like me.

"Just a little cross-chop," our helmsman Mike Shockley reassured. He expertly parried the waves, turned on a dime, and demonstrated "surfing" as we headed back by way of a sheltered cove where he pointed out the remains of an old Russian brick kiln.

Ask almost anyone about the night life in this robust, many-barred town and they'll probably direct you to several, from the B & B to a topless. Town friends say the B & B (for Beer & Booze) is the oldest, moved from downtown to a more convenient (for

Kodiak and offshore islands from Pillar Mountain. First capital when Alaska was Russian America; now fishing and king crab capital.

fishermen) waterfront location. They claim that Anna, the proprietress, personally prepares and distributes tasty fish hors d'oeuvres to her clientele on occasion.

The enthusiastic Kodiak Chamber of Commerce across from the museum is a good bet for information on tours, charters, lodging, food, entertainment, and current festival, including a new Russian one. Their "Welcome to Kodiak!" folder has a map, description of highlights, and a roster of clubs.

Note from the past: fellow travel writer Howard Clifford passed on a choice "brochure" from his files. It is a little booklet called *Where the Action Is!*, put out several years ago by the military's Special Services. Obviously intended to entice and hold servicemen, the skiing, hunting, fishing, etc., are described, and in addition "Special Services will lend you all the equipment needed for a prolonged hunting trip." 'Twas enough to encourage some tourists to enlist...on the spot.

KATMAI NATIONAL MONUMENT

The Katmai has changed the least in the past several years, not an adverse criticism at all, in this case. It was proclaimed a national monument in 1918, to preserve it for future visitors interested in having a close look at what happens when nature goes on a rampage. The big upheaval occurred in 1912 when volcanic Mount Katmai blew its top and shook the area for miles around. Over a period of four days the landscape of this isolated part of the Alaska Peninsula, fortunately sparsely populated, was radically changed. Where there formerly were green valleys, broad rivers of molten sand flowed from mountains that had been split apart. To some it must have seemed like the end of the world; repercussions were felt and seen in far-distant places.

Forty-two years later, Bob, in company with some California geologists, hiked in to photograph and study what had happened. They were somewhat later than the National Geographic Society, which waited for four years after the eruption for the land to cool down enough for exploration. The society continued to send in expeditions over several years, and named a fifteen-mile-long valley with steaming fissures the Valley of Ten Thousand Smokes. It was

Visitors hike mile and a half trail from bus to sandflow floor of Valley of Ten Thousand Smokes in Katmai National Monument.

owing to these studies that the valley, and a large surrounding area, was set aside as a national monument.

Bob was enchanted with the valley, rugged though it was, even though the name no longer applies, for the smokes have cooled down and now there are only a handful.

"It's like walking on the moon," Bob said. "Absolutely fascinating to come to a miniature Grand Canyon where the sand flow has been cut to a depth of a couple of hundred feet by a stream. Powdered pumice isn't the easiest substance to walk on, either."

Bob brought back some rocks for bath toys for the youngsters. They were fairly large, but light enough to float because they were made of pumice, fused by the intense heat.

Now there is a road to the valley's edge, and a bus makes a daily tour in summer. Wien Air Alaska's Brooks River Fishing Camp in Katmai National Monument overlooks Naknek Lake. The town of that name made news during the last hotly contested state election. Naknek is the hometown of a former legislator, conservation-minded Jay Hammond, reelected governor in 1978.

Wien also has some fly-in camps outside the Monument. There are package tours to all. Park Headquarters adjacent to Brooks Camp maintains a campground. For information on hiking possibilities, rules and regulations, and conditions to be expected, write the Park Superintendent, P.O. Box 7, King Salmon, Alaska 99613. Wien's three-day, two-night tour from Anchorage leaving daily June 1 to September 6 costs under $300 per adult (children about $50 less). It includes transportation, lodging, meals, activities around the lodge, and the day-long bus tour.

At King Salmon (a town) Brooks-bound travelers transfer to a real bush plane, a ten-passenger Mallard, amphibious relative of the Goose. No docks or landing strips at Naknek Lake; the plane puts down out from the shore, and then is towed in by motorboat—tail first (a little demeaning, we thought, for any "bird"). Then everyone walks the plank to shore for an on-the-beach briefing on bears by a ranger, before walking up to the lodge. The reason for the lecture became obvious on the way. We saw fishermen casting and catching large salmon from the edge of the lake. Just across the stream the bears were doing the same, only they waded right in and used their paws. And let us not forget, these are Alaskan brownies, big blood brothers to "South 48" grizzlies.

During our stay in the camp the bears moved in closer. I politely gave the right of way to one on the path to our cabin (modern, with shower) one late afternoon. By the beach, while sitting on a piece of driftwood watching the anglers, I noticed everyone disappearing from the lake edge, two blocks away. They were being replaced by a mother and cub. One evening Bob had a wonderful time stalking a mother and triplets. He was sure that the only reason he could be so persistent was that she had her paws full trying to supply herself and unusually large family with food and still keep and eye on her lively brood. Bob, standing behind a signpost perhaps forty feet from the lake, watched her parade her family along the waterline several times.

Backpacking into the valley is popular. A party of campers on the tour bus were also planning to climb one of the volcanic peaks. We were content with the drive down the narrow dirt road, which appears threatened with extinction by the forest crowding in on the sides. Along the way there were glimpses of wildlife, small streams to ford, and finally the magnificent view from the overlook. After a sack lunch, those who want to can walk down a gently switchbacked trail to the valley floor. Here the rushing Ukak River falls over green

Mother and triplets in the front yard of Brooks River Lodge share fishing rights at Naknek Lake with two-legged guests. Katmai National Monument.

shale, where fossils are found. The approximately three-mile round trip hike and poking around in the pumice give one the feel of the valley. Everyone went down (including the aforementioned one-legged lady).

Today's visitor may be interested in fishing too, but many are content just to watch the powerful eight-foot leaps of magnificent sockeye salmon up the falls in Brooks River, on their way to spawn. For many, the main objective is seeing the unique Valley of Ten Thousand smokes. Whatever your purpose in visiting the monument, you can be sure of discovering a most unusual and entirely different face of Alaska.

THE PRIBILOF ISLANDS

Before leaving the Anchorage area, we'll include one beyond-the-end-of-the-road trip especially for lovers: seal lovers; bird lovers; flower lovers; and if you are a lover lover, it would be hard to find a spot more remote, off-the-beaten-track, and away from it all in which to be alone together.

The Pribilof group of islands consists of St. Paul, St. George, and Otter, plus two rocky islets, Sea Lion and Walrus. They are dots on a map, in the Bering Sea, about three hundred miles off the west coast of mainland Alaska and two hundred miles north of the Aleutian Island chain. Reeve Aleutian is the "only way to fly," and they serve the remote communities to the far west three times a week.

We left early one morning, sharing a new Japanese-made jet with freight, and outnumbered by friendly Aleut natives of all ages headed for their distant villages. It seems that even the youngsters here are more accustomed to plane travel than most people from the "South 48" states. The flight traverses the Alaska Peninsula and skirts the Katmai National Monument. Our plane crew (which often includes a Reeve family member) was dedicated to this part of Alaska. Along the way, the captain mentioned everything he considered interesting, which ranged from the status of visible still-smoking volcano peaks to rusting debris left over from the Aleutian campaign in World War II.

Our trip started in mist and rain, but these high mountains conquer the clouds. Moreover, the plane flies low enough most of the time to note the contrast of low, marshy areas, rounded volcanic domes, old lava flow scars, myriad lakes, and grassy rolling mounds. Trees are replaced by tundra; dark and bright green grassy patches interspersed with rich reddish-brown volcanic dirt give the land the look of being cultivated. Over the Bering Sea leg of the flight our pilot kept an expert eye out for marine life below, dropping down for a closer look at sea lions and whales.

Headquarters for all travelers, birdwatchers, builders, and businessmen is the Aleut native-operated hotel on the biggest Pribilof Island, St. Paul. Our landlord was soft-spoken Terenty Philemonoff, a young-looking father of seven and grandpa of ten. He has a finger in almost everything that goes on in St. Paul, including managing the co-op store. The rooms have twin beds, a sink, and the rest of the facilities are down the hall. Everyone eats together at specific times. Meals, as is the case on most tours, are extra. If you want a predinner cocktail, you will have to BYOB from Anchorage. Ice is available from the hotel dining room. Or go next door to the friendly neighborhood tavern and join the townspeople.

Tours are met at the plane by a guide, most likely an Aleut with Russian background and name. Andrey Mandregan met us, prepared to dispense Pribilof history and show us his favorite places from one end of St. Paul to the other. He relishes his subject: from the time the first fur seal was seen and described, the later discovery of the breeding grounds in 1786 by the Russian navigator for whom the islands were named, the part the Aleuts played and their plight, to the present optimistic trends in the islands.

Bob's prime targets for photography are the easily accessible seal and bird rookeries. The world's largest fur seal herd, now over a million and a quarter, migrates and breeds here annually. It is a wild confusion of sight, sound, and smell, depending on which way the wind blows. A seal rookery is no place for Women's Lib. The eligible males weighing up to six hundred pounds return in late May and fight for their territory. Then they battle for the much smaller females who return in June. The polygamous winners called "beachmasters" collect their harems averaging forty "wives" each. The losers have to be content to hang around the fringes. The

Fur seal bull "beachmaster" gives instructions to his harem, averaging about forty cows. Large bird and seal rookeries in the Pribilof Islands are easily visited and photographed by tour groups.

females give birth and mother their pups. Playful seals of all sizes enjoy their water sports. All except the beachmasters, who don't dare to leave their domain for the duration, even to eat and drink, for fear of losing ground.

The rocky cliffs and lush grassy terrain (no trees) are a sanctuary for 176 (recorded) species of shore and sea birds. If you aren't a birdwatcher already, it is easy to succumb. Thousands of birds, some rare, nest in the large rookeries. Bob photographed them easily with plain or modest telephoto lens. And while Bob worked, I found that without budging from a comfortable viewing spot on the tundra, it was possible to count an amazing variety of tiny plant life within arm's length radius.

What about the controversial seal harvest? It is usually completed by the end of July, and is not included in the sightseeing. Visitors are invited to take an informative look at the processing plant, though, where the prime pelts are treated and packed for shipping. There are also allied industries. St. Paul's lucrative fur seal industry goes back to the Russian fur traders. They transplanted the closest available natives, the Aleuts, from their villages to harvest the seals to satisfy the demand for the lovely fur in the court of Catherine the Great, and others in Europe and Asia. After the Russians sold Alaska, the Pribilofs were neglected which allowed for overexploitation of the seals. The mammals were headed for extinction until the Convention of 1911 put fur seals under international protection.

Congress put the Pribilof Islands in a "special reservation." Funds are appropriated for research and the herds carefully managed. The seals are considered a renewable resource now, and are expected to maintain their present fine population level with continued care and strictly monitored harvest.

The Fur Seal Act of 1966 paved the way for special municipal grants. The almost five hundred residents voted to incorporate St. Paul as a "city," the better to develop new industry, principally tourism. Eventually this may involve more natives than the important sealing industry.

The Aleuts are well aware that nature is a prime commodity, but that visitors are also interested in their Russian-Aleut heritage. The last Russian church we'll mention is the most unusual. In the first place, its wood exterior was hard come by when you consider that the island is treeless, and the church was built in the early part of the century. It has the traditional shape, but the natives used considerable ingenuity to fashion the characteristic onion dome and cross. The dome is an outline made of a pliable metal and painted golden yellow. The cross above the gate is attractive, appropriate—and made of sections of plumber's pipe. The interior, one of the most beautiful and colorful we have seen (even in Russia), is proudly displayed by Father Michael Lestenkof, native Aleut priest.

Paroquet Auklet, one of many species of birds (some rare) photographed by tourists in teeming rookeries of Pribilof Islands.

We noticed attractive hand-crafted fur seal skin items for sale in the hotel lobby and co-op store across the street: handbags, hats, and even earrings. Townspeople hope to revive long-lost Aleut arts, such as basketry, which utilizes the island's plentiful long, tough grass.

As long as concern for preservation continues in the Pribilofs, nature lovers can count on seeing the annual May to September spectacular on land, sea, and in the air. Don't stint on your film supply. And bear in mind that those seals opt for the wild, windy, wet, foggy weather they thrive on. When we were there, nature threw the book at us, weatherwise, too. Avid nature watchers just dress for it and aren't hampered. They consider it part of the experience.

FAIRBANKS

Fairbanks calls itself the Golden Heart of Alaska. And it was, from its beginning until the 1930s. Then, gold—the substance—and everything connected with it dwindled in importance. Giant dredges and the smelter that fed on them closed down. Gold-panning and prospecting were viewed as being more for fun than for profit. In the latter 1960s, Alaska's second-largest city boomed over "black gold"—oil—as the hub for supplying the North Slope oil fields by air and by truck on the far north "Haul Road." Now Fairbanks is looking forward to Arctic gas line activity. Moreover, gold, which escalated in value, stirs renewed interest in mines and dredges in the vicinity. The over sixty thousand Fairbanks area residents are also aware of tourism gold, and the value of attractions such as the University of Alaska Museum's C. J. Berry Gold Room, endowed by his heirs. They wanted to memorialize their prospector forebear who struck it rich in the Klondike and kept it for his family.

Still, Fairbanks is entitled to its golden label, considered from a broader perspective. What is more golden than memories recalled and perpetuated mostly for the fun of it? In our opinion, Fairbanks is one of the choice places in Alaska where you get the full impact of the old rubbing shoulders with the new. Stashed in the shadow of tall modern buildings, where least expected, you can still discover small, original log cabins, more than likely still lived in. Then there are those long, warm, golden days of summer when, as if to make up for the short, cold winter days, the temperature hovers in the seventies (*above* zero). We hope that, in spite of the bonanza, the golden-hearted hospitality of the vigorous, friendly residents will continue when you visit there.

Travelers who drive the whole Alaska Highway to its official end at the sod-roofed log-cabin visitor's center on the bank of the Chena River, which flows through Fairbanks, have earned their feeling of accomplishment. A sign states they have covered 1,523 miles, just from northern British Columbia, and their adventures, if each were interviewed on arrival, would be as varied as an FBI fingerprint file. Depending on their experiences they may or may not be dreading the drive back down. Rarely will you encounter someone who doesn't think it is a great pioneering experience and worth doing— once. Mostly, these visitors will already be plotting how they can come again, but usually by going part way by sea or air, to cut down on the driving.

There are other ways of getting to Fairbanks than by car. You can go by the Alaska Railroad, by scheduled airlines, or by taking one of the fine bus tours and letting someone else do the driving.

Fairbanks began in 1902 after a lone immigrant miner, Felix Pedro, found some nuggets and staked his claim on nearby creeks. His discovery set off the usual stampede, ensuring a rapid population growth and setting town-organizing machinery to work. They didn't name the town after him; his name was given to the discovery stream, Pedro Creek. The rather staid name of Fairbanks was recommended by Judge Wickersham, then a solid Fairbanks citizen and leader, in honor of his friend Charles W. Fairbanks, U.S. senator who later became vice president of the United States under President Theodore Roosevelt.

Lodging and stores

Creature comforts come high in Fairbanks, whether you are a visitor or a resident. They have also come a long way in quality since our first visit many years ago, especially the hotels. Prepaid tour groups have come to expect good, attractive, and comfortable accommodations like the Golden Nugget Motel, the Fairbanks Inn, and the Traveler's Inn. On our own, we have paid $45 double, per night, and on top of this one has to eat. You may find some lower rates by shopping around and looking out of town. They say prices are "subject to change" in Alaska's main boom towns. To avoid overnight changes, independent lodgers should make and confirm reservations and prices ahead.

Those who have driven up the Alaska Highway usually have their own sleeping and eating arrangements with them, at least for emergency use, and there are several campgrounds and trailer and camper parks. Though people may feel ready for a good cleanup, and a little luxury (and maybe even want to kick up their heels a bit), it isn't a serious matter if they have to put in a reservation at the hotel of their choice and wait a day, if the town happens to be jumping at the height of the tourist season.

We are always happier when we can beat the cost of living by camping, mostly because there are so many of us. We aren't alone in this. When you camp, you keep running into the same familes all along the route. Comparing notes is fun. We especially remember one ingenious family of two adults and four young teen-agers who were traveling in an ordinary-sized family car, even into the wilds of McKinley Park by way of the Denali Highway. It was a sight to delight the heart of an efficiency expert to see the bunch pile out of the car toward evening, quickly select a campsite, put up the tents, and roll out the sleeping bags, while the food committee prepared space-saving freeze-dried meals, all labeled and packed ahead in family-size portions.

Fairbanks' water supply has improved considerably since our first visit, when we had to buy jugs of it from a well owner in order to have water that was both pure and palatable. In later visits the city water was judged pure enough to use from the faucet. We added some bourbon for predinner cocktails and the color was most unusual, a greenish-black gold. From then on, Bob has called his Fairbanks bourbon and water a Chena Slough Sling. The water is fine now, except perhaps in outlying districts where it may be healthy enough but has a brackish look and taste.

Fairbanks has all the other services you may need—dry cleaners (self-service and custom), laundromats, well-stocked supermarkets, department stores. However, you can count on the cost being a little higher than in other parts of Alaska, except the Arctic. A staff at the attractive Chamber of Commerce Information Building, near the bridge crossing the Chena River, gladly dispenses advice and folders to visitors.

Transportation

Fairbanks and vicinity is spread out enough so that a car is necessary to do very much exploring. This is no problem if a visitor is with a tour group. Good tours of the city are available, as well as trips farther afield. In fact, even if you have driven up with your own car, it will save time, and prove very informative, if you make arrangements to take one of the fine comprehensive tours. Then you can do revisiting on your own later.

Car and recreational vehicles can be rented—for a price—but better reserve ahead to be sure of getting one in busy Fairbanks. For short hauls there are taxis, but costs mount up in a hurry. Though we were aware that the life expectancy of a car is short in these stern northern climates, we marveled one year at the number of new cars. Even the rental cars were new. The reason was quickly deduced by our car expert, Terry. It was the year after the big flood when the Chena and Tanana rivers joined forces to make a river twenty-five miles wide. Many items, including cars, had to be replaced the following year.

Charter flights are available through many small airline companies. We like Fairchild's slogan: they claim they will fly "anywhere there is air." A popular short flight out of Fairbanks for those who yearn to cross the Arctic Circle is to the Indian village of Fort Yukon, well worth the time and cost.

Alaskaland

Spread out over forty acres, Alaskaland, originally Centennial "Alaska-67," is Fairbanks' newest, most ambitious project. To those used to viewing a New York or Montreal "World's Fair," Alaskaland may look pretty lean. Moreover, near the end of the 1967 Centennial summer it and the rest of Fairbanks were caught in a flood that almost swamped them permanently. Even with the help of all the rest of Alaska, it has been a struggle. A relatively few dedicated people and organizations have somehow managed to keep this worthwhile free visitors attraction going.

That is all the apology we intend to make for Alaskaland.

In our opinion, these Alaskans have done a great job gathering together items of the past in order to preserve them where visitors can easily and pleasurably view them. Some of the items were pretty big and awkward to set up: original log cabins, an old church, assorted stores and offices. They were gathered up in and around Fairbanks and are attractively arranged to give you the impression that you are walking the streets of an authentic, old-time mining town.

The smallest house in this gold rush frontier village belonged to Kitty Hensley, a sea captain's mistress. It looks like a two-story dollhouse, with a little bay window trimmed with some stained glass panes, and it is prettied up with petunias and sweet peas. Inside, the furnishings are in the style of the period, all donated or lent by many different families. The house is a Welcome Center and visitors can go in and look around, even up the little staircase to the bedroom. Posted outside the door is a prim and proper notice giving a run-down on Kitty and making clear that the house has been neatened up since Kitty lived in it. Moreover it points out that in no way does inclusion of the house imply approval of the former owner. Seems a shame to come right out and point the finger like that, after all these years. Being placed catty-corner across from the no-nonsense-style early church ought to restore a small aura of respectability.

We couldn't resist poking around the trading post, with old-fashioned practical items hanging on the walls and rafters and lining the shelves. We pored over old account books and price lists, and someone spotted an item still necessary to camping families with small children and asked if here was where we got the potty we used to use. Another shop, alluring to both kids and adults, is an old-fashioned ice-cream parlor, with its delectable list of goodies.

The native villages, Indian and Eskimo and Aleut, picturesquely situated by the river and including a fish wheel, are another exhibition area where you can lose yourself for hours. Here you will find native dances, blanket tossing, and craft work going on. There is a retail store for buying native items. A round-domed building is

A highlight of Alaskaland in Fairbanks is a gold rush frontier village, with original log cabins and a historic stern-wheel riverboat.

now the home of the original Eskimo-Indian World Olympics, started several years ago during the five-day Golden Days celebration commemorating the founding of Fairbanks. Though similar contests are given locally in the Arctic, too, just for the Eskimos' fun and competition, the main event is held here in July. The rule still stands that to compete seriously for the awards a contestant must be at least one-quarter native—for everything except the muktuk eating contest (muktuk is whale blubber).

Another interesting survivor of the past is the large sternwheeler *Nenana,* placed in its own lake at Alaskaland. An interesting photo subject from the outside, the *Nenana* houses a restaurant and a cocktail lounge.

Cruise of the *Discovery*

Some people are stern-wheeler fans, just as others can't resist old railroads. Even if you aren't yet hooked on stern-wheelers there is a trip we heartily recommend for a pleasant, enlightening, different look at the environs of Fairbanks. It's an excursion into the past; you'll follow part of the route the stern-wheelers used to take on their way to the mighty Yukon, the "marine highway" of the early days.

Good-natured, congenial Jim Binkley is skipper of the *Discovery,* a real stern-wheeler that takes visitors on a four-hour, twenty-five-mile "voyage," a unique experience in this day and age. His father, who came over the Chilkoot Pass in 1898, was a riverboat pilot. Jim's boys are following right after their dad; Skip, Jim Jr., and John already have earned pilot's licenses.

Jim's lovely and gracious wife, Mary, and twenty-one-year-old daughter Marilee also share the work of this family business. Jim and Mary are Alaskans from way back, and another example of teamwork between husband and wife. They met at the University of Alaska while Jim was studying engineering and Mary was studying fisheries. They pooled their interests by starting their Alaska Riverboat Excursions in 1950, now called Discovery Cruises.

An Eskimo girl and an Athabascan Indian girl are also part of the crew. We have met several over the years who have held this job. Usually they are students of the University of Alaska, and they are invariably intelligent, attractive, have a good sense of humor, and enjoy fielding questions "cheechakos" ask about their background. Many of these natives still depend a great deal on fishing, hunting, and trapping for subsistence.

There is a lot to see and photograph and the Binkleys won't let you miss a thing. They point out fish wheels, prize dog sleds, and beautiful log homes with flower gardens, many with a float plane parked in the river as commonly as you would park a car in the garage. They'll note almost-hidden Cripple Creek, the gold stream that delivered more than $100 million over 30 years, and the nearby new restaurant being developed from gold rush memorabilia. The highlight is passing close to a genuine trapper's home on a remote wilderness island. From the boat they'll describe the current activity, probably drying fish on racks for humans and dogs. You'll see bear and moose hides drying, and perhaps a new cache or cabin under construction.

Captain Jim Binkley's stern-wheeler *Discovery* passes Tanana River fish wheel traps on four-hour tour out of Fairbanks.

This stern-wheeler trip is more than just a tourist attraction to those who are interested in what happens to primitive people when outside elements start encroaching on their way of life.

There is an exceptionally good reciprocal feeling between Jim and Howard Luke, who is developing this land and gaining title under his aboriginal rights. Jim knows that it is good for his business to have a working trapper's camp located where it can be seen and described from the stern-wheeler. Many natives such as Howard are glad to be encouraged to keep on with the old ways, still practical for them.

So far the balance has been a good one. Jim encourages the Indians by helping them help themselves whenever the need arises. He goes to great lengths to understand and assist them, and the natives trust and respect him. This camp on the Tanana remains proud and independent.

The fare for this interesting afternoon stern-wheeler excursion is about $15 per person from the landing in the Chena River, a short distance outside of town. Transfers (additional) are available from points in Fairbanks. The price includes a coffee and doughnut break on the boat. Reservations are advisable; this trip becomes more popular all the time.

Captain Jim has been expanding his tours. He purchased the historic cargo ship M.V. *Yutana,* converted and restored it, and rechristened it the *Discovery II.* Now he can give more than twice as many visitors a taste of this colorful portion of Alaska transportation history.

Cripple Creek

If you are interested in ghost towns (or atmosphere), there is one you shouldn't miss while you are in the vicinity of Fairbanks. Cripple Creek Resort is eleven miles out of town on the road that passes the University of Alaska.

Cripple Creek was originally a company-owned mining town at Ester. The buildings have been preserved practically intact and include the Malemute Saloon, a tintype photo studio, a hotel, and a little gold mine. Don Pearson, unforgettable for his readings of Robert Service poems, is the host. We have rarely seen him out of character—bearded and fancy-vested—even when he has stopped by our home on his way outside.

We usually stay out here at Cripple Creek. We appreciate the false-fronted setting and also the fact that we can both sleep and éat for the price of most rooms in the city. The hotel, with rooms $17 single, $20 double, each with adjoining bath, are up an old-fashioned staircase. This building was formerly the mess hall of the mining camp. Meals are still served on the first floor, mess-hall-style at long tables with benches.'The food is good, with prices ranging from $7 for a buffet, and $9–$12 for crab, salmon, or steak dinners. Our kids thoroughly enjoy the style and food in the dining room. Bob and I like to sneak into the small adjoining Mine Room Steakhouse, where for only $10 you can get a really magnificent charbroiled steak. It's the darkest bistro we have ever patronized—

just loaded with mine atmosphere. We are grateful for the flickering candlelight—it's hardly enough to see by, but probably valuable as a warning should the oxygen content in our "mine air" suddenly lower. Recessed in the walls, spookily lit, are some very effective almost three-dimensional paintings of mine scenes. They were done by a young student, Galen Garwood.

The hotel has no bar, but the Malemute bartender is always happy to dispatch a waiter with your order up the short, dirt "main street." You won't find many night spots like the Malemute anywhere, and the entertainment, for sure, is live. It's hard to diagnose the attraction the show has, even for the townspeople who frequent the Malemute. The format and gags change little. You can't even say that it gets funnier after quaffing a couple. We have seen rather staid tour groups fractured by a jewsharp-and-skittles accompaniment to a ballad by Don Pearson and his red-bearded bartender—and the group was only on their second round of sarsaparillas.

The pianist who holds things together between shows is invariably good-natured, friendly, and a nimble-fingered whiz. From ragtime to Debussy, she can play almost anything you name and has a special knack for making out-of-state visitors feel at ease to the point of singing out lustily on old-time songs.

Don Pearson's renditions of Robert Service poems really steal the show. When the lights go out and he sits by the old round wood table next to the old-fashioned potbellied stove and starts reciting "The Cremation of Sam McGee" by lantern light, even the liveliest, noisiest audience quiets down. You could hear a nugget drop on the sawdust-covered floor. He may follow it with the humorous and lesser-known "Bessie's Boil"—or any of those Service gems that strike a mood. He knows them all, from the heart.

If you continue on beyond Cripple Creek about forty-eight miles, you will come to the river town of Nenana at the confluence of the Nenana and Tanana rivers. On the river here is where the official time of the annual big spring ice breakup is determined. Usually in early May, as Alaskans make bets and interest mounts, the ice starts to move, upsetting a tripod and tripping a shore clock establishing the exact official time. The winners collect sizeable sums of money. Keep on Highway #3 and you will arrive at Anchorage.

Don Pearson recites poems of Robert W. Service in Malemute Saloon at old ghost mining town of Ester, now a resort, a few miles out of Fairbanks.

Time was when you could stop on your way out to Cripple Creek and watch or take pictures of a huge gold dredge at work. Now, for signs of past gold history, drive out the Steese Highway from Fairbanks. Its terminus is at Circle City, 162 miles to the north on the Yukon River. The road passes through historic gold-mining country and you'll spot remnants along the way. The Eagle Summit, a little more than 100 miles from Fairbanks on this road, is noted as the only view site to which you can drive to see the midnight sun on June 21-22. There are campgrounds and places to stay, including a long-established hotsprings resort.

The University of Alaska

The University of Alaska is noted for being our country's northernmost university and for offering courses in subjects particularly related to its geographic position. Scholars are attracted here from all over the world to participate in research projects in geophysics, mining, anthropology, polar regions, fisheries, animal husbandry (including the prehistoric musk oxen), and subarctic agriculture. In connection with the latter, there is a nearby experimental farm, but all over the attractive campus are some obvious signs of the university's success with growing things. In its splashy-bright flower beds, you'll recognize many of the common summer blooms, only bigger than usual, thriving under the long, warm summer days.

The university combines the old and the new. Over sixty years old, and constantly growing, the building program seems perpetual. Enrollment (many of the students are native young people) is on the increase, and it is a busy place in winter. Just a temperature drop below zero, sometimes by many degrees, is never an excuse for interrupting schedules or extracurricular activities like cross-country skiing.

Old Alaska is exceptionally well represented in a fine museum containing examples of wildlife and native artifacts. It is open nine to five every day, including Sunday, for visitors to browse on their own, or follow along with a polite, well-informed, often native student guide. The museum staff is prepared to give visitor information, and it is worth inquiring at the front desk to see what is going on. There may be a walking tour of the campus or Alaskan films scheduled.

With Alaska tourism extending through winter, adventuresome visitors may like to include Fairbanks on their itinerary, just to get the feel, if only briefly, of what it is like to live in Alaska's northern interior. When you visit the campus in winter you'll note that those parking-meter-like stands are in use. They are plug-in engine warmers, an essential part of transportation in parts of Alaska where the winter temperature falls to fifty or sixty degrees below zero, mainly in the Interior and Arctic regions.

Fairbanks International Airport has long been a gateway to the Arctic, pioneered many years ago by Wien Air Alaska flying to Kotzebue, Barrow, and Nome in northwestern Alaska. But the city can no longer be considered a true "road end." The Elliott Highway extends beyond and meets the North Slope Haul Road that continues on to Prudhoe Bay of the Arctic Ocean. So far, the road has been closed to public use beyond the Yukon River bridge, 129 miles from Fairbanks, though it is now part of the state highway system. Meanwhile, tourism advocates are eyeing its possibilities, thinking in terms of bringing visitors by the busload. They hope to use the same facilities (now idle) built to keep pipeline workers comfortable and happy along the route.

MOUNT MCKINLEY NATIONAL PARK

"Is it worthwhile taking a side trip to Mount McKinley?" many summer visitors ask. We would have to answer yes. In fact, rather than a sidetrip, we would consider it a main destination, no matter how you are traveling. This is based on the assumption that some people may be making a one-time vacation trip to Alaska. If the visitor is interested in wildlife, vast Mount McKinley National Park is probably the best, most easily accessible area where one can really count on seeing animals.

The wilderness (summer only) Denali Highway, with its sparse traffic, is a good bet for seeing wild life of all sizes, including goats and sheep on the higher slopes. On the Anchorage-Fairbanks Alaska Railroad run in winter the engine may nudge a moose disputing the train's right of way on what any sensible moose can see is the best path when the snow flies.

Now that the last few miles of road connecting Fairbanks and Anchorage are completed there is an alternative to heading back down the Alaska Highway: State Highway #3, also called the George Parks Highway. We are partial to this shorter, more direct route to Mount McKinley National Park for purely personal reasons. As ex-mountaineers, it appeals to us because here was the starting point for the earliest conquerors of mighty Mount McKinley. The superstitious Indians left the peak alone. The first attempt to climb the mountain was made in 1903 by energetic Judge Wickersham.

But you don't have to drive to the park. Popular combination package tours make use of air and bus combinations as well as the Alaska Railroad, from either Anchorage or Fairbanks. The train trip takes four hours from Fairbanks; eight hours from Anchorage. By staying over at least a night in McKinley Park, people have the opportunity to see what they really came for: wild animals in their natural setting.

A "safari" takes off from the McKinley Park Hotel at 6:00 A.M., travels sixty-five miles to Eielson Visitor Center for lunch, and back in time to catch the late-afternoon train for Anchorage. Eielson is the first point in the park where Mount McKinley is visible. You may or may not see it, depending on weather, but with the help of the guide, even the most unobservant will see animals. Though it seems inhuman for humans to have to get up so early, this is when the wild ones are up and about. You may even see some rare sights like a mother Toklat grizzly bear training playful twin cubs.

McKinley National Park, about center-state, is a taiga forest with timberline around 3,000 feet. It is a wet alpine tundra region, permafrost underneath. Trees, principally spruce, poplar, birch, and aspen, are not very tall or thick-growing. Game is exposed, but it is surprising how well it is camouflaged, like the ptarmigan. It takes a little practice plus sharp eyes to spot animals as they stand perfectly still, blending in with the background.

The animal trek we remember best was in late summer, just before the park closed for the season. The signs showed summer was definitely on the wane and fall was fast approaching. There had been enough nippy nights so turning leaves of deciduous trees made a brilliant splash on the landscape. Even the muskeg was brightening up. The last of the wild flowers were gone, except for a few stalks of hardy, gone-to-fluff fireweed. We saw several willow ptarmigan beginning to assume their winter plumage. By snow time their feathers would be all white. In fact, all sorts of animals were out on this rather cloudy morning, big and small, as if they were desperately garnering the last of their winter's food supply. We saw caribou, bear, moose, a variety of squirrels, a red fox, rabbits, and a porcupine stripping bark off a tree. A large doglike animal furtively loped across the road and the driver verified the fact that we had indeed seen a wolf. This *is* unusual, for they are becoming very scarce and are extremely elusive.

We might well have taken a clue from those animals that it was time to head home for the winter. By the time we got back to the hotel light raindrops had turned to snowflakes. On the train trip to Anchorage it appeared that winter had now come to the high country. There was more than just a dusting of snow on meadows and rocks of the surrounding mountains.

Caribou poses near main road in Mount McKinley National Park. Big game is as great an attraction as the elusive peak itself.

Lodging and food

The McKinley Park Lodge burned down since we last stayed there, and we were curious about the replacement, not easy in wilderness areas. Though eventually it will be rebuilt completely, we were captivated by the imaginative way lodge planners swiftly stop-gapped the immediate problems of putting up people, including large tour groups. In fact, we consider the solution an improvement. They picked a clever and logical theme: "railroad," the mode of transportation long connected with visiting McKinley Park.

The hotel lobby, main dining room, and some adjacent sleeping rooms are prefabricated. The rest of the facilities are refurbished railroad cars, some of them historic. The coffee shop is actually a couple of rejuvenated diners. The bar is (of course) some genuine and colorful old-style lounge cars. The large lobby is personalized with vintage touches like wooden waiting room benches, old-fashioned hotel desk, potbellied stove, and overhead fans. Everything is only a short walk from the McKinley Railroad Station.

Expansion is planned, but only outside the park. McKinley Chalet continues to add rooms in its wooded setting overlooking the Nenana River. Just above it, by the highway, is the site earmarked for a big lodge, to be corporation-built and ready for use by 1980.

Enterprising individuals Linda and Gary Crabb advertise the "two best stays to visit" McKinley. One is the North Face Lodge, all the way through the park and in view of the mountain. The other is Mt. McKinley Village, just across the Nenana from the park. The Village is headquarters for some popular wild-and-wet float trips down the Nenana plus a bargain "Picnic by the River": under $5 for chicken or ribs, beans, salad, and beverage, served on a paper plate-lined souvenir frisbee.

Another couple, Corrine and Jerry Colrud, handle all that goes with operating a Kampground of America, and also offer an unusual, informative tour called "Hills of Fire."

Everyone knows about gold in Alaska, but it comes as a surprise to learn that, in these parts and all of Interior Alaska, coal has been the main energy source for about fifty years. The three-hour, $7.50 bus tour passes coal-vein-streaked foothills on the way to the Usibelli open pit coal mines. The mine management has been actively practicing extensive restoration and reclamation after mining. Visitors see, closeup, some giant earthmoving machinery in action, including the world's largest "cat." This mine is a model for the future. The large amount of coal reserves in the area is still being assessed. It is predicted that this particular type of coal, which burns with little pollution, could be a very important fuel for generating future electricity. The "Hills of Fire" refers to several spots where buried coal seams smoke from deep-down spontaneous combustion.

Several residents, including manager George Flaherty at the park hotel and KOA, praised the cuisine (homebaked goodies!) and wine at what they called the local "supper club." Local in Alaska can mean within a twenty- or thirty-mile radius. On our way back down the highway toward Anchorage about fifteen miles we saw the Jere-A-Tad, Supper Club, Chalet-Family Cottages, and Gas. We were far too early for the 5:00 P.M. opening of the "club," but we liked the atmosphere and the aroma, due to the fact that Elaine Pollock was just taking her daily bread out of the oven. Because it was too hot to cut, she insisted that we take a loaf with us. Delicious.

Greater choice of access to this once-remote National Park has necessitated revamping Park Rules and Regulations to keep shy wildlife in view of an increasing number of visitors. If you visit on a

Towering 20,320-foot Mount McKinley, with female moose browsing in glacial pond by Wonder Lake road.

package tour, you'll automatically follow the routine. If you intend to spend more time and camp or hike on your own, there are many brochures put out by the Park Service that spell out what you need to know.

The main thing to remember if you are camping is that you should take your supplies in with you. Small stores before you enter the park may be lightly stocked and expensive. Some service stations sell white gas for Coleman camp stove cooking. Firewood may not be available. Veteran campers will naturally have along a waterproof tent and rainwear, being suspicious of the wilderness, subpolar or otherwise. They also know all about bugs, and bring insect repellent. One other warning—this wilderness road can be unpredictable, with inclement weather.

Certain campgrounds within the park may require reservations. Though private vehicles are restricted, free shuttle buses allow visitors to travel the length of the park road, hopping on and off at designated stops and times. You may drive yourself if you have Park Headquarters authorization, a camp permit, or a reservation at Camp Denali, just beyond the far park boundary.

Camp Denali

At the McKinley Park road end, set ninety miles beyond the hotel, is a wilderness camp especially attuned to individuals who can take their outdoors unadulterated by the usual creature comforts. Not that a person won't be completely comfortable, well fed, and extremely well entertained. You just have to know beforehand what you can expect at Camp Denali, and be of a kindred mind with the operators. If you read their literature, if it intrigues you, and if you correspond concerning reservations, it is assumed that you will arrive eager to participate fully in some very wonderful wilderness experiences.

But Camp Denali isn't everyone's cup of tea. It was started by Celia Hunter and Ginny Wood, mentioned later in the Arctic section where we discuss their previous careers. Conservation-minded, they firmly believe *now* is the time to be preserving Alaska, especially if her future value leans toward being a "state of recreation" in an increasingly crowded world. For this reason, they kept the camp as close to nature as possible, adding only improvements that made maintenance easier.

It was a struggle to start Camp Denali in the early fifties, before there was a road traversing the park. Everything had to be backpacked or flown in, which these dedicated people did, as soon as they were able to whittle out an airstrip. It was even tougher keeping a seasonal, rather limited-appeal camp going in those lean years.

In 1973, Celia and Ginny were presented with a "Connie" Award from the Society of American Travel Writers. These are given annually to individuals who make outstanding contributions to a quality travel experience through conservation and preservation. The women received theirs for conducting notable wilderness treks and nature-oriented programs at camp.

We were reassured when Celia and Ginny told us to whom they were passing on the torch (or Coleman lantern) in 1975. A young couple, Jerri and Wally Cole, also well appreciate and cherish Camp Denali's unique wilderness qualities. As visitors again in late summer of 1978, we noted they have continued the traditions, adding homey comforts and conveniences for guests—but slowly. Even so, when you start describing the accommodations (in order not to mislead prospective visitors) the camp sounds quite rugged and primitive. Mainly it is the lack of traditional plumbing. Hoses bring pure, cold water as far as spigots on the corner of cabin porches, or they may stop a few feet short. They are sometimes chewed through by porcupines with a propensity for plastic pipelines. Community showers (hot) share the laundry building, labeled the Sluice Box. And you'd better believe it when they say every cabin has a private "path." That was the breaking point for one visitor who thought they meant "bath." Though it may be rather artistically built, and its open side faces the most beautiful mountain-view wilderness vista you have ever seen, the private path leads to a small building which is undeniably an outhouse.

Inside your cabin you light your own lantern fixture as needed and build your own fire in the Yukon stove. Though there are some regular beds now, more likely you'll have a bunk, supplied with a sleeping bag and a warm, changeable liner, cozy during chilly nights. And don't expect resort-type luxury, such as special room service, or a bar. This doesn't mean that you can't bring your own to mix with some of that pure, cold water if you wish, however. Just gauge your cocktail time by the dinner hour.

The less-than $100-per-day charge includes lodging; nutritious, family-style meals; pick-up and return to McKinley Station (180 miles round trip with the accent on observing and photographing wildlife coming and going); guides and gear as needed for activities in and out of camp; and that hardest-to-measure intangible: Individual Treatment. Jerri attributes that to the flexibility at Camp Denali.

"The activities of the day depend on what we can psyche-out that our guests want. Then we help them do it," she says.

As the Coles and their nature-oriented staff ferret out interests and make suggestions, guests fall into smaller groups for fishing, canoeing, hiking, or "shutter-bug" safaris, guided by a staff member who knows the birds and plants. Everyone's favorite excursion is panning for gold in a stream beyond ghost town Kantishna, once a gold camp. Their formula seems to be working well. A growing number of outdoor enthusiasts are willing to waive the fancy trimmings and pay the necessary tariff, reassured that here nothing will be added to detract from a true wilderness atmosphere. In not too many years, it is entirely possible people will be waiting in line or have to make reservations far ahead for the chance to vacation in similar surroundings.

A peculiar-to-Camp-Denali-setup known as "Bedrock" is still available. We are sorry to learn that the management saw fit to more than *double* the price since last we inquired. Bedrock now costs $4 a night. They describe these tent accommodations as "inexpensive minimum shelter for those traveling with their own camping equipment (sleeping bags and cooking gear), willing to rough it in order to save money." Bedrock began as a special concession to Celia's and Ginny's many mountain-climbing friends. But anyone from all over the world with kindred outdoor tastes and a slim pocketbook is welcome. Space is limited and on a first-come basis.

"Some of our best camp help has been recruited from Bedrock," states Wally. "They come to see the country, stay on, or make arrangements to come back and work next summer."

We find Camp Denali entrancing partly because of the amazing variety of people who pass through. They usually decide to come after listening to a friend's enthusiastic report. The camp is a great leveler. Millionaires, statesmen, teachers, scientists, mountaineers, valleypounders, businessmen, musicians, artists, photographers, tradespeople, housewives, people of many foreign countries, all find a common ground. Some stimulating conversations have started at the family-style dining hall and continued on at the lodge around the fireplace. The songfests are fun, too. Depending on the current clientele, the songs are likely to be folk variety, but the folks singing them may be singing in any language from Japanese to Swahili.

Reservations are definitely necessary, partly because space is limited, but also because the remoteness of the camp and the sometimes capricious nature of the environment in general necessitate planning ahead on pickups, if needed, from park headquarters. The address is P.O. Box 67-S, McKinley Park, Alaska 99755. Phone (907) 683-2290 (summer) or (907) 683-2302 (winter).

Though Camp Denali is least suitable for infants and young children, who need a lot of watching because of its wilderness nature, older ones who are used to camping and the outdoors fit right in. Also, we should not imply that a person has to be extremely rugged to enjoy it there. An example is our previously mentioned almost Alaskan one-legged lady. For three weeks one summer we watched her traversing the uneven surrounding hillsides, picking berries, studying wild flowers, and practicing falls on the protecting, bouncy tundra.

"Might as well have magnificent scenery and convivial company while getting used to a fake underpinning," she commented as she left. "It's a great spot for rough-terrain practice!"

5 The Arctic

THE burning question asked by would-be adventuresome travelers to the Arctic used to be *"How* do we get there?" Now it is *"When* is the best time to visit the Arctic?" The answer to both questions relates to the development of transportation, as with all such questions in Alaska. Sightseeing in the Arctic has had to wait on improvements in air travel, which have been phenomenal in the last few years.

Alaska's outer rim, bordering the Arctic Ocean, the Bering and Chukchi seas, and including the northernmost tip of the North American Continent, has always stirred people's imagination. Words that come to mind are Eskimos, snow, ice, tundra, sleds, husky dogs, igloos, parkas, mukluks, reindeer, polar bears, seal, walrus, whale, skin boats and northern lights, for a starter. Beginning around 1800 a large number of outsiders infiltrated the Arctic, returning with stories of adventure, as well as the furs and other wealth they were seeking. Others headed to the Arctic for philanthropic purposes, such as establishing churches or teaching. The mode of travel was by ship, which was time-consuming and required a fully organized expedition. The only time to travel far northern seas was while they were liquid. If you stayed too long, you had to winter with the Eskimos. If you started too late, you would be turned back by ice, or perhaps stuck in it.

World War II focused attention on all of Alaska, as the United States realized that its Achilles heel might very well be that piece of real estate up in its far northwest corner. The Arctic was valuable for air bases built with Eskimo help in record time, and as a midway point for ferrying aircraft to our Russian allies. Under the circumstances, it is understandable that sightseeing was still in second place. Transient and longer-term visitors there had a job to do. The military learned much about survival tactics from the hardy Eskimos, while the adaptable natives cheerfully learned mechanical and technical skills and helped man the operations in these outposts. They are still carrying on today.

Now, finally, the sightseer has a place. Wien Air Alaska pioneered summer tours in the Arctic in the early 1950s. Traffic grew as the word spread and as air travel continued its rapid growth and improvement. Alaska Airlines innovated winter tours in the late 1960s, as well as summer tours. Airlines, tour operators, and travel agents organize the expeditions. All a traveler has to do is to fit them into his time and money budget. It is possible to catch a fair glimpse in as little as one day, departing from certain Alaskan points, but to most people that short a stay would be just a teaser.

Summer used to be the tourist season. Some visitors were intrigued by the late, fleeting, soggy, but often beautiful Arctic spring. Others might hang on into fall, pleasantly surprised at bright colors in the tundra. In general, though, unless you were a hunter or had work to do, the three summer months were best. The ice was going or gone. The ground was firm, and the Eskimos were well engrossed in their summer's work of preparing for the inevitable survival challenge of the Arctic winter. You were welcome to watch, as long as you didn't hamper the operations.

Now, having taken advantage of the year-round choice available and having seen the Arctic in most of its moods, we still hesitate to give a pat answer. We might steer people away from May. Usually sometime during that month the breakup occurs, and for reasons peculiar to the region, people need time to tidy up before entertaining guests. The best answer we can come up with, if pressed, is: "See it *now*!"

The Arctic is unique, but rapidly changing. Natives are loath to give up the old ways entirely. Yet, being practical and most

Eskimos Chester and Helen Seveck in wolverine-ruffed parkas. For many years he herded reindeer near Kotzebue.

adaptable, after centuries of survival in their particularly rugged environment, they are also receptive to the new. Moreover, they are very quick to adopt those innovations for which they see a practical purpose, and which fit in well with their way of life. Thus you are likely to see ready-made clothing and lined rubber boots ordered from Sears, rifles instead of harpoons, outboard motors on skin boats, and even TV dinners stashed among the frozen seal, fish, and reindeer meat in their homemade perma-frost lockers.

How long it will take the pendulum to swing toward complete modernization is anyone's guess. Meanwhile, we find the changing times utterly fascinating, no matter what time of year we visit.

To see the most in the shortest time, sightseers would do well to buy a package tour. Travel agents will have up-to-date information on costs and tours, or will help you plan your own.

Just because package tours are well planned does not mean that they are inflexible. The whole group might be routed to some unexpected spot, if something unusual comes up on the spur of the moment. Chasing reindeer near Nome is a good example, for these wild creatures are quite unpredictable. When word comes through that a large herd is in an accessible spot for viewing and photographing by a busload of tourists, that's where the whole tour heads. Time allowance is made for shopping and poking around on your own, and if you have something in mind you would especially like to see or do, it can usually be arranged, even if it means staying over an extra night or so.

But we have another reason for recommending a tour for first-time visitors. Popping in as a visitor for a few hours or a couple of days is not the same as living and working with people or, for that matter, gradually getting to know them through recurring visits over a period of years. A lone, hurried stranger *could* be considered rude for having the curiosity to want to see how natives live, possibly snap some pictures, chat with children or adults, and otherwise interrupt their activities. It is helpful to be with someone who knows the people. As guest of a guide on a first visit, a certain amount of shyness on the part of both visitor and resident is dissipated.

Our own work depends on our getting acquainted and becoming friends with people in the places we visit and Bob photographs. In the Arctic we started cold—as tour members. Now, many years and many visits later, when we go back we're among friends. We have learned that showing genuine interest (you don't have to be nosy) and a friendly pleasant attitude elicits a reciprocal response. And we have to give credit to our three youngsters, who are usually with us. They have been invaluable icebreakers because they invariably and quickly gravitate toward youngsters their own ages. Eskimo people love children, their own and everyone else's. They take their kids with them when they travel. Apparently, without realizing it, we ourselves have been observing an old Eskimo custom.

CLOTHING

Do you ordinarily wear long johns while vacationing? Do you carry cold-weather gear—boots, pants, parkas, earmuffs, and mittens—to insulate you against -52° temperatures? Few people do. But if you plan to travel in the Arctic you *may* need some of them, some of the time.

There is no need to invest in out-of-the-ordinary clothing. The airline lends you a warm, colorful Eskimo-style parka as soon as you arrive. In summer, these parkas with fur-ruffed hoods are sufficient for all conditions, including rain. In winter, the airline stands ready to outfit its tour guests in anything they might need in the way of extra cold-weather garb. The fit may not be custom, but well over a thousand Alaska Airlines guests blessed this aspect of tour travel the first season the winter tours were offered!

Otherwise, clothing is informal, with the emphasis on comfort and warmth. We swear by slacks and a layer or two of sweaters topped by the borrowed parkas. Our family looks forward to picking our colors from the parka room on arrival. Someone among us is always required to choose red; Bob's orders. Besides the considerable comfort they offer, the parkas add a necessary touch of color to a sometimes monotone landscape. Some visitors consider wearing the hoods devastating to hairdos; they add their own headband or scarf as protection against the sea breezes and use the fur ruff as a neck warmer. We have seen tourists sporting all sorts of footwear in the Arctic, including open-toed sandals and high heels. We recommend comfortable walking shoes, plus a handily stored pair of slipover plastic boots, in case it is damp underfoot.

SUMMER VS. WINTER

The phenomenal summer-winter contrast in the Arctic can be dramatically illustrated by comparing some landmark, say the Bering Sea, at six-month intervals. In midsummer, on June 21, it is noisily liquid, with waves whipped up by a brisk wind washing down a seawall, or rolling over a beach. In midwinter, December 21, the Bering Sea is a prisoner, locked in ice. It shows evidence of a tremendous struggle before giving in. It is the epitome of sculptured movement, in repose, its restless upheavals frozen in pressure ridges. Its voice is gone, except for an occasional loud crack of ice. The sea is a silent frozen mass as far as you can see.

There are other sharp contrasts, too. Just north of the Arctic Circle at Kotzebue there is a great deal of difference in the amount of light on those two dates. In winter the sun hardly rises above the horizon for eighteen days before and for eighteen days after the shortest day. In summer, the sun stays above the horizon or barely sinks below for the same length of time before and after the longest day. The temperature can vary well over a hundred degrees between winter and summer. We have experienced a chilly -52° and a balmy +65° in a one-year period of traveling to Arctic points. People in the Arctic are energetic and busy summer or winter, but we think they seem more relaxed and have more time to visit in winter. The dog population, for sure, is happier. Tied up with little to do in summer, and too warm if it gets much above 50°, they get bored. The coming of winter, the time when dogs have useful work to do, invigorates them. Their coats become glossy and their eyes bright.

We have long been sold on summer visits to the Arctic. When Alaska Airlines pioneered winter tours, we debated whether we might be interested. Their arguments *for* seeing the Arctic in winter sounded just like the image of Alaska we, and most of the tourist industry, had been trying to shed. The "snow and ice" concept started in bitter congressional debates over the original Purchase more than a hundred years ago. Some impressions are tough to live down and can be most disparaging. The airline's bright thought was to play up this image as *the* unique feature of the Arctic, with winter the only time to see it thus. They gambled on the idea that this aspect of Alaska might mean intriguing adventure to travelers.

Sun does not set above Arctic Circle (here at Kotzebue) in midsummer. Multiple exposure taken every fifteen minutes on June 21.

Their gimmick was to make it possible for people to see it in utter comfort.

We discovered new things to appreciate on our first winter trip. Bob, as a photographer, was entranced with the subtle lighting. It provides long shadow patterns, warm color schemes, and ever-changing lighting effects. We like the aesthetic improvement the snow cover makes on unpainted, weathered houses, which lurch this way and that because of periodic freezing and thawing of the ground under them. Even the stark cemetery near a town and the rolling tundra has a softer look in winter dress. Gay parkas and the cheery friendliness of people stand out even more. It must have been after a trip to the Arctic the hymn writer Frances Wile wrote his "All Beautiful the March of Days." Surely the line "the flowing waters sealed" refers to the Bering Sea or the Arctic Ocean. And "the solemn splendors of the night burn brighter through the cold" could only be the northern lights!

Our general opinion (shared by a few thousand other winter Arctic visitors) is that *anyone* can go to the Arctic in summer and find plenty of adventure. In winter, it goes beyond adventure and becomes an experience...a conversation piece for a lifetime.

GETTING THERE

We always enjoy coming to the end of the road and heading for the Arctic. There are no more anxieties about driving, busing, railroading, or boating. We can park our extra gear and take to the air, relaxed and expectant. Whether our point of departure is Anchorage or Fairbanks, if we want to visit Eskimo country we *have* to take a plane. According to experts in transportation, air travel is likely to continue as the cheapest and most practical way to bring in both supplies and visitors to Arctic regions for the next thirty years, at least.

In the Arctic, it was not only the development of better, swifter aircraft that was important to tourism development. These aircraft had to have a place to land. Building and maintaining adequate airstrips, like roads, is a continuous job, but possible. At least landing fields are measured by a prescribed number of feet, not in hundreds of miles. A fearless leader of summer Arctic tours in Kotzebue some twenty years ago recalls that the first landing strip measured about two thousand feet. The wings of the plane hung over the lagoons on either side as the pilot held his plane to the straight and narrow and stopped in that distance. Flying was incredible in those days, and it still is. The pilots now around who can still talk about the old days were, of course, the most skillful of the lot.

To reassure travelers to the Arctic, we should point out that even small Arctic towns manage to whittle out, fill in, and pave the prescribed number of feet in order to have jet service. Moreover, the natives are thoroughly intrigued with these big propellerless planes. They ride them as often as possible and turn out regularly to watch the landing, unloading (of both visitors and freight), and takeoff. Even the older Eskimos who have never seen a train or driven or ridden in a car take jet travel in their stride.

Terrain from the air

The change of Arctic terrain is noticeable soon after leaving Anchorage. Whether you have flown, driven, or cruised to that point, you have already been well indoctrinated with the mountain-islands-water-trees aspect of Alaska. The first things you will probably miss, looking down over a seemingly infinite expanse of land, are the trees. Below is tundra—from a Russian word meaning "where the trees are not." The terrain is not completely devoid of high spots. You will see Mount Iliamna and Mount Spur in the distance and other volcanic peaks, some of which have erupted fairly recently, dumping ashes on Anchorage. Mount McKinley is often out in top form, especially in winter. The flight deck is sure to point out any landmarks that can be seen.

The farther north and west we go the more land seems to blend into one flat Arctic plain. The winter snow cover helps to highlight any slight elevations. Aimlessly wandering, stagnant and sluggish rivers—even the mighty Yukon and Kuskokwim—are completely immobilized in winter. They look like a maze of giant white worms, or highways laid out with no thought to destination or plan. Where the landscape is dotted with lakes in summer, there is just a white jigsaw pattern of tundra and frozen water in winter. Overall, it is a cold-looking wasteland below.

An announcement says the jet is landing at Unalakleet, and though you may not figure out quite where the airstrip lies, you can pick out trails marking the snowy landscape and finally a bit of a town on the edge of Norton Sound. This part of the Bering Sea is frozen. In winter and on a midafternoon landing on a sunny day, the surface glistens like seven-minute cake frosting. Unalakleet is a hunting and fishing village, with a population of about 500. A sign next to the neat new airport building informs anyone interested that this is the "Fishing Capital of the Arctic." The plane is there only long enough to exchange passengers (probably fishermen in summer) and freight, which now is likely to be transported to and from the jet by a snowmobile pulling a sled, rather than by a dog team.

ARCTIC MODES OF TRANSPORTATION

Though sightseers are limited in choice of transportation getting *to* the Arctic, after arrival they are given a chance to sample a variety. As in other parts of Alaska, people walk a great deal, wearing adequate footgear for current conditions. Many a visitor has succumbed to purchasing his own pair of mukluks (almost knee-high, lined, walrus-hide-soled, fancily trimmed boots). If his home is where snow and cold can be expected in winter, the mukluks will come in handy. Otherwise, people hang them for wall decorations, saving them for their next winter trip north.

On winter tours visitors are transported in warm, comfortable buses to most of the activities. They also have a chance to travel by dogsled and snowmobile. Even reindeer sleigh rides may be added some day. There is talk of reactivating the "Curley-Q Railroad" that used to take passengers to the 1900 gold fields. Instead of from Nome to Kougarok, about eighty miles, it would take visitors one way to the Basin Creek gold diggings.

Taxis are available for Arctic transportation. They keep their motors running perpetually, to ensure prompt starting in below-zero temperatures, a necessary maneuver unless a battery and engine warmer is used. If you see a cord stretched across the snowy

Teammates in front of the Nome Nugget Inn. In winter, the Bering Sea is frozen. Fine examples of Alaskan husky dogs.

sidewalk from a building to a car or truck, it is to keep the vital parts of the vehicle defrosted. We have noted some engines left on in summer also, either from habit, or perhaps because cars become temperamental in Arctic climate.

The favorite new form of transportation, though, is the snowmobile. It has caught on too widely to be considered merely a fad. Even in the farthest out places it is giving dog teams stiff competition. Die-hards claim that it will never entirely replace the husky dog, considering it a poor substitute for snuggling in case of a blizzard or breakdown. Others prefer gassing a snowmobile (over 70 cents a gallon) to expending the effort it takes to dry fish enough to fuel a dog team. They reason that they have to "feed" a snowmobile only when it's *working*. My personal opinion is that it is much more exhilarating to ride in a sled behind a sleek-looking team of peppy dogs yipping with joy occasionally than to be bounced on a mechanical monster smogging up the clear air and deafening everyone within earshot.

The machines are handy and easy to use, though, and you see even youngsters driving them. Like all new means of transportation they cause problems, which the legislature tries to solve through passing bills to register and regulate them. One amendment, approved under fire, said towns under five thousand people should be exempt from the section that prohibits operating snowmobiles on public highways. The Arctic towns gain from this. For example, the Nome-Teller road sees infinitely more snow vehicles in winter than standard vehicles over the same route in summer. Meanwhile, Nome holds snowmobile races in early spring. Festivities the first year included the "first known snowmobile float parade," according to *The Nugget*, Nome's local paper. Kotzebue claims the "Indy of the North," the Archie Ferguson Memorial Snow Machine Race. In memory of a well-known local bush pilot, it's held on Memorial Day weekend and attracts racers from all over the Arctic.

The antidote to the snow machine races is an annual sled dog classic held in March. It is supported enthusiastically by the Nome Kennel Club, of course, which has been reactivated after being dormant for a number of years. The route follows the historic Iditarod Trail, one thousand miles from Anchorage to the Nome finish line. It's a "killer" race, they say, which soon separates the dogs from the puppies. So far the best time is fourteen days, but even the fastest teams and toughest "mushers" (drivers) prepare to spend almost three weeks on the trail. They're still talking about the 1978 win, by a nose—literally. Crossing the Front Street finish line, only a second separated number one from number two.

Some Eskimo youngsters get around fast by using ice skates all over town and out on the Bering Sea. They also pull each other in stateside-type sleds.

All year, scheduled and bush planes serve smaller communities. In summer you'll see kayaks and oomiaks. In the old days, Eskimo families plus all their belongings piled into oomiaks, large bearded-sealskin boats, and hand-paddled their way across broad expanses of open sea to summer camps or to visit relatives. Some places they still do, but the oomiaks are powered by outboard motors now.

All the comforts of home

"In your Alaska travel book be *sure* to tell what these Arctic towns are like," said my companion on the tour bus, as we were returning from the Eskimo dances.

She and her husband were from a neat suburb in a medium-sized midwest town, and they had traveled by camper to Anchorage. After talking to a couple in the trailer park who had just returned from the Arctic, they had decided, on the spur of the moment, to take the two-day tour.

I admitted that hopping from large, cosmopolitan Anchorage, Alaska's biggest city, to some of the smallest was quite a contrast.

"Oh, it's not really the *size* so much—we're used to small frontiersy towns where we come from. It's just that they are so—" she hunted for words—"so *bleak!*"

I knew what she was trying to say. *Any* Arctic town, looked at objectively and for the first time, is a shock. Even the largest, Nome, from a tern's-eye view on the landing approach, appears to be a very minute bit of civilization perched on the edge of the Bering Sea. Behind it the wide-open spaces stretch to infinity.

Houses are small, close together, and mostly unpainted. They don't sit squarely on firm foundations because they are built on ground that stays permanently frozen beneath the surface, called permafrost. The top layer thaws and shifts with the seasons and the heat of the buildings so houses have to be constantly jacked up here and there to keep them more or less level. Some homes are two-story and the family might move upstairs for the cold winter, occupying the whole house only during the warmer months. Sometimes they don't bother with foundations, but build the house on skids, moving it around to different locations. There is one charming small house with weathervane and Russian-style cupola that we always look for when we visit Nome. If it is not where we saw it last, we ask someone, and they tell us where to find it.

Arctic communities continue to make improvements, for which we can't conscientiously blame them. Progress and convenience are inevitable and right. Nevertheless, we miss the atmosphere lent by an unpaved main street bordered by historic boardwalks in Nome. However, we understand that certain visitor-minded factions (such as Nome *Nugget* editor Albro Gregory) are contemplating relaying the boards over the cement!

There are no trees, no lawns, no flowers, almost no yards around the town houses. The snow cover in winter helps soften the appearance of a row of houses that look as if they were constructed by a carpenter in his cups. To anyone seeing for the first time a small Arctic town clinging tenaciously to life in an unsympathetic environment, the overall picture is drab. Visitors soon get over their first shock, however, and become caught up in the history, spirit, and activities of the town, and the warm hospitality of its permanent residents.

After our realistic description of the appearance of Arctic towns, we should hasten to reassure prospective visitors that looks have no relation to the amount or kind of creature comforts available. Generally speaking, the farther out in primitive or wilderness directions a person travels, the fewer creature comforts he should expect. The Arctic is definitely an exception now, especially in the main towns. If there are discomforts, it is unlikely that visitors on tour will experience any. In the tradition of airlines flying to other parts of the world, the airlines serving Arctic Alaska recognized the need and have provided their own hotels. They may be a far cry from Inter-Continentals or Hiltons to sophisticated eyes, but they are clean, comfortable, and attractively decorated—and, most important, adequately supplied with plumbing. Speaking of such, we noted the rest rooms earthily labeled "Standups" and "Sitdowns" at one of the older hotel bars.

PIONEER SUMMER TOURS

To appreciate today's luxuries in the Arctic you would have had to be along on an early tour. We regret missing them. By the time we first traveled to Kotzebue in 1952, Wien Airlines had a hotel built and operating. Water was still delivered by trucks and purified in buckets, and the toilet (with elegant spotted-sealskin-trimmed seat) was primitive and serviced by the "honey wagon." But traffic was growing and everything was pretty well organized. It would have been fun to have experienced some of the growing pains of those first tours, as described by a couple of early "operators."

According to Celia Hunter and Virginia Wood, who began their Arctic tours in 1949, there had already been a start. In 1947 there were four tourist flights to Kotzebue and in 1948 about sixteen. They were on sign-up basis. If enough people were interested, a flight would be scheduled, and someone would check to be sure there was a place to stay. If you were the type to take a trip on that basis, you were likely to enjoy the activities available, which was mainly joining in or observing the normal routine of the busy Eskimo town during summer. Celia and Ginny, both expert pilots, had visited there one February after World War II and had been weathered in. Tourist possibilities occurred to them as they watched Eskimo dances, games, and hunting, and generally became acquainted. They talked some schoolteacher friends into a charter trip the following summer. They loved it, and went home loaded with ideas and teaching materials.

A young flyer, Chuck West, just starting in the travel industry, was also aware of Arctic tour potential. He had flown the "Hump" in World War II and was one of the early advocates of polar flights, when many were still debating whether or not that might be a practical route. His base was Fairbanks, and he was looking for someone to help take on "grass-roots" Arctic tours. He recognized a couple of kindred souls as soon as he met Ginny and Celia. They were certainly qualified for whatever might come up, having ferried everything from multi-engine transports to P-38's from Alaskan bases in World War II, and later bush-piloting in the area.

"Chuck chartered a DC-3 from Wien and made arrangements for use of their pilots, and we were in business," recalled Celia. "We started the trip as stewardesses on the plane, which was nothing like today's craft, as you can imagine."

She mentioned the box lunches and thermos coffee, the spartan seating, the delivery of laundry and other supplies, plus the length of time it used to take. After they arrived at a destination the two women were hotel operators, cooks, guides, and Jills-of-all-work. In spare time they flew bush charters. Trips were conducted once a week, with an overnight stay arranged for by verbal agreement with a local store owner who had rooms above his store. There was a fine rapport between the two women and the townspeople, and all went well until one memorable experience. The store owner, miffed at friction with military personnel, lowered the boom on Ginny and Celia, who were already on their way with twenty-one guests. On arrival the store and rooms were locked up; he was through with the transient trade.

"People who came on those early tours had a real desire to see the Arctic," say Ginny, "and they were wonderfully good sports." Though the predicament looked grim, the hilarious aspects took over, and it proved to be one of those rare experiences that will probably (unfortunately) never be repeated. They found space in someone's upstairs to accommodate ten, though it took a full-scale cleaning. Cots were set up and enough bedding purchased from the mercantile. They stashed the others around with whoever had a spare bed. Some of these people claimed they had the most fun of all. They awakened to find a ring of small, curious, and friendly Eskimo youngsters surrounding them. The kids stayed on to watch them dress and eat breakfast. By tour-of-the-town time they felt like part of the family. Celia says she slept on a huge bear rug in someone's cabin. Even the Catholic priest gave up his bed for the emergency. Everyone rose to the occasion in true Alaskan style.

By August of the same year, Wien's hotel was ready for business. Celia and Ginny activated it on arrival Saturday along with their guests, and then put it in storage condition before they left Sunday, a monumental weekly chore.

"We aren't sure whether the early tourists were reassured or worried to see our faces showing up like Jerry Colonna's in every single capacity connected with their trip and overnight stay in Kotzebue," Ginny reminisced. "Actually, those first visitors were the lucky ones—the Arctic can never be quite that way again."

The two women laid a firm foundation for Wien's tours. The airline, started by three Wien brothers, won fame for its pioneering in aviation in Alaska. One of its bush pilots, Frank Whaley (now retired), became their chief tour promoter. But those early adventuresome flights are another story, well told in a company centennial booklet by Alaska newspaperwoman Kay Kennedy.

Wien's tours have now expanded materially and geographically. Their 1978 summer schedule listed service between Chicago, Portland, Seattle, and Whitehorse. Tour destinations include wilderness Katmai and the Valley of Ten Thousands Smokes; Kodiak of Russian Alaska fame; and even Point Barrow and Prudhoe Bay, at the top of the continent, scene of North Slope oil activity.

We can't leave these three enterprising Alaskans, Chuck, Virginia, and Celia, dangling in the Arctic. They are typical examples of the multiple-career success stories that seem common in Alaska. You should never be surprised to run into someone whom you have not seen for a few years completely engulfed and happy in a flourishing new endeavor—especially when it is related to tourism. Though we knew each separately, we might never have known of their mutual efforts in the beginning of Arctic summer tours except for a picture of the three of them together in Chuck's office in Seattle. From modest beginnings he became one of the major tour operators in Alaska and the Yukon, incorporating cruise ships, a fleet of buses, and hotels.

Celia and Ginny, to whom we have already introduced you at Mount McKinley Park, have clung to the wilderness. Since Camp Denali days and its "vacation in depth," as Celia puts it, they've been working full tilt at Alaska conservation and preservation projects.

ARCTIC INNS

Speaking of enterprise related to accommodations, Alaska Airlines' Nome Nugget Inn Two, overlooking the Bering Sea, is a product of a rapidly growing airline and free-wheeling, original thinking by Alaskan characters. It is completely modern, and is unique on at least two counts: it is probably the first fly-in hotel and it was constructed in the record time of six weeks.

It had to be done in a hurry. The landmark Bering Sea Hotel, which originally occupied the site, burned, causing an acute shortage in tourist rooms. Alaska Airlines bought the property and, between May 1, 1966, and the hotel opening on June 17, had sixteen twin rooms decorated and outfitted. The secret was prefabrication. Hercules air freighters flew in units that had been barged as far as Anchorage, and a crew was ready to fit them together, with plumbing, electrical work, interior finishing, and finally furniture as each room was completed. They needed to expand by the next season, and flew in additional units the same way, a process that may be repeated many times to keep up with the growth of Arctic travel.

The airline's first Nugget Inn is still used, too. It was barged in and put together in 1964, also prefabricated. It was located about town center on the main street, next to a sign saying how many miles it is to other world points, and the direction to take. Heading west it is only 162 miles from Nome to the U.S.S.R. Now Nugget One has been moved next to Nugget Two. Both inns are changing hands, and more building is in the planning stage. Natives here appear to be following the pattern of those farther north who are already in the hotel business.

FOOD AND DRINK

Meals on the ground are not included in airline tour fares, and they could add at least $25 per day to the cost of your Arctic stay. Places to eat vary from season to season in both quantity and quality. Restaurants open and close, cooks come and go, service is minimal, the surroundings the plainest, and the menu variety dependent on current sources of supply. However, if you are not too fussy, and if you are willing to try new things, the food can be interesting and tasty. Arctic eating places may feature Alaskan specialties to some degree, if available, as well as traditional restaurant food. We've tried reindeer steaks and chops, Arctic sheefish, char, seal liver, spider crab, and even muktuk (black, chewy whale skin).

In Nome, tour directors point out the eating possibilities on a swing around town on the way to the hotel, and guests are then on their own. We'll opt for most any dining room next to the sea wall, and with a fine view of the Bering Sea. We stumbled onto the Polar Cub behind Front Street. It was serving that along with breakfast and lunches (only).

Consult a local resident and you can count on getting an honest, completely frank appraisal. Ernie Gustafson's Ft. Davis Roadhouse, three miles out of town, features steaks (including reindeer), Cornish game hen, and prawns fried in beer batter. "It's good—and expensive, like maybe $12 or so," volunteered our local source. "The more sophisticated and well-bred drunks hang out there...." A restaurant in town was described as "clean, food is good...uniquely and cleverly decorated." But the outside is likely to look "like a garbage truck just turned over...."

"Leonard's" lives only in legend now. We first discovered Leonard Trento de Venezuela when we wandered in for lunch at the Polaris Hotel a few summers ago. In no time at all we learned he was an exiled Venezuelan chef (famous) who would feed hungry-looking tourists because we were there. However, Leonard's heart was really in preparing gourmet food for workers in big oil and gold exploration and construction companies in Alaska, a number of which have headquarters in Nome.

Easter dinner, 1969, was a memorable one for our family, as well as tour group members. We found Leonard in his own small building, down an alley behind C. J. Phillips' Liquor Store. There, elbow to elbow, family-style, visitors along with townspeople had a delicious ham or roast turkey dinner, starting with a vegetable (all canned) compote appetizer. Leonard said the town was out of lettuce and eggs. Well, he said the eggs were still around, but being Easter, they were all hard-boiled, dyed, and hidden. Our chef made the dinner festive with champagne (on him) which we had to drink up during the main course, for he needed the glasses for his crowning achievement—Cherries Jubilee. The group burst into applause as Leonard, attired in one of his colorful chef's costumes, brought in the flaming dessert.

All during dinner, Leonard kept us entertained with his tales of life as a chef, teased the young people, and needled one of his competitors who was having dinner there. When we showed interest, he displayed and explained his whole wardrobe of chef costumes and posed cheerfully for the photographers to snap pictures. We lost track of time and had to scramble to pay the bill when the tour bus showed up. The check, that day, for all the fantastic food, plus Leonard's floor show, was very un-Alaskan— only $4 a head!

The one stable item you can count on in the Arctic is liquid refreshment. Some towns (Kotzebue for instance) vote bars and liquor stores in and out periodically, depending on the need for revenue. In Nome, though, it is fairly certain the bars are there to stay. If you plan to research Nome's night life in notorious places like the Board of Trade with its old newspaper-lined walls and other relics of the old days, better add a few dollars to your additional expenses.

Roadhouse bartender (and ex-Nome mayor) Bob Renshaw, identifiable by his well-waxed handlebar mustache, has whipped up a couple of specialties worth trying. The first is rightly named a Tanglefoot and is a martinilike drink more than one of which is apt to cause tangled-foot-in-mouth problems. One member of our party after her first experience with this potent beverage was heard asking for a child's portion the next time around! The other is a frothy confection called a Bering Ball. Bob gives his recipes for both on request. Apparently his only secret ingredient is a generous lacing with grain alcohol, which is sold in Alaska liquor stores.

That just about sums up the accommodations, inner and outer, in the Arctic. We have bypassed one form of accommodations much used in other parts of Alaska—camping. We would be the last ones to say it is impossible. Natives visiting in the summer and hardy old-timers think nothing of camping, carving, fishing, and otherwise carrying on their activities on the beaches. At the turn of the century, Nome was a tent city of twenty thousand or more gold seekers, stretched thirty-five miles along the busy beach. Separated only by a shovel handle's length, people sifted the sand for gold as fast as they could pan. They say mail was delivered by passing it hand to hand till it reached the addressee, in about three days.

For the casual flying visitor, camping is hardly feasible. The closest we've come to roughing it in the Arctic is to buy supplies (don't compare costs with home!) in the general stores and have a beach picnic, sharing our snacks with all the kids and dogs that accumulate. It's a great way to get acquainted.

ARCTIC TOUR TOWNS

The Artic's three major cities, Nome (actually in western Alaska with Arctic leanings), Kotzebue, and Barrow, are reached by regularly scheduled jet flights. From these points flights may be made to more points: Prudhoe Bay, Point Hope, Wales, Gambell, Shishmaref, Teller, Golovin, Bethel, and Nunivak, to name a few. You can go down the line still further, by bush flights, and pick out some interesting-sounding names like Eek, Egegik, Ugashik, Chukfoktulik, Tachykagamuit, Hoholitna, and Anaktuvuk, if they appeal to you.

When you compare travel brochures and releases put out by Arctic-serving carriers and agents you'll note considerable similarities in the tour offerings. They are all good tours, and a conscientious effort is made to deliver what they promise. The main difference is in the timing and where a visitor chooses to spend the night. You are bound to see more of Kotzebue and its people if you spend the night there. The same is true of Nome or Barrow.

Whichever route you go, you will have been exposed, in greater or lesser degree, to various native activities like Eskimo singing and dancing, games, blanket tossing, dog sledding, and skin-boats; and also museums. Somewhere along the line you will have had occasion to cross the Arctic Circle. The pilot flashes the "fasten seat belt" sign, warns you to hang tight, and then at the approximate spot salutes it with a dip of the plane. Later everyone is given tangible proof of this achievement, an Arctic Circle Certificate. Each town has its own particular attraction, though, as you will discover in even a small sampling. Which town will be the most intriguing and appealing depends entirely on the visitor and the type of adventure he is seeking. We can honestly recommend spending a night in each of the three biggest towns, if you can steal the time.

BARROW

Barrow's main distinction is its location. The fact that it is only twelve hundred miles from the North Pole and is the northernmost point on our North American continent attracts many people. In summer, when visiting is possible, the days are longer there, for the sun doesn't bother to set for eighty-two days. There is always something going on, day or night, under the midnight sun. Though exposed to outside influences, some of them drastic, for over a hundred years, Barrow is far enough out to remain unsophisticated and predominantly Eskimo. Though they may work at other jobs, the Eskimos still depend on hunting and fishing for most of their livelihood, and Eskimo is the main spoken language.

Like all Arctic towns, Barrow is growing and changing, however. It had an Eskimo name which meant "the point," but was renamed for an English polar explorer, Sir John Barrow. The population now is over two thousand. The few surrounding nomadic Eskimos have gradually moved to Barrow to settle and to take advantage of civilization's comforts: schools, jobs, and health services. One recent innovation has done much to take the town out of its primitive state: hooking up to a vast Navy petroleum reserve nearby so that natural gas can be used for cooking and heating. It has upgraded the living standards of the whole community.

The government continues to depend on Barrow for various projects, and many of the employees are natives. After World War II the DEW line (Distant Early Warning system) was started there. Today it is headquarters for the Naval Arctic Research Laboratory, and important for the servicing and supply of several research stations on floating ice islands.

Trying to help the Eskimos use up their summer "surplus"— daylight—is tough on tourists. The youngsters merely play until they drop asleep; their parents may be working at any hour. Visitors, who cannot tell when it is time to go to bed, run the risk of round-the-clock sightseeing.

Everyone wants to stay up for that spectacular late late show, starring the "midnight sun." Photographers can snap pictures every few minutes of a never-ending sunset, as the sun circles the sky completely. At "night" it arcs from west to east, never dipping below the horizon until mid-August.

Visitors in early June may get in on the whaling festival. Bringing in bowhead whale, long an Eskimo staple, is the town's first good excuse to celebrate after the long winter. Eskimo delicacies, like whale or seal meat, stew in the pot, and there are contests of derring-do and skill. Later tour groups are shown an excellent narrated slide show, which tells all about the whaling. They can count on seeing traditional Eskimo dancing, accompanied by drum and chant. Their costumes are parkas, mittens, and simple masks.

On the "city tour," it is evident that Barrow still has one foot in the past. Women mend nets, go fishing, and use their ooloos (sharp, curved knives) to carve seal meat, filet fish, and prepare seal skin storage pokes. Skin boats on the beach, caribou and reindeer antlers, walrus heads, with tusks still intact for future carving projects, and husky work dogs are still part of the scene.

The tour bus heads out of town to "The Point," a finger of land that gives way to a sandy spit before trickling off into the Arctic Ocean. In summer a tent camp is set up here. Grandparents and older kids take care of the little ones while their parents are out fishing and duck hunting. Visitors may be surprised to hear preschoolers and elderly Eskimos speaking Eskimo. There are good opportunities for pictures against the Arctic Ocean background: kids; fish and seal meat drying on racks; and husky pups. By mid-summer, the ice pack retreats to the distant horizon. The water is a milky sea green on a sunny day, contrasting with the deep-blue sky. You can walk out on the furthermost tip of the United States while breathing the "purest air in the world," a fact determined by the nearby Naval Arctic Research Laboratory. Researchers claim there is little dust to begin with; pollutants caused by vehicles, fires, etc., are quickly whisked away by Arctic winds.

At Brower's Trading Post you will find bargains such as fine white fox furs. Browsing in "Browerville," dating from the 1880s when Charlie Brower, adventurer and trader, was "King of the Arctic," turns up mementos left by famous explorers who stopped by. A picture of Will Rogers on the wall of the Trading Post is a reminder of the 1935 plane crash that took the entertainer's life and that of his pilot, Wiley Post. An Eskimo witness ran the fifteen miles to town and broke the news that shocked the world.

With the settlement of native land claims leading to revenue from oil production, the economy is flourishing. The regional Native Corporation has been busy sprucing up, straightening streets, and building new housing, including the farthest north prefabricated hotel, located almost on the edge of the Arctic Ocean. It is another case where progress is necessary and inevitable. Barrow will, no doubt, continue to be an interesting place to visit. We can only hope that there will always be some people interested in preserving the old culture and skills, so "cheechakos" can have the thrill of a glimpse of what is was like "in the old days."

PRUDHOE BAY

Barrow's top-of-the-continent neighbor is Deadhorse, near Prudhoe Bay on the North Slope. A few years ago, this was the scene of the world's greatest airlift, probably greater than Berlin's. Passenger-size to super-cargo Hercules jets were landing there, stock-piling equipment and supplies for the development of the oil and natural gas potential. In the winter of 1968-69, Bob had an assignment to take pictures there, in the coldest, darkest part of winter. It was so cold that he worried about his camera functioning, even though it was winterized for many degrees below zero.

We might have continued to rate Deadhorse below zero as a tourist destination, if we hadn't seen it recently in summer. The contrast was unbelievable. Easily a hundred varieties of flowers were in bloom: fluffy Alaska cotton, yellow poppies, buttercups, wild roses, assorted daisies and many other Arctic wild cousins to field flowers "at home." And Deadhorse is definitely for the birds: snowy owls, gulls, ptarmigan, loons, terns, assorted ducks, and sandpipers were spied easily.

Our favorite small game were unlimited frisky ground squirrels alerted to the tour bus and visitor treats. They developed "mumps" before our eyes, as they stashed all they could hold in their cheek pouches and then dashed off to hoard it in their burrows.

How are larger animals affected by all the activity? The usual thousands of caribou still meander over time-worn trails. Even after the main summer migration, hundreds may be seen scattered over a large area, wandering among the far-flung development sites and grazing in the Brooks Range foothills. In August, stragglers were still hanging around, hunted and shot—by photographers. We saw them grazing unconcernedly near buildings and truck traffic. Honking the bus horn in hopes they would raise their antlered heads for pictures seldom fazed them.

Large Eskimo family and belongings takes off in oomiak for month-long fishing trip out of Barrow.

The overall impression of the Prudhoe Bay area is that of a flat desert region, dotted with myriad treeless oases. Snow melt fills shallow indentations in the tundra, perfect nesting grounds for an amazing variety of birds. The lakes and flatness are slightly offset by tundra-covered frost cones, called pingos.

In the Arctic, old lakes (like previously mentioned old soldiers, bush pilots, and ferryboats) also never die, but fade away, after thousands of years, into pingos. By a complicated process of freezing and thawing and moisture percolating through accumulated lake sediment, the frosty mounds gradually push up from below. The tallest pingo in the area, having achieved an elevation of maybe twenty feet, is of course named "Mount Deadhorse." It even has a "timberline." Looking closely, we could see its "national forest," a number of twenty-to-thirty-year-old willow trees, about six inches tall among the tundra grass.

Tourists are not at first attuned to subtle Arctic terrain, but what appears stark and barren often comes alive on close examination, perhaps on hands and knees. I think we saw, and Bob photographed, everything possible during our short stay, from pipe to sandpipers. Our guide was Ernie Aufenkamp, who obviously loved his complex, controversial "beat." The tour bus jogs down expensively built ($200,000 a mile!) roads, gravel-padded up to five feet thick. All the buildings are on gravel pads, too, otherwise they would sink where come-lately construction has caused the first thaw in thousands-of-years-old permanently frozen ground.

Are there tundra scars? There are some from earlier exploration. Even slight impressions destroy a certain amount of the diversity of tundra plants, many not easily replaced. Now large fines are levied, encouraging much research in prevention and counteraction. For example, we were shocked to see a huge machine rolling across the tundra. The "Rolligon," though, leaves a barely perceptible track, because its 26,000-pound weight is distributed four to six pounds per square inch as it rides on mammoth air-inflated rollers. They say it can run over a man without harm. In its experimental stage there were only six: three in Prudhoe, two in Canada, and one in Saudi Arabia. Twelve more were scheduled for the North Slope. A half million dollars has been invested in finding the best-growing grass for reseeding. The brightest, greenest grass we saw was some that had been treated with a petroleum-based by-product. A hardy sedge grass that is used as a fill is also a feed for caribou, along with lichens.

We saw almost two hundred miles of pipe ready to be laid in 1975. The Prudhoe Bay docks, ice-free for a short period in summer, were loaded with supplies being barged in from supply ships. The "Christmas trees" we saw in the tundra are no poems here...that's oil jargon for capped wells. Their pipe "branches" and "trunk" elbows and valves are more like a plumber's nightmare. Along with the wells, flow stations, drilling sites, and self-contained oil company complexes, we were impressed with the long- "frozen assets" at idle work camps: all sorts of heavy equipment poised for the action that began in 1974 and '75.

Whether the long-contested, eight hundred-mile Alaska pipeline over Arctic wilderness to seaport Valdez is to be or not to be is no longer the question. It is finished. Will the ecology really survive the extraction of those fuel staples considered so important to today's life-style? Anyone interested in seeing first hand what is being done to preserve and protect the flora and fauna of a fragile area can get it straight "from the horse's mouth." At Deadhorse.

Caribou graze without concern near Prudhoe Bay oil company housing complex. "Eternal flame" is natural gas burnoff.

Otherwise, those traveling the Richardson Highway, particularly the section leading to Valdez, can watch for signs of the pipeline path, as we did.

KOTZEBUE

Kotzebue's main attraction is its beach, which is probably the most unusual main street you will ever see. It's where the action is, twenty-four hours a day in summer. The best way to observe it is to saunter along, flanked on one side by the town and on the other by Kotzebue Sound.

Kotzebue is a place to appreciate with all your senses. You will absorb a variety of impressions, most of them entirely unlike any you may have had before. Some may seem a little ripe or raw to sensitive noses and eyes of city people accustomed to gracious living. Take the smells, for example. You may be able to sort out such odors as fish, dogs, Clorox, waste (human, animal, and vegetable), and you will be lucky if it is not too warm and if the breeze whips in from a direction enabling you to stay on the fresh side.

We never think of Kotzebue as drab, at least along the beach. The bright-colored parkas lent to tourists by the airlines, the gay print parka-dresses worn by the Eskimo ladies and children, the racks with strips of rich red salmon and black seal meat drying in the wind, along with the general hustle and bustle, leave a generally colorful impression. There is a happy cacophony of sound— children playing, pups barking, and boats being beached or launched. It is not a town for queasy people, at times. Over many visits we have been lucky and have seen about everything being done on the beach from a hunter hanging a set of antlers to dry in the breezes, with bloody top of head still attached, to a crew butchering a freshly caught beluga (white whale) or skinning a seal—a real blood-and-guts operation.

For the first quick once-over, you may be lucky enough to have an Eskimo bus driver and guide; his English will be excellent, but he will have a touch of accent and an unusual twist to expressions that are a dead giveaway that he learned the Eskimo language first. He will admit that he understands Eskimo fine, can still speak it, but that all the kids these days are speaking English. Of the eighteen hundred or so population, five hundred are kids in school. Eskimo is likely to be a lost language here in another generation or so. After pointing out the highpoints from the bus, the guide will turn you loose to explore on foot, but he stays available to answer questions and act as liaison between townspeople from time to time.

He will warn you against approaching and petting the dogs tied on short chains on the beach. These are winter work dogs, fed scanty rations when not working in the summer, and they are warm, uncomfortable, bored, and often mean. They are smart, though. It is rumored that some sit on the four-foot chains to make them appear shorter, just to snag an unwary tourist and break the monotony! The pups roam freely, and are hard to resist. In fact, we never feel like maligning huskies since we have one ourselves. Treated well, they make wonderful, intelligent, and gentle family pets.

It is surprising that Kotzebue still manages to keep so much of its Eskimo flavor, with its continuous infiltration by Russian, Siberian, Norwegian, fellow American, and now tourist outsiders. Situated about twenty-six miles north of the Arctic Circle, it was a favorable location for trading, and it has been known as an Eskimo trade

Activity-filled main street of Kotzebue follows beach. Pups are friendly, though dogs chained on beach in summer may *not* be.

center for centuries. It lost its tongue-twisting Eskimo name and was named Kotzebue in honor of a Russian naval officer who wandered there in search of a northeast passage in the early 1800s. These adaptable, predominantly Eskimo (though probably there is no one left who can boast he is a *pure* Eskimo) townspeople take it all in stride. They reflect outside influences and at the same time hold on to many of their old ways, so far.

The larger, newer Nul-Luk-Vik Hotel, owned by the Northwest Alaska Native Association (NANA), has Kotzebue Sound view rooms, a dining room, and cocktail area. It also boasts telephones and colored TV, which of course boosts the price. The other choice is our long-time favorite, the Wien Arctic Hotel. It can take in half as many at about half the price and baths are shared, but customers are 100% satisfied with the homey atmosphere and excellent family-style meals.

The Arctic winter tours, which overnight at Nome, touch down briefly above the Arctic Circle at Kotzebue. Wien's summer tour hotel was boarded up in winter, we noted, on a quick stop in February. The days are still short then, and there was time only for a quick look while the jet took on passengers and freight before returning to Nome. The temperature was −52°, the sun was out, but there was little activity along the beach. Even the dogs were burrowed in the snow, their tails curled around their noses to keep them warm. A month later, though, the temperature was a balmy 15° above. Visitors watched Eskimo children in their shirt sleeves playing baseball on frozen Kotzebue Sound in front of the village.

POINT HOPE

Point Hope, Eskimo whaling village on the northwest fringe of the coast, has been moving to safer ground nearby, because of encroachment by the sea. This long-inhabited site has been a favorite destination for hardy adventurers. At this writing there are no organized tours going there. However, it is possible to visit and stay overnight in this primitive, friendly town by making arrangements through airlines that fly there. Many people (mostly Eskimos) converge there for the whaling festival following the successful spring whale hunt. The date hangs loose, usually "sometime in June."

On our first visit to Point Hope, in 1973, we were too late for the festival, but decided to fly there from Kotzebue, stay overnight, and then continue on to Nome by bush charter. When the town is full of whaling teams, Eskimo celebrants and families crowd in with friends and relatives. Others, like us, can stay at the limited, but comfortable, native-operated hotel, which we dubbed the "Airport Hilton." We couldn't complain about commuting time to the hotel. It is just off the landing strip. With doubtful plane weather next morning, we slept until we heard the plane actually coming in, hopped out of bed, dressed, closed our suitcases, and still didn't keep the pilot waiting.

Our host in charge of the lodging saw that we got around to noteworthy points of interest: a photogenic whalebone-rib-fenced cemetery and the whalebone-rimmed festival grounds; the hogan-like sod igloos now used as whale meat lockers; and the native store where we found excellent porous bone masks and ivory carvings. He took us to meet a sweet, elderly Eskimo woman still living in a sod igloo. It was surprisingly cozy and cheery inside. Tourists are still rare enough in Point Hope that as we walked around we soon accumulated a following of Eskimo children, a favorite photo subject of Bob's.

Eating places are limited, too, especially in menu choices. We sampled the only open possiblities, the Rock Lodge and Nick's, settling for a hamburger at each, same price $1.25, coffee free. We learned from Pete, our guide, that people could bring along their own food, and then someone (like his mother) would be willing to cook it for them.

The action in town that night was a bingo game in the smoke-filled community hall and library. At least one hundred souls, three-quarters of the population, were concentrating on the well-used cards with beans for markers spread out on the tables and overflowing onto the floor. The spell of the game was broken by chuckles when the caller said something in Eskimo as Bob snapped a flash picture. The jackpot that night was $41.50, and is often much higher during whale festivals, or dog mushing competitions, we were told. Everyone was obviously pleased to have us drop by. The caller hospitably offered to call in English as well as Eskimo, if we cared to join in.

Unique and historic whale-rib-marked cemetery at Point Hope. Yearly whaling festival in June draws visitors, especially Alaskans.

We intended to get back for the whale festival the following year, but by the time the flexible date was determined and we got the word, we were already committed elsewhere. Next time, at the first inkling, we intend to do as the Eskimos do: drop everything and go.

NOME

Nome, along with having the King Island Eskimos, has the added glamour of gold rush history, so recent that there are people still around to talk about it. Moreover, it appears that the search for gold will never really be given up. Though the glitter is not very apparent, and the shape of the town has changed at least twice from being destroyed by fire and flood, there is still plenty of atmosphere between Front Street and the Bering Sea. People still pan, including tourists. There is speculation on the amount of gold still left in the Seward Peninsula and lying under the shallow Bering Sea. The present upsurge in the price of gold may set off another gold rush. We hear that some long-idle giant dredges near Nome are rehabilitated and operating.

If gold had been discovered by the famous Three Swedes any other place on the Seward Peninsula, Nome would probably have been founded in that spot instead. Don't try to figure out a translation for its name. The story is that in the hustle and bustle of the frantic gold search, a mapmaker wrote in "Name," indicating that the matter was not yet decided and intending to fill it in later. His "a" looked like an "o" and later it was too late—the name stuck. It seems to fit the place. As any resident will tell you, "There's *no* place like Nome, it's a way of life."

The Eskimos did not start coming to Nome from their home on King Island until after it was established as a white man's town. Then they came by skin boat and set up summer fishing camps on the beach, returning to their island for winter. Because they were isolated until fairly recently, the King Islanders are possibly the purest Eskimos left. Only a little over twenty years ago they settled permanently at King Island Village, adjacent to Nome. They followed the same trend as other Eskimo villages to the north. Families, in their transitional period, changing from the old life to the new, need to be near schools, hospitals, and work. Today, about 80 percent of Nome's combined twenty-eight hundred population is Eskimo or part Eskimo. Many of the King Islanders adapt readily to tourism. They are still interested in carrying on their old skills and are noted for their ivory carving. They are fine dancers and are top competition at Eskimo get-togethers.

LIFE AND CUSTOMS IN THE ARCTIC
Eskimo dancing

Eskimo singing and dancing are an essential part of the entertainment in Arctic tour towns. Visitors are joined by most of the Eskimos, who enjoy the program as much as their guests. Part of

Beachcombing and wave-jumping on famous golden sands of Nome, on shore of Bering Sea.

this may be due to the audience participation. After performing for the guests, the Eskimo master of cermonies will invite (or draft) the visitors to try, providing them with an Eskimo teacher. All they have to do is concentrate on the simple steps and motions. There is a chorus in the background lustily chanting (in Eskimo) the un-harmonized melodies based on a primitive scale, while four or five drummers keep the beat. The drums are flat and circular, with a driftwood rim and walrus-stomach covering stretched taut. From time to time the drummer moistens the skin with water to keep it stretched tight and in tune.

The women's dance differs from the men's; it is less active. Women are required to keep mukluks on the floor, but a man is allowed to stamp one foot vigorously and occasionally leap a little. Women's motions are subdued and graceful and they keep their eyes demurely downcast. Men's dances often tell a story, which allows for appropriate action. Many of the dances you see are ancient ones handed down from generation to generation, but there are also new ones being composed, depicting today's happenings. Like popular songs, the good ones will probably be handed down as long as the culture is. They continue to follow the same distinctive patterns, but we detected a deviation in a special song composed by the King Islanders for the birthday of Bob Giersdorf, a well-liked visitor and Eskimo dance buff. Their offering broke him up. In keeping with the occasion, it had a "South 48" beat, and with many happy smiles and greeting handclasps the dancers indicated just how they felt about him.

Though there was no doubt on this one, we have reason to believe that the English interpretation of some of these Eskimo popular songs loses something in translation, as rendered by the master of ceremonies. The Eskimos have a great sense of humor, and from sly glances and giggles, we suspect the natives are aware of every comic nuance.

All ages join in the dances in summer. In winter, many of the teen-agers are away at school, and the older grade-school children are busy with homework. But from the oldest to the youngest they enjoy performing, in their colorful parkas and with hands always covered with mittens. The ancient reason for this custom seems to have been lost. There is a lot of toe-tapping going on among visitors, and by the end of the dances, they are caught up enough with the spirit so that the ones chosen are willing to give it a try. They are obviously among friends, and the atmosphere is relaxing, with the orchestra and chorus at one end, behind the dancers, and the other three walls and benches lined with audience. Visitors are easily identified by their cheery Easter-egg-hued borrowed parkas.

Besides the dancing, a carver demonstrates how to drill holes in ivory with a primitive bow drill, and one of the women shows samples of her craft, skin sewing. Then they put forth their wares, which may be purchased at reasonable prices. Whether one buys or not, everyone is welcome to examine and talk with the natives, who by now are beginning to seem like personal friends. Moreover, you may recognize some you saw working at summer chores and assorted jobs around town.

THE ISLAND ESKIMO DANCERS

Age-old chants and dances are performed for visitors on Arctic tour in Nome.

Blanket toss

The blanket toss is to contemporary Eskimos what certain logger skills are to the timber industry in this modern age—no longer needed, but perpetuated in festivals and for fun. In the old days, when they hunted with harpoon and hand-paddled kayaks and oomiaks, it was much trickier to spot game in a vast expanse of uneven ice, let alone stalk it. The hunter with the best eyesight needed a vantage point thirty-five to forty feet up.

Blanket toss is test of skill and for fun now. Hunters once were tossed aloft in order to spot distant game.

Natives today perform the blanket toss in the age-old manner, but instead of just hunters, women and children also enjoy this Eskimo version of the trampoline. The blanket is a circular walrus or caribou skin, with sinew or rope handles threaded around the edge. Everyone, including visitors, grabs a couple of loops, one of the Eskimos explains the game, and a bright-eyed little miss in parka and mukluks hops on. After some preliminary testing, the caller gives a count of three, after which comes a mighty heave and an extra leap by the jumper, and she goes high in the air. She lands on her feet, all set to play again. If there is any wind, it sometimes requires some fancy footwork by the blanket holders, who, like firemen, rush to be sure the net is under the jumper.

The toss presents a few extra problems in winter, of course. It has to be done outside, because no ceiling is high enough. The skin has to be kept in a warm place or it freezes stiff. Even so, when it is exposed again to below-zero temperatures, it can soon freeze again, so the tossing is brief. In winter, the Eskimos wear their beautiful warm fur parkas; in summer they wear lighter-weight ones with some fur on the inside, but the outside is made of gay cotton, colorfully rick-racked and stitch-trimmed. Like their "South 48" counterparts, the kids in summer swap their mukluks for sneakers. Usually in summer the toss is performed just before the evening dances, but in winter it is dark by then. Moreover, it is hard to get a quorum of performers, for the children are in school and the parents at work during the day. And so they settle for Saturday and Sunday turnouts, and as the days get longer in spring, after school, to keep in practice.

There is one story that will probably become a legend: how the blanket toss saved the lives of some King Islanders as well as Alaska Airlines personnel. A group of dancers was invited to Tokyo, and on the last performance Frank Feeman, Alaska Airlines' interline vice president, volunteered to try his skill. To see a novice try the toss is always amusing to the Eskimos as well as to other spectators. It is a great way to lose your dignity, and unfortunately also to acquire a broken bone. (Because of this, they now discourage amateurs.) Frank was game, though, and the inevitable happened: he broke both heels. Though they were scheduled to take off on the next plane, the whole troupe voted to stick with Frank and his bed of pain. It was a lucky choice. The plane ditched in Tokyo Bay with total loss of life.

Other games

Some contests of skill had their beginning in the past when they were part of Eskimo survival training. Today, in farther outposts, many of them may still be practiced for real.

At festivals, such as over the Fourth of July in Kotzebue, the competition is keen and we have seen everything from muktuk-eating contests to seal skinning, a gory contest for women. Both whale and seal are important to the Eskimo economy—to their survival. They are permitted to subsistence hunt as did their forefathers, and they do so as humanely as deer hunters...or modern butchers. No part of the animal is wasted. As this is still a basic skill, the contestants are expert. With only the ooloo, a small, razor sharp metal (formerly stone) knife with a curved handle, a winner can complete the job in less than five minutes. In between are dance contests and feats of derring-do: wrestling, knuckle walking, arm carry, finger pull, neck pull, and high kick. We also saw these feats demonstrated by a group of Explorer Scouts in Nome, whose project is learning and mastering these rugged skills of their ancestors. They seemed to particularly enjoy the high kick, and were amazingly adept. It's not what you think. In the Eskimo version, a seal skin is tied to a pole that is raised higher after every try, and to qualify, *both* feet have to hit the skin at the same moment.

We saw the first Eskimo Olympics, held in a Fairbanks ballpark several years ago. They followed the format of the Greek, but with variations that were pure Eskimo. Though he had probably flown in on a jet, the runner sprinted breathlessly into the arena holding a flaming seal-oil torch and lit the lamp, an ancient Eskimo one, also fueled by seal oil with a moss wick. With applause and cheers, these informal Olympics were formally opened after a welcome speech given first in Eskimo, then English. Now they are the "Eskimo-Indian World Olympics," held annually in midsummer at Alaska-land. Besides appropriate native contests including dance, there is a queen contest. The winner, an attractive native girl, wears a regal and real ermine crown and native dress as she rules over the festivities.

Chasing reindeer

Being able to view Alaska's wild animals in their natural habitat is high on the list for most visitors. In the Arctic, it is polar bears, caribou, walrus, whale, and seal that they hope to see. But it is most likely that the only live animals they will see are the imported, semidomesticated herds of reindeer, especially near Nome.

In the hunting season, sea creatures, which still play an extremely important role for Eskimo living, are brought to shore and butchered, and the skins are prepared for use. To "South 48" sensibilities some of this is much too earthy. But we can heartily recommend the reindeer—both winter and summer—with one exception. Those with weak stomachs should avoid visiting Golovin (or any other such place) during the early spring roundup and butchering.

Reindeer are unique to the Arctic, though the Alaskan variety were originally transplanted from Siberia in the late 1800s. Because of the rampant exploitation of game in the Far North, the food supply of the Eskimo was becoming depleted. Besides a hunger stopgap, it was also hoped that the reindeer would multiply, and eventually a productive northern industry would evolve. It has been a long struggle, a story in itself, but today it appears to be nearing reality. Herds have ranged from Point Barrow to the island of Kodiak, with the heaviest concentration on the Seward Peninsula. Much experimental work is being carried on at Nunivak Island. In the Nome area, plans are under way for a meat-processing plant, to prepare steaks, "jerky" (dried, salted meat strips), and smoked delicacies. Skins and antlers have already been used successfully for clothing and accessories. It is now getting down to the point where use can be made of almost every bit of the animal.

Nome was not quite prepared for the impact these animals might have on visitors. Maybe it goes back to childhood, Santa Claus, and Rudolph, but from the oldest to the youngest traveler, once they hear there are reindeer in the vicinity, they *have* to see them. The tour guide goes all out to see that people have the chance, though it plays havoc with plans. The reindeer movements are quite unpredictable, and the herd has to be somewhere near a road so a whole busload of people can be transported. Guests are warned to be ready, and away they go at the drop of a rumor, or a summons from Larry Davis, a personable Eskimo who owns a herd ranging near Nome.

Larry knows a great deal about reindeer, and obviously enjoys them and his work. He'd have to; they are skittish, wild, unreliable, and at times ornery. But they are magnificent, too, especially when you see five hundred or so coming across the tundra. To say he herds them is using the term loosely. Actually, he follows them and keeps track of them, confining them to his specified rangeland. In summer, they range farther and faster, and he has helpers on snowmobiles which track over the tundra almost as well as they skim over the crusty snow in winter.

Larry has been trying to train some more amenable reindeer to the harness, hoping eventually to hitch them up to a sleigh, but success has been only moderate, so far.

"The Laplanders have been domesticating them for centuries," Larry points out. "Guess I'll have to go to Lapland and learn some of their secrets!"

Personally, we are not sure whether he'll ever domesticate his reindeer—after all, they have been Alaskans long enough now to develop stubborn traits all their own. Meanwhile, we'll settle for chasing them, and a choice time is in winter. Arctic winter tours are still so new that problems like how to find a herd within commuting distance are still worked out on an individual basis. If it is possible, they try to figure out how to take people there.

Our small group was exceptionally fortunate. It was a gorgeous sunny day and at –25° the diamond-sprinkled crust gave just enough support for snowmobiles to skim along at a fine clip. Keeping pace was Larry Davis with his open-air snowmobile and sled, followed by his constant companions, a pair of Australian shepherds, a hardy, intelligent dog used in the Arctic for herding reindeer. They happily raced along behind for several miles, but as they tired, Larry picked up first one and then the other in his lap, where they snuggled down gratefully for the last couple miles, blending right in with his fur parka.

Though the days are still short in February, at late morning it was very light and the sky was an intense blue. The snow cover reflected light also, and our driver, Thor Weatherby, pointed out that it was only about a foot deep, though probably "drifted deeper up toward yonder hills." We had thought the snow would be much deeper, but he pointed out signs like a deserted miner's cabin where it came up only to the front step. The other giveaway was the low-growing willow bush (no trees, of course). My sister-in-law, Kay Fish, whose husband, a writer, rode in the snowmobile ahead with Dick Burchell, remarked that the rolling terrain gave a western-rangeland look to the whole scene. After all, we were in hot pursuit of a herd, and it would have been easy to imagine other similes, except for the

Frank (seated) and Ursula Ellanna (both with fur parkas) visit with guests while fishing through holes in Bering Sea ice, near Nome in winter.

cold and snow. Reindeer depend on foraging in the prairielike tundra for their food, even in winter, and Thor pointed out some spots where they had smelled out and pawed down under for some favorite shoots or roots.

"They can paw through a couple feet of packed snow, or three feet or so of loose snow for forage," said Thor. "But if it forms a hard crust, the whole herd has to be moved."

We gobbled up the eight or ten miles in no time at all, entranced with the signs of life Thor pointed out, and which soon our city eyes began to pick up on their own. A white Arctic owl flew low looking for a lemming, the small short-tailed rodent noted for its suicidal drive into the sea at certain times of the year. A fox, well warned by our noisy machines, confidently trotted off in the distance. And then, shortly after crossing the frozen Nome River, we spotted the reindeer.

The herd is accustomed to Larry's snowmobile, and he worked freely among them, corralling them for picture taking. Our noisy transportation was parked and turned off some distance away, and it was then that we became aware of the unusual sounds that go along with this most exhilarating sight. As the nervous herd mills one way, and then the other, there is an oddly disturbing clicking tinkle. We thought it was hooves against the icy crust, but apparently it is their noisy ankle bones clacking away. "New Dimensions in Music" composers should record this and use it! There are grunts, coughs, pants, and calls, plus the musical chime of the belled ones, too.

When disturbed, reindeer react somewhat like sheep, charging thoughtlessly and en masse after any few that strike out from the main herd, but moving much faster. Larry's job is to outguess and outrun them in his vehicle; they are just as quickly convinced to dash in the other direction. In appearance they are most like caribou, but smaller, about 150 to 200 pounds, wilder and with a more solid-looking set of antlers. They vary in color from a few all-white ones to the more usual Alaskan brown and gray. Both males and females shed and replace antlers each year in late spring and June, which is also calving time. The rest of the year they are fully antlered, fine-coated creatures, and a sight to set both amateur and professional photographers mad, winter or summer, when displayed in herds. Photography is fairly simple in summer, but in winter shutters are likely to stick. Movie cameras, though winterized, pose problems at times. Kay, still intrigued with the similarities of reindeer herding and steer roundups, thought still photographers could be compared to quick-draw cowboys. They whipped their cameras out from under the warmth of their parkas only when ready to shoot. The other main complaint (strictly from writers) was that their ball-point pens froze, making note-taking impossible. We finally wised up and kept our tools of the trade inside our warm mitts, or in an inner pocket, next to our hearts.

At dinner the night before, we had all ordered huge, delicious reindeer steaks, which we consumed with gusto. That was before we had stalked these magnificent creatures in their natural setting and learned about them from Larry, Thor, and Dick. In some sort of mutual tribute to an unforgettable snowfari and some critters we felt we had come to know rather intimately, *this* night we all ordered seafood.

Teammates

All over Alaska, husbands and wives pitch in together and do the jobs that need doing. Perhaps we are more likely to be aware of this because that is the way Bob and I have always worked. In the larger Alaskan cities, couples follow separate careers, but adults (as well as youngsters) everywhere appear to be compulsive workers. Our theory is that the whole northern aspect encourages a more vigorous life. Alaskans will agree, and add that it oftens takes two workers in the family to beat the high cost of living. Whatever the reason, we are much impressed with the way people work together. In smaller towns and outlying settlements a man and his wife function as a team, often in an unusual type of business.

Much of our insight into Alaska life has been gained over the years through keeping in touch with them. Somewhere on an Arctic tour you are likely to meet the following, or their counterparts.

This is the way it was in the old days...

Ursula and Frank Ellanna, an Eskimo couple, are grandparent age, but they look younger—smooth sun-and-wind-tanned faces under dark, shiny hair. They wear beautiful fur parkas and warm mukluks. Whether you step into unaccustomed below-zero chill in winter or the unusually brisk air of summer, those parkas and mukluks look like the most desirable wearing apparel in sight.

Frank is from King Island; Ursula, from farther north, joined him there when they were married in 1929. This sea stronghold was home for a proud and independent community. They built their houses precariously on stilts on impossibly steep cliffs and survived for centuries on the bounty of the sea. Expert seamen, they roamed and visited widely, but always returned to their island. They started coming to Nome after it was established as a white man's town, and the gold fury had subsided. It took as long as thirteen hours by skin boat to cover the distance that a bush plane covers in about half an hour. The Eskimos were not interested in gold; just the fishing and hunting and garnering their winter food supply. When the Bureau of Indian Affairs condemned and closed their school on the island in 1959, the villagers moved to Nome permanently. Even so, for several years, diehard hunters always went back for the winter season, Frank and Ursula among them. Some still do, principally to get walrus for ivory carving and skins for boats. Frank and Ursula still have a home there and talk of going back to move it to a better position for withstanding the elements in winter.

Ursula is an especially charming and articulate Eskimo woman with only a slight accent. Frank is willing to leave the talking up to Ursula. He understands English, but prefers to converse in Eskimo or remain silent, though obviously proud of his wife and happy with his role in the demonstrations. However, just strike a subject dear to his heart, and he opens up, making himself understood adequately. These two delightful people adapt readily to many situations, including trips "outside." They lend their talents to Alaska promotional projects or visit friends and relatives with equal aplomb.

The Ellannas as well as other Nome friends had been urging us to visit Nome in winter. The ice and snow were not to be dreaded; they were the essence of the Arctic. Only by coming in the winter could one get the true feeling of this unique part of Alaska. As a clincher, everyone guaranteed Bob that he would have even better picture weather. Though days are short in dead of winter, they are often sunny.

Fishing through a hole in the ice of the Bering Sea is a fine time to discuss everything from Eskimo philosophy of life and customs to igloos. The Ellannas had prepared several holes and fastened colorful lures to barbed lines made of nylon, because it stays pliable instead of freezing. A small long-handled dipper was kept handy to remove the ice as it threatened to clog the hole. As we waited, Frank and Ursula carefully explained the sport of tomcod jigging. The idea is to jiggle the line just enough to attract the eye of the small fish and help snag him.

"A little too early," said Ursula. "We'll catch some, but next month, when its warmer, they'll come close. Very good to eat."

Frank and Ursula, and occasionally one of us, with beginner's luck, caught enough to keep interest alive, but there was hardly enough action to interfere with our conversation. In the winter sunlight, out on the ice pack, there was a feeling of unreality. Farther out, protected by half-igloo shelters, other groups were fishing for large crabs. An occasional sharp cracking sound made us wonder if what we were depending on was really as solid as it appeared. Someone asked what happened when the ice started to melt.

"There are signs," said Ursula. She explained that "leads" (cracks farther offshore) developed, and then the hunting was good. Along the shore a crack would widen, and they would watch it daily. Then, a slight tide variation plus a warm day would suddenly start the whole mass moving swiftly and silently out to sea.

"What happens to the people who are out fishing and hunting and the children who might be caught while playing?" we worried.

"We watch," she said, and Frank nodded in agreement. "The kayaks and oomiaks are ready. We go pick everybody up. No one is afraid."

Living in a harsh environment where survival depends on his own ingenuity and self-sufficiency in cooperation with nature, the Eskimo belief in the immortality of spirit was enough to sustain him from fear, especially of death. This applied to the animals they killed, too. Even today some hunters give a freshly killed seal a drink of water, so that his spirit will return to other seals and say that it has been well treated. Thus the living might be inclined to come and get killed by these hunters, who need them for sustenance. It was common to give names of the recently deceased to the newly born. It could be the spirit returning for another turn on earth.

We were curious about the status of women, recalling bits and pieces of old Eskimo lore, like girl babies and grandmothers being the first to be put out on the ice when there were too many mouths to feed.

"Maybe a long time ago, and in very poor places when hunting was bad for many months," Ursula conceded. "We always had enough. And if a child lost his parents another family wanted him. He was the same as their own."

She reassured us further by explaining how important women were always considered in their community, on King Island. "The men had to hunt, and the women had to take care of the food and see that clothes were made and mended. Even a little tear in a mukluk or mitten is very bad. A wife went along on hunts to help with these things," she added.

"What if a man didn't have a wife, or was visiting far from home? How about that custom of wife lending—or was it swapping?" someone asked slyly.

"Oh, long before *our* time—before missionaries, too," countered Ursula. Frank said something in Eskimo, and Ursula laughed, but didn't translate. Maybe he was cursing the missionaries who spoiled things.

Dog-sledding is definitely improved in winter, the Ellannas pointed out. For one thing, the beautifully marked, highly intelligent dogs take it more seriously. They go along with the idea in summer, tolerate having their pictures taken, and muster up enough enthusiasm to haul passengers a short distance over the tundra. But winter is their season—when they are essential to the work to be done, and they know it. Besides, it means lots of activity and there is no comparison between a tundra demonstration (intriguing as it is to visitors who have not seen this before) and skimming over real snow and ice. Howard Farley, who raises and trains dogs, commuted between the Nugget Inn and our fishing holes, so that everyone had a ride in his sled.

Along the way we saw kids on ice skates, residents dashing about on snowmobiles, more fishermen, and people out walking, taking advantage of the ice imprisonment of the usually restless Bering Sea. Bob found some ice formations and was all set up with his camera, ready to shoot the dog-sledders and team against an already waning sun. People-models are used to Bob's taking several exposures, and patiently pose for "just one more." Three times around and Marrow, the lead dog, had Bob's number, and it was up. Marrow looked at his master and then at the photographer with a "he must be nuts" look and flopped. Only the word "home" brought him to his feet. He grudgingly let Bob aboard the sled and away we flew to the Nugget Inn.

Between the inn and the Bering Sea was the only igloo we have ever seen in the Arctic. It was built for fun by Explorer Scouts of Post 63, Nome. This same bunch keeps fit by competing in age-old games, handed down from a rugged derring-do heritage, in which they take pride. Naturally, the igloo was a conversation piece. No matter how many times people are told otherwise, when they come to the Arctic they hope to see this architectural symbol. It is part of

King Island Eskimo hunters with rifles and skin oomiak follow leads in ice of Bering Sea in early spring, near Nome.

the image. Snow igloos, practical, simple shelters, quick to build when you know how, were built for survival on long journeys or when hunting parties were caught by storms. Another use, ancient and now obsolete, was a final shelter for an old person, no longer able to do his bit in a community with dwindling food supply. There he waited, apart from the village, for his spirit to be freed from his no longer useful body.

Perhaps the igloo myth persists because of its distinctive shape, or the romance of its survival use: man against the elements able to create a dwelling out of the only materials available. At any rate, Eskimo homes now are made of wood, often driftwood, insulated with sod, though the trend is now toward modern insulation materials when they can get them. In more primitive settlements, they may be igloo-shaped.

Eskimo boats

Boats are on display various places, in both winter and summer. Kayak frames are of driftwood, the rest is skin, and each is made to the personal measure of the person using it. The scale for the various parts of the boat pattern is designated by so many hands and thumbs, not inches. A walrus-gut watertight cover is added to keep the boater warm and dry. There are places for storing lines, floats, harpoons, and other essentials, all made out of natural materials. Eskimo raincoats, also made of walrus gut, are items most people might see only in a museum. There are painstakingly sewn from seal intestines, three inches in diameter but many feet long. When split open there is a six-inch-wide strip to work with and be sewn together with watertight stitches. When not in use, the hooded parka-style raincoat looks like a crinkled, dried-up skin. It becomes pliable when soaked in water before use, and is very efficient as a windbreaker, too.

One summer, guests went to a nearby lagoon and took turns piling into a large outboard motor-powered oomiak, the same kind the King Islanders used to paddle from their island home until a few years ago. Dominic Thomas, Eskimo of many hats, including master of ceremonies at the dances, was the operator and thoroughly delighted in the comments of his passengers. He understood English well and spoke it as Eskimos do—when they have something to say. One prim lady was hesitating, and Dom wasn't sure whether it was lack of faith in his oomiak or his driving. He finally decided getting in and sitting down was the problem, and with typical native dispatch went to the bottom of it. He gave her a hand, indicated a seat, and said, "Put it there!" She put it—and for the rest of the stay the catchphrase for that particular bunch of visitors was "Put it there!" at every appropriate opportunity.

Our Eskimo friends seem to enjoy adapting to a new industry like tourism. Many a visitor has gone home richer in the knowledge of things Eskimo after their short stay in the Arctic, and their association with couples like the Ellannas.

Gold!

Among our treasured husband-and-wife teams, there was one triangle. It was the couple you would least suspect—the Engstroms, married half a century, grandparents, and obviously devoted to one another. But for years, Elsie put up with her husband Herb's infatuation for a gold digger!

Most of the year the affair was kept under control, but once the snow started melting, the streams thawed, the robins returned, and the squirrels started frisking, Herb's thoughts turned to what he had been thinking about all winter, his gold digger—a dredge. With more patience and understanding than most wives, the three of them lived in harmony, mining their Basin Creek diggings, fifteen miles from Nome, every summer until they retired a few years ago.

"Herb got gold fever when we first came to Nome," said Elsie. "He filed his claim at Basin Creek, but in those depression days he used his mechanical skills to earn our living. Then he fell for my rival when he saw her at Tajara Creek, thirty-five miles across the mountains."

With bulldozer and skids he dragged his dismantled darling all the way to Basin Creek, put her together, and started searching for the rich strike (dream of every gold miner), managing meanwhile to wrest a living from the frozen earth.

Besides the dredge, Herb's gold mine consisted of a diesel-powered hydraulic hose to wash down pay dirt, some small "rockers" for preliminary washing, and gold pans. Though it was Herb's "work," this easily accessible operating gold mine looked like fun to vacationers. Neighbors and others had been dribbling by for years lending a hand for the fun of doing a little gold-panning. They were as interested as Herb in the chance that he might one day make the big strike.

Alaska Airlines wondered if maybe Herb and Elsie could use a little more free help—say a busload or so at certain times. Hospitable Alaskans have trouble saying no, and Herb's small mining operation became threatened by a rare occupational hazard: too much free help. By the time the sightseers had passed through Nome's famous gold country during the fifteen-mile ride to the Engstroms, gold fever was rampant and spreading. As they went for the pans and rockers, it was easy to imagine what it must have been like during Nome's turn-of-the-century stampede!

Herb put his gold-contaminated guests to work. He fired up his diesel engine and hosed down fresh pay dirt from the stream bank. Though they were interested in his dredge, and though he pointed out that panning is a hard way to make a few cents per day "with no time out for coffee breaks," no one listened very hard. They wanted to do it themselves: children, grandparents, booted men, and ladies (some in high heels)—many standing in the icy water. Frankly, we'll never forget the first real flakes *we* panned out, their particular luster standing out from the residual sand in the bottom of the gold pan.

We can't resist trying our hand at panning whenever we are in Nome, still called "Gold Rush Capital" of northwestern Alaska. Tours now are instructed by Nels Swanberg, born and reared in Nome, the son of gold rush parents. He knows and tells all about panning, sluicing, and dredging in a room lined with heirloom photos of early Nome, before he and his wife Margaret lead you to the action next door.

Somewhere along Nome's notorious beach, the bus stops and lets people out for a close-up look and a sample of the famous golden (actually it's more of a garnet red) sand. We'll swear the bus was several pounds heavier when everyone got back on, clutching whatever container they could muster, full of sand for panning out later. The rough water of Norton Sound off the Bering Sea stirs things up enough that dreaming of finding some "dust" or a nugget isn't too far out, however.

Besides some idle dredges and one that is working far off in the distance, visitors are exposed to gold-rush lore at Virginia and Willie Brown's Nomerama Theater. A narrated slide show describes the frantic era, after which Virginia introduces the "voice," Brownie himself. For years we've been intrigued by Brownie's fantastic tales of the old days, and also his description of some newer "old days"— before planes, especially jets. The living was rugged and Nome was isolated, the ice-locked Bering Sea keeping ships out for at least eight months of the year. Fresh supplies were nonexistent. Eggs were already old by the time they got there. The arrival of the first (perhaps only) boat was a time for celebration. Everyone turned out to see what new things people had ordered as the cargo was lightered in by barge. The Bering Sea is too shallow for a good harbor at Nome, and ships have to anchor out in deep water.

Small wonder the Boeing 727 jet arriving daily summer and winter, laden with supplies as well as visitors, always attracts a crowd of greeters. This super-bird is one of the Arctic's modern miracles.

Longtime miners Herb and Elsie Engstrom pan for gold at their Basin Creek diggings out of Nome.

Bush flying

Joyce and Dick Galleher have the most glamorous team business connected with tourism in Nome. They'd be the last to call it glamorous, but bush piloting earned the name when air travel in Alaska was just beginning, around 1924. There are plenty of legends aired about fantastic achievements in those early flying days. Though many of the original bush pilots are now grounded, a steady stream of young pilots keeps the honor of the profession flying high. The main difference now is that instead of supplying prospectors and homesteaders in the bush, the modern planes are the supply line for remote villages, geologists, and other scientists searching for signs of natural wealth for the government or private business. Bush flying is also in great demand because of the rapidly increasing influx of recreationists and sightseers.

Dick Galleher came to Alaska for the same reason most young pilots do—to seek a place to live and work in an air-minded area. In the early 1950s the Gallehers headed north from Bremerton, Washington. Dick bush-piloted in remote areas: Red Devil, King

Salmon, Katmai, Bethel, Dillingham, and Sleetmute, to name a few. After about ten years in smaller towns the couple bought a steadily growing but still small bush operation, Munz Airways. Now as Munz Northern Airlines, and scheduled, its growth has been phenomenal in the last three years. In the Alaska tradition, Joyce, petite and pretty, has worked right along with Dick while rearing three children.

Munz is a working airline, but visitors who have a yen to visit almost anyplace on the Seward Peninsula while they are in Nome should talk to Dick and find out when he will be flying there. Arrangements can be made for staying overnight, if desired. A charter cost is calculated on an hourly basis, the total divided among the number of passengers. At one time visitors were allowed to go on working bush trips only on a space available basis. That meant they would have to wait for the next plane if the current one filled up with freight, such as a load of reindeer meat or something else more essential than a sightseer. Now, for round-trip excursion fares that range from $50 to the closest towns to $90 for distant ones, you may choose to stick with the pilot, or be dropped off some place that suits ·your fancy, to be picked up on the way back.

Some sightseeing excursions may take all day and cover the most westerly fringes of Alaska. The plane touches down to deliver people, freight, and mail to isolated communities close to the International Boundary, which is also the International Date Line. Passengers can peek into the future—"tomorrow"—as well as the Soviet Union without leaving the United States, and no visa required.

A two-hour stopover in Shishmaref, hospitable Eskimo village on a low, narrow island just off the coast of the Arctic Ocean, allows time for sightseeing. The homes, school, church, and fishing camp down the beach are all within walking distance of the landing strip. Along with Eskimo kids and other assorted plane greeters we hitched a ride on the waiting freight and mail pickup truck. An Eskimo guide pointed out the summer activities, mostly gathering and preparing food for the winter, and making clothes and shelter. We took pictures, talked with the residents, shopped for some intricate beadwork and a finely etched ivory bolo tie, and were invited into two homes for coffee while making the rounds.

Bush pilot Dick Galleher and his wife, Joyce, of Nome.

Nomeward bound, the pilot flew at "see"-level; beachcombing, he called it. Tin City, location of the only tin deposits in the United States, was a fly-by, but we made a short stop at Teller, now connected to Nome by road, and at Brevig Mission, a reindeer station, where there are old corrals and remains of camps along the beach. Nome's easy-to-recognize landmark, Sledge Island, so-named because of its shape, stood out against the late summer Bering Sea sunset. Deserted now, the island was once a quarantine station.

You may have to arrange to stay an extra night in Nome if you are serious about flightseeing, and want to visit places like Gambell, Savoonga, and the Diomedes.

"No two trips are ever the same," Dick claims. We agree with that, having checked it out on his Diomede Island flights. Since our first flight to this part of the Arctic was in midsummer and the second in midwinter, the contrast was even more obvious.

The flight was a charter, though, as usual, Dick had a pickup here and there. The idea was to prove that we could see two continents, two seas, and two days—all in two hours. We might have made it within the time limit if we had left the photographer at Nome. The first hangup was rocky King Island, original home of the Eskimos at Nome. It was a photographer-frustrating sunless day, but the subject matter was one of Bob's favorites—a real ghost town. We saw the deserted frame houses on stilts clinging to the rocky cliffs, as Ursula Ellanna had described them. Seeing the island, though, we wondered how the villagers ever survived there. It was hard to imagine that the rugged bit of land rising in a restless sea provided an adequate living over the centuries. Though the moorage and launching problems appeared insurmountable to us, we could well believe that the skilled King Island mariners migrated as they pleased in many directions in their skin boats.

The village looked ghostly enough in summer. It was even more so in winter, as Bob kept us churning in tight circles until he was satisfied he had the jagged outlines of the cliffs with their stone outcroppings on top plus the rickety-looking houses on film. Half a dozen nervous passengers held on while our pilot tried to point out the caves which served as natural walk-in freezers where the Eskimos used to store their walrus meat. Seattle *Times* columnist Byron Fish noted poetically that the outcroppings in winter snow and ice reminded him of a "Stonehenge built by abominable druids." Either we all shut our eyes at that point, or it was invisible in the ice, for no one located a five-foot bronze statue of Christ high in a rocky crèche, though a King Islander in Nome had told us to be on the lookout for it.

Everyone could make out Cape Prince of Wales, most westerly point on our continent, as well as the East Cape of Siberia. The two neighboring seas were the Chukchi, part of the Arctic Ocean, and to the south our familiar Bering Sea, separated by the fifty-four-mile Bering Strait.

Most imagination-provoking, however, was the thing we could not see, the International Dateline, which separates today from tomorrow. Or from yesterday, depending on which side you live. It runs between the two Diomede Islands, less than three miles apart. Big Diomede belongs to Russia, Little Diomede to the United States. On a map you can see that the imaginary line jogs, in order that this far-west section will be on the same day as the rest of our country. In summer there was no sign of life on the Russian

Diomede, but the whole town came out to wave at Dick on Little Diomede. They recognized his plane, and besides his regular supply stops, he is much appreciated for many mercy flights.

"Big and Little Diomede natives are interrelated," said Dick, "and they used to visit back and forth. Now the Russians have evacuated their island; no one knows what happened to the natives."

On the basis of this, the winter flightseeing group, though well away from the boundary, begged for a closer look, and their adventure took on an added flair—a real one. From "deserted" Big Diomede rose one flare, and then another. It could have been a friendly greeting, or a warning. With a plane full of writers and one photographer, even though strictly travel-motivated, our pilot wasn't about to wait around and find out!

There are bush flights out of other points besides Nome, of course. If you have time, make a short stop somewhere on your own, to be picked up on the pilot's return trip. It can be a very rewarding experience. We especially remember a brief flight we took on our first trip to the Arctic, out of Kotzebue, in 1952. What we found then is probably typical of many a small community today, if you wished to do the same.

Sheshaulik is just a short flight across Kotzebue Sound. It is the summer home of the people of Noatak located about forty miles up the Noatak River. We visited the camp for only an afternoon, by small plane. Our view of native life at Kotzebue had been revealing and photographically rewarding. At Sheshaulik, though much of the same type of winter preparation work was going on, we felt projected back even further in primitive times.

On this particular jaunt, Bob and I were on our own. Our native pilot, after introducing us to a group who came to meet the plane, took off to visit friends. We didn't even have three-year-old Terry, usually in charge of public relations, with us. Irene Cornue (now Morgan), Wien Airlines' tactful tour hostess, had already convinced us that Eskimo people, by nature, are hospitable and inclined to be friendly—at least until *you* prove otherwise.

We were well aware that the long summer days at this camp were

Deserted village on King Island in Bering Sea about thirty air minutes from Nome looks even more ghostly in winter. Villagers now live in Nome.

busy ones. Everyone was occupied with some essential task connected with garnering an adequate winter food supply. We had no intention of intruding or interfering in their work.

Even the children were busy, but being children, they were also curious. They found time to follow us as we wandered around trying not to get in the way, but stopping to pass the time of day and ask a question now and then. Though many were not adept in English, we felt entirely welcome, and Bob always asked if they minded before taking pictures of specific people. The youngsters shared a sample of muktuk with me, and I found part of a chocolate bar for them. I was relieved that the delicacy made from whale skin, though chewy, didn't have the fishy flavor I was anticipating. Even so, to my taste, they got the best of the exchange.

A pleasant-looking lady named Nellie Wood, dressed in a gay cotton-print, long-waisted summer Eskimo dress, spoke English. She seemed inclined to talk as she fileted fish and strung them over head-high racks to dry in the wind and sun. After a few minutes she tossed me a flat little mat made of bird feathers and invited me to sit down. She was interested to learn that summer was our busy work time, too, and that our visit to their camp was really our work. She may not have believed it, though, until we sent her a black-and-white glossy print, for which she thanked us in a beautifully handwritten letter some months later.

We were beginning to feel quite at home when the time came to take off for Kotzebue again. Our hosts politely invited us back and suggested that an even better idea would be to stay over till the men caught another whale or some seal, as that work was interesting, too. Observing a small primitive community busy in their important tasks for making their existence possible, and as yet barely touched by another intruding culture, provided a fascinating interlude. We wonder if it has changed much, and wish we could have spared more time there.

Somewhere along the line, if the budget can stand it, every visitor to Alaska should take a bush flight or two. It's more than just a trip from here to there. The Arctic has a variety of unexpected sights to watch for: old reindeer stations, quonset huts, small cabins, and a surprising number of wrecked military planes from World War II. (We delivered the planes to Nome for the Russians to pick up and fly on to their country.) There are all sorts of natural fascinations, too, over land and sea: lava flows, cinder cones, hot springs, sporting whales, seal, walrus, polar bears, swans, and reindeer. A bush pilot doesn't just fly over these things. He is as interested as his passengers and zeros in for a closer look. Our best advice is to take a look at a map complete enough to show even more out-of-the-way places like Akiak, Aniak, Sleetmute, Igiak, Kwikpuk, Alakanuk, and that jawbreaker Chukwuktolagamute. If they appeal to you, talk it over with the airlines and local bush pilots serving the Arctic to find out when and how you can go there and perhaps stay with a native family. Bush flights run both winter and summer. The only time things are bogged down is during spring breakup, usually a short while in early or mid-May.

Arctic shops and museums

What kind of souvenirs can I buy—*good* things, not junk or imports? This is a common question asked by visitors.

In the Arctic, some of the finest, most authentic and worthwhile mementos are still available. They are created in various materials: ivory, furs, gold, bone, jade, stone, teeth, skins, and even from unlikely sounding parts of the anatomy like nerve centers of walrus tusks and baleen, the plankton-straining strips from a whale's mouth. The latter comes in black strips ten to twelve feet long, up to five hundred from a single whale, and it can be shredded and woven into baskets or carved into jewelry. Eskimos are noted for their fine carving and sewing and ingenuity with available materials.

Many visitors are surprised to find the Eskimos' carving so meticulous. When you consider their background it is logical that they should finish even miniatures down to the minutest detail. Observation has often been a keynote to survival. In an area of vast, frozen terrain, a hunter has to be alert to all possible deviations, just to find his way back again. All clues to the route, no matter how slight, have to be noted. Judgments of time, distance, animal habits, and appearances are essential skills in an Eskimo's life. And so you'll find that tiny black baleen eyes inserted in animal carvings and cribbage board figures are minutely accurate. It is the same with drawings on skins and other media.

It means a great deal to some people to buy directly from the natives, and this is possible from Barrow to Nome. Usually after the dances, wares are spread out and people can look at them, talk with the artists and craftsmen, and buy if they wish. Prices are fairly assessed, we feel. These are all custom-made items and the exchange is dignified, not based on haggling. Usually an artist will carefully etch his name on his carving. We were amused to see one with the zip code carefully and delicately added, also.

Other shoppers would rather browse through the shops for their souvenirs. There is a great deal of choice in all kinds of materials, as well as artifacts. If the town is very small, like Teller, everything will be together in a general store. We found some mostly whole (except for a handle) stone ooloos (woman's knife) to add to our collection by looking through a box of artifacts on a counter. At Kotzebue, and other townsites, kitchen middens (piles of debris) build up from centuries of Eskimos living in one area. People interested in such things spend a lot of time digging down and studying the discards to learn about the past. Today's Eskimos are interested in these primitive garbage dumps, too—partly to supply museums, and partly because pushovers like my husband are intrigued with small items that the diggers are willing to part with for cash. The children, especially, are on to him. One of his treasures is a small valve carved of bone that was probably used long ago to keep a bladder float inflated or plug a sealskin poke. Other more impressive items are sometimes discovered. In a shop off the lobby of the Nugget Inn Three in Nome we saw an old seal-oil lamp for sale for $75. It was a flat stone bowl which needed oil and moss wick to make it operative. The lamp would probably work just as well as it ever did in its Eskimo dwelling, no telling how many years ago.

Excellent shops and museums complement each other in Barrow, Kotzebue, and Nome. In the museums, put together by people who are truly interested in such, you can learn what is good. In the shops, you can sometimes buy it. Making the rounds is easy, and comparison shopping is fun. To start you out, the museums are pointed out or visited, and a shop or two is usually included in town tours. Then you are on your own.

There is a fine museum at the Naval Arctic Research Laboratory adjacent to Barrow. NARL is noted for its work with T-3, the ice island, oil exploration, polar bear research, and Arctic living experiments. The researchers' stomping ground is very old, and long inhabited by men and animals. As artifacts turn up they are carefully studied, catalogued, and placed on display. Some thousands-of-years-old relics are of men and animals, long obsolete. There are also exhibits of Arctic plants and specimens of animals. Among the blue Russian trading beads, masks, women's knives and scrapers, we found a "bush guitar" made out of rusty tin cans, an "artifact" of sorts from a more recent age. Along a hallway is a wing section of the Will Rogers plane. A caseful of Greenland Eskimo "tupilaks," tiny, imaginative carvings of people and animals, are charming and intriguing. They were meant to represent the souls of the dead. Long-ago carvers considered them evil spirits and harmful ghosts; today they are considered good luck.

In Kotzebue, the community museum is called *Ootukahkuktuvik* which means "place having old things." Unusual items here are dolls with old-style bird-feather parkas; a bone comb-like berry picker to speed up the transfer of small Arctic berries from bush to container; and a tiny primitive diaper, made of skin, trimmed with fur, and with a disposable moss liner.

In contrast, Kotzebue's large, modern-style NANA Living Museum of the Arctic is hard to describe. We never expected to see such a slick production there near the top of the world. It answers just about everything you might think of to ask about Arctic life, from the magnificent stuffed animals in the lifelike dioramas to the live Eskimo part, with the dancing and demonstrations woven into the sound-and-light show.

There's also a jade workshop adjacent to the museum. For many years a tons-heavy slab of native Alaska jade from the Kobuk River Valley lay by the road in Kotzebue, ignored by the residents, but pointed out to tourists. It was ordered by Peron for a statue of Eva, but never delivered. You may still see some of it along with other huge boulders brought from Jade Mountain to be cut up, carved, and polished in the shop. Some may be on sale in gift shops and old-time stores along the main street, such as Rotman's and Walsh's, well-stocked with souvenir items made of gold, ivory, skin, and jade.

In Nome, Howard and Mary Knodel's Arctic Trading Post faces Front Street; the entrance to their Eskimo Museum is around back.

Dennis Corrington shows Russian trading beads to visitor at the Arctic Trading Post and Eskimo Museum in Nome.

They claim the "finest collection of ivory carvings, old and contemporary" inside the "farthest west Eskimo Museum." The Museum was begun by previous owner Dennis Corrington, who used his talent for trading in far-out villages to collect choice items for the Trading Post and for his next venture in Skagway, where we saw him last.

The Museum is included in the Nome package tour and the Knodels have kept the displays imaginative and informative. To set people straight time-wise, we recall a glass case of dirt layers. Planted at appropriate intervals were items suggestive of times in history, from 5000 B.C. to contemporary, represented by a bottle cap. A life-size diorama of a house interior has Eskimo models with faces beautifully carved in soapstone by Harry Koozaata. He is one of over sixty-five Bering Straits carvers whose works in various media, particularly ivory, are on display. Weaving baleen baskets is almost an obsolete art now. For the huge one on display, Mary estimates the weaving time at about eight hours for each square inch.

Prime furs are often for sale in all-purpose, general merchandise trading posts. There are red fox and mink from the Nome area; beautiful white fox from St. Lawrence Island; huge Arctic wolf; wolverine, which is used next to the face on parkas because it doesn't freeze from breath condensation; beaver from Unalakleet; hair seal, mostly spotted, but also some of the rare white and brown ribbon seal. And there are furs from nearby Siberia, which come via New York! Other interesting materials used by the Eskimos: walrus tusks and stomach, seal intestines, baleen, mammoth ivory and mastodon teeth from fifty thousand years ago. The last is likely to be found anywhere in the Arctic, often in caves. It is much prized for carving because of its beautiful colors, absorption of iron phosphate and other time-wrought color changes, and it makes most attractive jewelry.

Seeing an ancient mammoth relic reminded me of a more current mammoth invasion: Annabelle, the only elephant in Alaska. Our youngest, Tracy, had read in her school *Weekly Reader* that a baby elephant living in Anchorage visited Nome. Naturally, she checked right away with her Eskimo buddies, Karen and Florence Thomas and Anita Serloak, on the accuracy of the report. It was true, and the girls vowed it was the strangest critter they had ever seen under the midnight sun. They loved every minute of Annabelle's visit, in a terrified way, amazed at everything about her except her four feet encased in mukluks and the fact that she had traveled to Nome by jet. After all, wasn't she an Alaskan now? And *all* Alaskans fly, as often as possible!

No one is very surprised at anything freighted in by jet these days. Bob has a photograph of a big new tour bus being unloaded at

Nome that looks as if it were being hatched by the Hercules jet freighter. He says he expected it to sprout wings and take off after its "mother." Arctic airline purchases (other than aircraft) are unusual, too: walrus stomachs for skin drums, dog teams, and oomiaks, for example. And so are some of the passengers (besides tourists): natives making trips outside for medical care or other reasons. A small child or an elderly, Eskimo-speaking grandparent will have a little tag attached and will be looked after every step of the way until met at his destination. In fall and spring, there will be groups of students coming or going, aided by someone from the Bureau of Indian Affairs. Or whole dance groups and high school ball teams will be airlifted to their competition grounds.

CONCLUDING THOUGHTS ON THE ARCTIC

Our Arctic roundup would not be complete without taking a look into our crystal ball and making an attempt to predict the future of travel there. This is risky. Anyone writing about the Arctic as it is now may have his copy outdated before it is printed. A prediction or two that we thought original has already been thought of, namely, driving to Europe from Alaska via a tube across the Bering Strait. Someone thought that possibility should be explored as long ago as the early 1900s. Open up Alaska's Arctic through extension by road and rail? There is already a task force working on this. The expensive Alyeska Pipeline Service Company-financed access road to Prudhoe Bay has now become part of the State Highway System, use only by permit, so far. What a legacy for tourism. . . . It passes through a vast wilderness once traversed by primitive man. Archaeologists along the route have first rights. They have been patrolling along with construction crews, salvaging and cataloguing over ten thousand invaluable items from over two hundred dwelling sites that were occupied in the far distant past.

It is also hard to keep ahead of merged airline plans for new and interesting routings. Name it, and they have probably already filed for it. Oil is the catalyst for interchange flights between Alaska Airlines and Texas-serving Braniff International. They call it the "Pipeline Express." Continental and Western Airlines also interchange, funneling traffic through Anchorage via the Seattle gateway. Though these interchanges were initiated for business reasons, expanding traffic is also due to tourist interest. They appreciate the direct link with Alaska from the Southwest.

Two Hawaii-Alaska triangle flights have been popular and prospering. One has been for Japanese only, interchanging Japan Air Lines with Western Airlines so that the Alaska-Hawaii leg is almost free. The Alaska-Hawaii-California triangle was a great deal for Americans, too, until spoilsports pointed out that only *Alaska*-Americans and *California*-Americans were getting to Hawaii for next to nothing. Even if it costs proportionately more now, that triangle tour possibility is a winner. Imagine taking off for Alaska in the dead of winter. First stop is the Arctic with its dogsledding and ice-fishing. Swap your parka for a bikini for the next stopover: surfing, swimming, and sunbathing in Hawaii. Then back home! What a contrast!

From 1970 through 1972, Alaska Airlines started a new westward movement, flying summer charter tours from Anchorage to two gateways in the Soviet Union. One went west, out the Aleutian Chain to land in Khabarovsk, in the Soviet far east. The other route was directly over the North Pole to Leningrad, half a world away. Aeroflot, the only way to fly in the U.S.S.R., and Russian Intourist then guided the package tour groups from one end of the Soviet Union to the other. We found the tours to be revealing and fascinating overtures—enough to put together a travel picture book on the subject. It is expected that the western approach from Alaska will be renegotiated and resumed...someday.

Meanwhile, there are rumors of Eskimo "summit meetings" on the Bering Sea ice in winter, and stories of friendly exchanges between Russian and American scientists on Arctic ice islands, along with signs of political detente. Perhaps the next friendly gesture may be an Alaska-Soviet sister city program. How about Nome and Siberia's Provideniya, separated by only about 250 miles of Bering Sea?

As you must have gathered by now, the Arctic is one of our favorite destinations. There, in comfort, visitors are kept busy absorbing this different face of Alaska. It is a rare person who feels he didn't get his money's worth—and then some. Since visitors to the Arctic are already beyond road ends and off the beaten track, they have to return via their main point of departure, Anchorage or Fairbanks. No matter where they choose to travel next in Alaska, even a kaleidoscopic experience of life in the Arctic is a tough act to follow.

Epilogue

KEEPING a finger on the pulse of Alaska travel is like trying to contain a blob of quicksilver. This "update" comes almost nine years after our book's first publication. The keynote continues to be growth, in development of resources and in population, now estimated at over four hundred thousand.

Guesses and rumors are rampant concerning Alaska's future. Anyway you shake it—by flood, earthquake, oil eruption, or population explosion—the state is bound to change. It will take a long time to make much of a dent in Alaska's vast wilderness. People are something else. Lots more of them in certain areas may take a toll; some places may never be the same again. Not necessarily defined as "worse" or "better"; they'll just be "different."

Based on our travels throughout the state during the summer of 1978, by cruise ship and ferry, by bush planes and jets, and driving and camping in an RV, our advice is still: See Alaska *now*. We're convinced that travel in Alaska, under almost any conditions, will be rewarded by unique and satisfying adventure.

Alaskans, accustomed through history to boom and bust, are looking to the future. Astute and flexible members of the already important tourist industry realize that quality travel can be maintained if carefully nurtured now. We found more and better hotels in the cities, and also in way out places: the Glacier Bear Lodge in Yakutat, the Land's End at the tip of Homer Spit on the

Kenai Peninsula, the Top of the World at Barrow, and Kotzebue's newest native-owned Nul-luk-vik Hotel, for examples.

Besides being attracted to Alaska's open spaces, future visitors may travel there to enjoy the world's best music, art, dance, sport—you name it. If oil revenues reach the expected potential, the state will be able to afford to present the tops in entertainment.

During the next busy years, perhaps prearranged, prepaid package tours are the best answer to assure good itineraries and creature comforts with the fewest surprises in cost. However, we see no reason to discourage independent travel, using either public or private transportation. An Alaska-wise travel agent can be your best friend. The services travel agents offer are free, and they can come up with alternatives if space is tight at certain times in certain cities. You won't want to skip visiting where the action is, but it's possible to sightsee during the day and aim for a remote, less-congested place to spend the night. Make reservations as far ahead as you can, but remember that old Scout motto: "Be Prepared."

In conclusion, though we have been photographing and writing about Alaska for a number of years, we feel we have only begun to cover the subject. We hope that this picture-and-word "preparation piece" encourages people leaning toward travel in Alaska to stop dreaming and do something about it.

Perhaps by now our magic word "Alaska" has begun to awake genes endowed in you by some pioneer ancestor. No longer dormant, they hauntingly suggest that the adventure *you* seek may still be found in Alaska.

Meanwhile, our favorite places draw us back, and new, thrilling possibilities entice us like a siren's song. We suspect we will continue to be chronic and enthusiastic Alaska travelers until we die (with our mukluks on, of course).

A Transportation
and Information
Round-Up

W<small>HEN</small> we have questions, we ask for help from tour operators, travel agents, various transportation media, and public information services. We have relied on many of the following sources for current up-to-date travel information or help in planning a trip. We have also read a lot. In this round-up first we'll generalize; then add some specific sources; and finally make a few suggestions for further reading on our favorite subject.

GENERAL INFORMATION

The State Highway Map locates and describes campgrounds and also tosses in considerable general information. For Alaska highway information write: Department of Highways, P.O. Box 1467, Juneau, Alaska 99811. They issue a periodic report on state highway conditions. Visitors can also pick up the most recent report as they pass through Tok Junction, at the Visitors' Center.

We frequently consult the Alaska Division of Tourism (DOT), Pouch E, Juneau, Alaska 99811. Write for the state-sponsored booklet "Discover the Worlds of Alaska," a very comprehensive round-up of information with a valuable Travel Index. Editor Diana Murphy updates annually such general planning helps as information sources, visitor services, and an unbelievable number of entertainment and recreational possibilities. All kinds; all over the state.

Statewide chambers of commerce are good bets for all sorts of on-the-spot information, especially regarding hotel, motel, lodge, and restaurant facilities. You may not get replies to written queries. The offices are busy and the staffs are usually small. But people are friendly and willing to help when you stop in. We always check the visitor information center or chamber of commerce in each town, as a matter of course.

For information on outdoor recreation and available wilderness cabins, write the U.S. Forest Service, P.O. Box 1628, Juneau, Alaska 99802.

Hunting and fishing regulations: It is a good idea to know the rules, which may be obtained from the Alaska Department of Fish and Game, Subport, Juneau, Alaska 99811.

AIR TRAVEL

Several international airlines operate through Anchorage: Air France, British Airways, Japan Air Lines, K.L.M. Royal Dutch Airlines, Lufthansa German Airlines, Sabena Belgian World Airways, Scandinavian Airlines System, Northwest Orient.

Queries to most airlines serving Alaska are usually answered promptly with enticing, complete, and colorful brochures on the areas they serve. For both interstate and Alaska flights try the following for information: Alaska Airlines, Seattle-Tacoma International Airport, Seattle, Washington 98158; Western Airlines, Seattle-Tacoma International Airport, Seattle, Washington 98158; and Wien Air Alaska, 4100 International Airport Road, Anchorage, Alaska 99502.

Smaller scheduled airlines cover their regions, flying from principal cities. Some we've sampled while in their air space are: Munz Northern, out of Nome, Kotzebue, and St. Mary's; Reeve Aleutian, from Anchorage; and Kodiak Western, Kodiak. And among bush and charters: Channel Flying and Eagle Air (helicopter and float plane), Sitka; Glacier Bay Airways, Gustavus; L.A.B., Juneau and Haines; Flair Air, Klawock near Ketchikan; Cook Inlet Aviation and Maritime Helicopters, Homer on the Kenai; and Denali Flying Service, Mount McKinley National Park. And there are others; some two hundred certified air taxi operations in various towns, cities, and recreation areas. If you set your mind to it, we'll wager you can find a way to go *anywhere* you want to visit.

If you want to fly your own plane, write for information to the General Aviation Office, FAA, 1515 East 13th Avenue, Anchorage, Alaska 99501.

LAND TRAVEL

Bus through Canada to Alaska

Alaska Hyway Tours, 100 West Harrison Plaza, Seattle, Washington 98119

Alaska-Yukon Motorcoaches, 2434 32nd Avenue West, Seattle, Washington 98199

Greyhound Lines-West, 8th and Stewart, Seattle, Washington 98101

Trailways, Green Carpet Tours, 345 N.E. 8th, Portland, Oregon 97232

Railroads

Alaska Railroad, Traffic Division, Box 7-2111, Anchorage, Alaska 99510

White Pass & Yukon Route, 1314 Joseph Vance Building, P.O. Box 2147, Seattle, Washington 98111

Car and camper rentals

Major airlines feature fly-drive Alaska trips and most Alaska cities now have car rental service. You'll find Avis, Budget, National, and Hertz at airports and downtown offices. For campers and RVs, it's Number One Motorhome Rentals, 515 East 6th, Anchorage, Alaska 99501. Better make reservations ahead; they're popular in summer, especially during those long, light weekends.

SEA TRAVEL

Ferries

The Alaska Marine Highway System, State of Alaska, Division of Marine Transportation, Pouch R, Juneau, Alaska 99811, and connecting British Columbia Ferries, 2631 Douglas St., Victoria, B.C., Canada V8T 4X7, issue schedules in current use and other necessary information. It is essential to consult them when planning a trip. Double check at points of departure well ahead of time to be sure there have been no changes.

Steamships

Travelers are rediscovering the relaxing pleasure of this method of travel—ideal for exploring the beauties of Southeast Alaska. Combination air-sea-land tours are popular. Compare brochures, available for the asking, from any of the following. This growing, competitive travel market offers a variety of tours, ships, and a myriad number of departures.

Canadian Pacific Railway Company, Foot of Granville St., Vancouver 2, B.C. Canada. (T.E.V. *Princess Patricia*)

Holland America Line is parent company for Westours, 100 West Harrison Plaza, Seattle, Washington 98119. (M.S. *Prinsendam,* S.S. *Veendam,* and the M.V. *Fairweather* which makes excursions on Lynn Canal between Juneau and Skagway)

P. & O. British Cruise Lines is the parent company of Princess Cruises and Princess tours, 727 Washington Building, Seattle, Washington 98101. (M.S. *Island Princess, Sun Princess,* and *Pacific Princess*)

Royal Viking Lines, One Embarcadero Center, San Francisco, California 94111. (*Royal Viking Sea*)

Sitmar Cruises, 3303 Wilshire Boulevard, Suite 444, Los Angeles, California 90010. (T.S.S. *Fairsea*)

TRAVEL AGENTS AND PACKAGE TOUR OPERATORS

There are many more than the ones we list here, and the number is growing. These are friends, through which we have been gleaning information as needed over the years. Some cover Alaska in general, and some operate in local areas, or cater to specific interests.

At the top of the list, because they stay on top of all Alaska travel news, is Alaska Tour & Marketing Services, Inc., Suite 312, Park Place Building, Seattle, Washington 98101. Their staff can tell you all you want to know about travel in the far north (and don't be afraid to ask). They've added a toll-free phone: 800-426-0600.

AAA, American Express, and Ask Mr. Foster are nationwide; consult the nearest branch office.

Alaska Air-Sea Tours, 1205 Vance Building, Seattle, Washington 98101

Alaska Riverways, Box G, Fairbanks, Alaska 99708. (*Discovery Cruise*)

Alaska Travel Bureau, 1030 Washington Building, Seattle, Washington 98101

Alaska Leisure Corporation, 207 Main Street, Ketchikan, Alaska 99901

Atlas World Travel, 4038-128th S.E., Bellevue, Washington 98006

Atlas Travel Tours, Ltd., Travelodge Mall, Box 4206, Whitehorse, Y.T., Canada Y1A 3T3

Audubon Ecology Workshops, International Audubon Society, Harwinton, Connecticut 06790 (For the birds!)

Cartan Travel Bureau, One Crossroads of Commerce, Rolling Meadows, Illinois 60008

Evergreen Travel, 19429 44th W., Lynnwood, Washington 98036. (They also handle Alaska travel geared to handicapped persons, both individuals and groups.)

Grand Circle Travel, P.O. Box 150, Long Beach, California 90801. (They book AARP and NRTA tours to Alaska.)

Johansen Royal Tours, 1410 Vance Building, Seattle, Washington 98101

Kneisel Travel, Inc., 345 N.E. 8th, Portland, Oregon 97232 (Also handles American Sightseeing of Alaska.)

Knightly Travel Service, 1200 Westlake Avenue North, Seattle, Washington 98109

Lincoln Tours, First National Bank Building, P.O. Box 81008, Lincoln, Nebraska 68501

Maupintours, 900 Mass Street, Lawrence, Kansas 66044

Percival Tours, Inc., CNB Building, Suite #1516, Ft. Worth, Texas 76102

Pressley Tours, Route #1, Makanda, Illinois 62958

Princess Tours, 727 Washington Building, Seattle, Washington 98101

Questers Tours, 257 Park Avenue South, New York, New York
10010 (Nature-oriented)
TravAlaska Tours, Inc., 4th & Battery Building, Suite #555, Seattle,
Washington 98121
Westours, Inc., 100 West Harrison Plaza, Seattle, Washington
98119 (Also handles Gray Line of Alaska)

SOME ADDITIONAL READING (prices given as of 1978)

The Milepost, Alaska Northwest Publishing Company, Box 4-EEE,
Anchorage, Alaska 99509. $5.95 (add current postage). Covers the
state mile-by-mile. Crammed with essential information, and
illustrated, it is so revered that it has been referred to as a highway
travelers' "bible."

The Alaska Travel Guide, Box 21038, Salt Lake City, Utah
84121. $4.95 p.p. Editor and publisher Larry Lake keeps it compact
and easy to use. Has an Alaska/Yukon Hotel and Motel Directory,
and an excellent color section.

These guides are liberally laced with ads, information and
pictures of points of interest, and they are updated yearly. They are
especially helpful to car travelers.

The Alaska Magazine, edited and published by Bob Henning, is a
typically Alaskan publication for Alaskans and friends of Alaska.
Articles and pictures give a cross-section of life then and now. You
can learn a lot about Alaska without even going there by
subscribing for $15 a year. It will put you in the proper frame of
mind for your visit to Alaska. The same Alaska Northwest
Publishing Company responsible for *The Milepost* (address above)
publishes the magazine, and also a growing library of Alaskana
books, listed in the magazine and in its book catalogue.

We would also put in a good word for some excellent regional
books by Mike Miller, published by Alaskabooks, Box 1494,
Juneau, Alaska 99801; and an "Exploring" series: *Mt. McKinley,
Katmai National Monument,* and *Prince William Sound* by
Richard Montague of Alaska Travel Publications Inc., P.O. Box 4-
2031, Anchorage, Alaska 99509.

Then there is *The New Alaskan,* Route 1, Box 677, Ketchikan,
Alaska 99901, Bob Pickrell, Editor. This is a newsy, almost

monthly, monthly that is especially geared to what's happening in Southeast Alaska. We enjoy it for its highly original advertisements, as well as its slanted (Editor Pickrell's enthusiastic) recommendations of places to visit—especially those off the beaten path. 40¢ a copy.

Index